Presence

Exploring Profound Change
in People, Organizations, and Society

Presence

*Exploring Profound Change
in People, Organizations, and Society*

Peter Senge

C. Otto Scharmer

Joseph Jaworski

Betty Sue Flowers

NICHOLAS BREALEY
PUBLISHING

LONDON

First published in Great Britain by
Nicholas Brealey Publishing in 2005
Reprinted in 2005

3-5 Spafield Street
Clerkenwell, London
EC1R 4QB
Tel: +44 (0)20 7239 0360
Fax: +44 (0)20 7239 0370

100 City Hall Plaza, Suite 501
Boston
MA 02108, USA
Tel: (888) BREALEY
Fax: (617) 523 3708

http://www.nbrealey-books.com
http://www.presence.net

ISBN 1-85788-355-1

Managing Editor: Nina Kruschwitz
Book design: Chris Welch
Coltsfoot illustration: Diane Leonard-Senge

British Library Cataloguing in Publication Date
A catalogue record for this book is available from the British Library

Printed in Finland by WS Bookwell

Dedicated to the memory of Francisco J. Varela
(1946–2001)

Contents

Part 4 Meeting Our Future

Introduction

It's common to say that trees come from seeds. But how could a tiny seed create a huge tree? Seeds do not contain the resources needed to grow a tree. These must come from the medium or environment within which the tree grows. But the seed does provide something that is crucial: a place where the whole of the tree starts to form. As resources such as water and nutrients are drawn in, the seed organizes the process that generates growth. In a sense, the seed is a gateway through which the future possibility of the living tree emerges.

Introduction

Although the four of us come from quite different backgrounds, we do share one thing in common: we have all been part of extraordinary moments of collective awakening, and seen the consequent changes in large social systems.

One of those moments occurred in South Africa in 1990. Peter was in the hill country north of Johannesburg, coleading a three-day leadership workshop that had been offered for fifteen years, but never in South Africa. His colleagues included a black South African and a white South African who were being trained to lead the program on their own in the future. There were thirty people attending; half were white business executives and half, black community organizers. Many took personal risks to participate in the program.

On the last day of the program, the group heard that President

F. W. de Klerk was going to give a speech, so they took a break and gathered in front of a television set to watch. This turned out to be the famous speech that set into motion the ending of apartheid. In the middle, de Klerk began to list all the previously banned black organizations that were now being "unbanned." Anne Loetsebe, one of the community leaders, was listening with rapt attention. Her face lit up as de Klerk read the name of each organization: the African National Congress (ANC), the Pan Africanist Conference, and so on. Afterwards, she said that as each organization was mentioned, she saw in her mind's eye the faces of different relatives who had been detained and would now be coming home.

After the speech the group reconvened and completed the program as usual. Later that afternoon, they watched, as was the custom in the program, a video of Martin Luther King, Jr.'s "I have a dream" speech. This had been banned in South Africa and many of the participants had never seen it before. Finally, the program closed with a "check-out" that gave each person a chance to say whatever he or she wanted. The first four people made lovely comments about how meaningful it had been for them to be there and what they had learned about themselves and about leadership. The fifth person to speak was a tall Afrikaans business executive. This man, like many of his business colleagues, had been reserved and shown little emotion during the program. He now stood and turned to look directly at Anne. "I want you to know that I was raised to think that you were an animal," he said. And then he began to cry. Anne just held him in her gaze and nodded.

"As I watched this," says Peter, "I 'saw' a huge knot become untied. I don't know how to describe it except to say it was as if a rope simply became untied and broke apart. I knew intuitively that what had been holding him and so many others prisoners of the past was breaking. They were becoming free. Even though Nelson Mandela was still in the Robben Island prison and free elections were still four years in the future, from that moment I never had any doubt that significant and lasting change would occur in South Africa."

For many years, we four have shared a common desire to understand better how such moments and the underlying forces for change they signal come about. We felt that what we had written in the past, at best, described the words but left the music largely in the background. Contemporary theories of change seemed, paradoxically, neither narrow enough nor broad enough. The changes in which we will be called upon to participate in the future will be both deeply personal and inherently systemic. Yet, the deeper dimensions of transformational change represent a largely unexplored territory both in current management research and in our understanding of leadership in general. As Otto puts it, "This blind spot concerns not the what and how—not what leaders do and how they do it—but the who: who we are and the inner place or source from which we operate, both individually and collectively."

Of Parts and Wholes

Everything we have to say in *Presence* starts with understanding the nature of wholes, and how parts and wholes are interrelated. Our normal way of thinking cheats us. It leads us to think of wholes as made up of many parts, the way a car is made up of wheels, a chassis, and a drive train. In this way of thinking, the whole is assembled from the parts and depends upon them to work effectively. If a part is broken, it must be repaired or replaced. This is a very logical way of thinking about machines. But living systems are different.

Unlike machines, living systems, such as your body or a tree, create themselves. They are not mere assemblages of their parts but are continually growing and changing along with their elements. Almost two hundred years ago, Goethe, the German writer and scientist, argued that this meant we had to think very differently about wholes and parts.

For Goethe, the whole was something dynamic and living that continually comes into being "in concrete manifestations."[1] A part, in turn, was a manifestation of the whole, rather than just a component of it. Neither exists without the other. The whole exists through continually manifesting in the parts, and the parts exist as embodiments of the whole.

The inventor Buckminster Fuller was fond of holding up his hand and asking people, "What is this?" Invariably, they would respond, "It's a hand." He would then point out that the cells that made up that hand were continually dying and regenerating themselves. What seems tangible is continually changing: in fact, a hand is completely re-created within a year or so. So when we see a hand—or an entire body or any living system—as a static "thing," we are mistaken. "What you see is not a hand," said Fuller. "It is a 'pattern integrity,' the universe's capability to create hands."

For Fuller, this "pattern integrity" was the whole of which each particular hand is a concrete manifestation. Biologist Rupert Sheldrake calls the underlying organizing pattern the formative field of the organism. "In self-organizing systems at all levels of complexity," says Sheldrake, "there is a wholeness that depends on a characteristic organizing field of that system, its morphic field."[2] Moreover, Sheldrake says, the generative field of a living system extends into its environment and connects the two. For example, every cell contains identical DNA information for the larger organism, yet cells also differentiate as they mature—into eye, or heart, or kidney cells. This happens because cells develop a kind of social identity according to their immediate context and what is needed for the health of the larger organism. When a cell's morphic field deteriorates, its awareness of the larger whole deteriorates. A cell that loses its social identity reverts to blind undifferentiated cell division, which can ultimately threaten the life of the larger organism. It is what we know as cancer.

To appreciate the relationship between parts and wholes in living systems, we do not need to study nature at the microscopic level. If you gaze up at the nighttime sky, you see all of the sky visible from where you stand. Yet the pupil of your eye, fully open, is less than a centimeter across. Somehow, light from the whole of the sky must be present in the small space of your eye. And if your pupil were only half as large, or only one quarter as large, this would still be so. Light from the entirety of the nighttime sky is present in every space—no matter how small. This is exactly the same phenomenon evident in a hologram. The three-dimensional image created by interacting laser beams can be cut in half indefinitely, and each piece, no matter how small, will still contain the entire image. This reveals what is perhaps the most mysterious aspect of parts and wholes: as physicist Henri Bortoft says, "Everything is in everything."[3]

When we eventually grasp the wholeness of nature, it can be shocking. In nature, as Bortoft puts it, "The part is a place for the presencing of the whole."[4] This is the awareness that is stolen from us when we accept the machine worldview of wholes assembled from replaceable parts.

The Emergence of Living Institutions

Nowhere is it more important to understand the relation between parts and wholes than in the evolution of global institutions and the larger systems they collectively create. Arie de Geus, author of *The Living Company*[5] and a pioneer of the organizational learning movement, says that the twentieth century witnessed the emergence of a new species on earth—that of large institutions, notably, global corporations. This is a historic development. Prior to the last hundred years, there were few examples of globe-spanning institutions. But today, global institutions are proliferating seemingly without bound, along with the global infrastructures for finance, distribution and supply, and communication they create.

This new species' expansion is affecting life for almost all other species on the planet. Historically, no individual, tribe, or even nation could possibly alter the global climate, destroy thousands of species, or shift the chemical balance of the atmosphere. Yet that is exactly what is happening today, as our individual actions are mediated and magnified through the growing network of global institutions. That network determines what technologies are developed and how they are applied. It shapes political agendas as national governments respond to the priorities of global business, international trade, and economic development. It is reshaping social realities as it divides the world between those who benefit from the new global economy and those who do not. And it is propagating a global culture of instant communication, individualism, and material acquisition that threatens traditional family, religious, and social structures. In short, the emergence of global institutions represents a dramatic shift in the conditions for life on the planet.

It may seem odd to think about titanic forces such as globalization and the information revolution as arising from the actions of a new species. But it is also empowering. Rather than attributing the changes sweeping the world to a handful of all-powerful individuals or faceless "systems," we can view them as the consequences of a life-form that, like any life form, has the potential to grow, learn, and evolve. But until that potential is activated, industrial age institutions will continue to expand blindly, unaware of their part in a larger whole or of the consequences of their growth, like cells that have lost their social identity and reverted to growth for its own sake.

The species of global institutions reshaping the world includes nonbusiness organizations as well. Today, for example, it's possible to enter an urban school in China or India or Brazil and immediately recognize a way of organizing education that has become completely taken for granted in the West. Students sit passively in separate classrooms. Everything is coordinated by a predetermined plan, with bells and whistles marking time, and tests and plans to keep things moving like one giant assembly line throughout each hour, day, and year. Indeed, it was the assembly line that inspired the industrial age school design, with the aim of producing a uniform, standardized product as efficiently as possible. Though the need to encourage thoughtful, knowledgeable, compassionate global citizens in the twenty-first century differs profoundly from the need to train factory workers in the nineteenth century, the industrial age school continues to expand, largely unaffected by the realities within which children are growing up in the present day.

As Buckminster Fuller pointed out, a living system continually recreates itself. But how this occurs in social systems such as global institutions depends on both our individual and collective level of awareness. For example, each individual school is both a whole unto itself and a part, a place for the "presencing" of the larger educational system. So, too, is each individual member of the school: teachers, administrators, students, and parents. In particular, adults carry the memory, expectations, and emotions of their own experience as schoolchildren. The same holds true in businesses: the organization's members become vehicles for presencing the prevailing systems of management because those systems are most familiar. As long as our thinking is governed by habit—notably by industrial, "machine age" concepts such as control, predictability, standardization, and "faster is better"—we will continue to re-create institutions as they have been, despite their disharmony with the larger world, and the need of all living systems to evolve.

In short, the basic problem with the new species of global institutions is that they have not yet become aware of themselves as living. Once they do, they can then become a place for the presencing of the whole as it might be, not just as it has been.

New Ways of Thinking About Learning

Our actions are most likely to revert to what is habitual when we are in a state of fear or anxiety. Collective actions are no different. Even as conditions in the world change dramatically, most businesses, governments, schools, and other large organizations, driven by fear, continue to take the same kinds of institutional actions that they always have.

This does not mean that no learning occurs. But it is a limited type of learning: learning how best to react to circumstances we see ourselves as having had no hand in creating. Reactive learning is governed by "downloading" habitual ways of thinking, of continuing to see the world within the familiar categories we're comfortable with. We discount interpretations and options for action that are different from

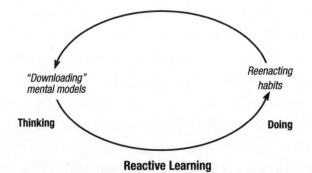

Reactive Learning

All learning integrates thinking and doing. In reactive learning, thinking is governed by established mental models and doing is governed by established habits of action.

those we know and trust. We act to defend our interests. In reactive learning, our actions are actually reenacted habits, and we invariably end up reinforcing pre-established mental models. Regardless of the outcome, we end up being "right." At best, we get better at what we have always done. We remain secure in the cocoon of our own world-view, isolated from the larger world.

But different types of learning are possible. More than seven years ago, Joseph and Otto began interviewing leading scientists, and business and social entrepreneurs. Those interviews—which now total more than 150—often began by asking each person, "What question lies at the heart of your work?" Together, the two groups illuminated a type of learning that could lead to the creation of a world not governed primarily by habit.

All learning integrates thinking and doing. All learning is about how we interact in the world and the types of capacities that develop from our interactions. What differs is the depth of the awareness and

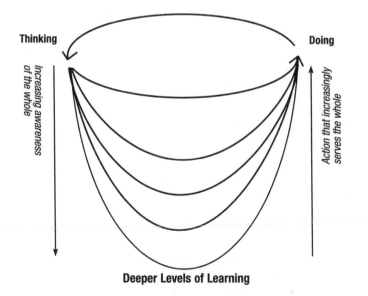

Deeper levels of learning create increasing awareness of the larger whole—both as it is and as it is evolving—and actions that increasingly become part of creating alternative futures.

the consequent source of action. If awareness never reaches beyond superficial events and current circumstances, actions will be reactions. If, on the other hand, we penetrate more deeply to see the larger wholes that generate "what is" and our own connection to this wholeness, the source and effectiveness of our actions can change dramatically.

In talking with pioneering scientists, we found extraordinary insights into our latent capacity for deeper seeing and the effects such awareness can have on our understanding, our sense of self, and our sense of belonging in the world. In talking with entrepreneurs, we found extraordinary clarity regarding what it means to act in the service of what is emerging so that new intuitions and insights create new realities. But we also found that for the most part, neither of these groups talks with the other. We came to realize that both groups are really talking about the same process—the process whereby we learn to "presence" an emerging whole, to become what George Bernard Shaw called "a force of nature."

The Field of the Future

The key to the deeper levels of learning is that the larger living wholes of which we are an active part are not inherently static. Like all living systems, they both conserve features essential to their existence and seek to evolve. When we become more aware of the dynamic whole, we also become more aware of what is emerging.

Jonas Salk, the inventor of the polio vaccine, spoke of tapping into the continually unfolding "dynamism" of the universe, and experiencing its evolution as "an active process that . . . I can guide by the choices I make."[6] He felt that this ability had enabled him to reject common wisdom and develop a vaccine that eventually saved millions of lives.

Many of the entrepreneurs we interviewed had successfully created multiple businesses and organizations. Consistently, each felt that the entrepreneurial ability was an expression of the capacity to sense an emerging reality and to act in harmony with it. As W. Brian Arthur, noted economist of the Santa Fe Institute, put it, "Every profound innovation is based on an inward-bound journey, on going to a deeper place where knowing comes to the surface."

This inward-bound journey lies at the heart of all creativity, whether in the arts, in business, or in science. Many scientists and inventors, like artists and entrepreneurs, live in a paradoxical state of great confidence and profound humility—knowing that their choices and actions matter and feeling guided by forces beyond their making. Their work is to "release the hand from the marble that holds it prisoner," as Michelangelo put it. They know that their actions are vital to this accomplishment, but they also feel that the hand "wants to be released."

Can living institutions learn to tap into a larger field to guide them toward what is healthy for the whole? What understanding and capacities will this require of people individually and collectively?

Presence

We've come to believe that the core capacity needed to access the field of the future is presence. We first thought of presence as being fully conscious and aware in the present moment. Then we began to appreciate presence as deep listening, of being open beyond one's preconceptions and historical ways of making sense. We came to see the importance of letting go of old identities and the need to control and, as Salk said, making choices to serve the evolution of life. Ultimately, we came to see all these aspects of presence as leading to a state of "letting come," of consciously participating in a larger field for change. When this happens, the field shifts, and the forces shaping a situation can move from re-creating the past to manifesting or realizing an emerging future.

Through our interviews, we've discovered similarities to shifts in awareness that have been recognized in spiritual traditions around the world for thousands of years. For example, in esoteric Christian traditions such shifts are associated with "grace" or "revelation" or "the Holy Spirit." Taoist theory speaks of the transformation of vital energy (qing, pronounced "ching") into subtle life force (qi, pronounced "chi"), and into spiritual energy (shin). This process involves an essential quieting of the mind that Buddhists call "cessation," wherein the normal flow of thoughts ceases and the normal boundaries between self and world dissolve. In Hindu traditions, this shift is called wholeness or oneness. In the mystic traditions of Islam, such as Sufism, it is known simply as "opening the heart." Each tradition describes this shift a little differently, but all recognize it as being central to personal cultivation or maturation.

Despite its importance, as far as we know there is relatively little written in spiritual or religious traditions about this shift as a collective phenomenon or about collectively cultivating the capacity for this shift. Yet many of our interviewees had experienced dramatic changes in working groups and, in some cases, in larger organizations and social systems. Some of the theorists had even developed ways of thinking about this that transcended the dichotomy between individual and collective.

In the end, we concluded that understanding presence and the possibilities of larger fields for change can come only from many perspectives—from the emerging science of living systems, from the creative arts, from profound organizational change experiences, and from direct contact with the generative capacities of nature. Virtually all indigenous or native cultures have regarded nature or the universe or Mother Earth as the ultimate teacher. At few points in history has the need to rediscover this teacher been greater.

About This Book

The four of us were drawn to work together from different directions. Building on his earlier work on organizational learning, Peter has devoted his energies for twenty-five years to encouraging learning communities—developing capacities among diverse organizations to collaborate in order to accomplish changes that would be impossible for those organizations to achieve individually. Otto's initial experiences with large-scale change date to his efforts as a grassroots activist during the latter days of the Cold War in Berlin, engaged in establishing networks of relationships across the East-West divide in Europe. Joseph has been an entrepreneur for much of his life, cofounding a major law firm and then devoting his energies to creating the American Leadership Forum, a national network for developing servant leaders. He later was responsible for scenario planning at the Royal Dutch/Shell Group of Companies, where he first worked with Betty Sue. Betty Sue's lifelong interest has been the power of the stories we tell in shaping the reality we experience. As a professor of English literature and a specialist in myth, she has undertaken diverse projects such as collaborating with Joseph Campbell and Bill Moyers on the well-known *Power of Myth* television series, and working with Shell scenario writers in creating evocative stories of the future to help managers see their present reality more clearly.

As we talked and shared our stories, we came to believe that a growing number of people in diverse institutional settings were having similar experiences of profound collective change, and were asking similar questions. In part, we came to this belief when we began to study Otto and Joseph's interviews together in the fall of 2000. Gradually, we realized that the interviews offered both significant corroboration and, more important, clarification of our firsthand experiences. A theory Otto had been developing on "presencing" of different levels of perception and change[7] began to merge with Joseph's ongoing work on "sensing and actualizing new realities,"[8] and eventually a number of working and technical papers were produced.[9] But, most important, the theory started to come to life as we found ourselves drawn into a web of synchronous events that were difficult to explain. It seemed as though we too were becoming part of a future "seeking to emerge."

In organizing this book, we have sought to convey the experience of our work together as well as the results. The four of us often appear as "characters" talking with one another, telling stories, and exploring our different points of view, woven together with ideas and perspectives from the interviews conducted by Joseph and Otto. All quotes that are not referenced come from those interviews.[10] The flow of ideas more or less traces the flow of our conversations and experiences and the theory, or way of seeing, that gradually emerged from those conversations. But while the conversations themselves took place over a year and a half, it took close to two more years for the four of us to write this book.

The first three parts of the book correspond to the process of deepening collective learning as we have come to understand it. This starts with learning to see, moves on to opening to a new awareness of what is emerging and our part in it, and finally leads to action that spontaneously serves and is supported by the evolving whole. The fourth and final section places this deeper learning in the context of a more integrative science, spirituality, and practice of leadership.

Above all, this book is about a theory and our journey to understand that theory. Midway through our work together we began to understand the theory more clearly. When this happens, authors, especially authors of books or articles about leadership, organizations, and social change, usually choose to spare their readers the messiness and uncertainty of their journey. Instead, they lay out all their ideas up front and then progress very logically through exposition, illustrations, implications, and conclusions. We chose not to do that and instead have left the chronology of our experience roughly intact—in part to keep touch with a journey that continues and in part because to do otherwise would suggest a level of understanding that we cannot yet claim.

In blending our theory and our story, we hope to encourage others to join in the journey with curiosity, skepticism, and vulnerability. We don't have answers. After much effort, confusion and ambiguity remain—undoubtedly in part because of our own ignorance, but perhaps also because of the timeless mystery that sits at the heart of what we have learned.

Part 1

Learning to See

1.

The Requiem Scenario

November 2000

The four of us were sitting in a circle in the study of Otto's home on Maple Avenue in Cambridge, Massachusetts. Outside, a light snow was falling. Inside, under the windows, Otto had placed bright red poinsettias. The walls were covered with charts, several with a large U drawn on them. Books were neatly stacked everywhere, and in one corner a computer hummed quietly.

"When Otto said that *Jurassic Park* was written in this house, I couldn't help thinking how ironic it was, given our conversations," said Betty Sue. "Now here we are sitting in the 'house of the dinosaurs' talking about a real-life nightmare scenario: the destruction of our environment; the growing social divide between rich and poor; the potential dangers of things like biotechnology; and escalating violence around the world."

"Isn't it ironic the way people talk about dinosaurs?" Peter said. "Today we say an organization is 'just like a dinosaur' when we mean it's slow and can't adjust to change. But you know, the dinosaurs did manage to survive over a hundred times longer than humans have so far. Whatever beings might take our place here in the future will probably say, 'Just like the human beings—too bad they didn't have the adaptive capabilities of dinosaurs!'"

Betty Sue shuddered. "Hearing human beings talked about in the past tense like that is terribly chilling. I guess we all know that since we have the means to destroy ourselves, it's possible that we will. The unthinkable is possible, but it's still very difficult to consider. The poet Auden said, 'We must love one another or die.' No one thinks we're very close to loving one another just yet, but we also don't seem willing to consider the consequences of not doing so."

"And that's why we don't change," Peter replied. "I was speaking at a conference on business and the environment last week, and stayed at a conference center that I first visited twenty years ago. This center hosts a conference every year at which a prestigious environmental sustainability award is given, so you would expect it to be a showcase for environmentally sound practices, but I'm sure this place generates more waste per customer than they did twenty years ago.

"Everything is individually wrapped—coffee, sugar, shampoo— and each container will be thrown away. The materials used in the room were no more environmentally sound then they had been twenty years ago—the wood hadn't been sustainably harvested, the plastics and materials couldn't be recycled, and the appliances couldn't be remanufactured. I had asked for a room where I could open the windows. They didn't have any because they relied on central air-conditioning and heating. The electricity that drove the air conditioning undoubtedly came mostly from power plants that burned coal and other fossil fuels—heating up the earth in order to cool off our rooms. Then I saw this silly little bar of soap, individually wrapped. Somehow it epitomized the whole situation.

"Those soaps end up being ninety percent wasted—waste that is completely unnecessary. They could easily be replaced by liquid soap dispensers that create almost no waste. There are even biodegradable liquid soaps now. One is manufactured by a supplier in Sweden, partly owned by Scandic, which has gone from a mediocre, financially strapped business to one of Sweden's most financially successful hotel chains, in part through its commitment to 'the sustainable hotel room.' There's no reason being environmentally smart can't be good for business as well—at least in Sweden.

"So I stood there looking at this little bar of soap, listening to my air conditioner whir in the background, feeling angrier and angrier, and wondered why this American conference center still hadn't learned in twenty years what the Swedish hotel chain had learned in a few years. Why were we even still bothering to hold conferences about environmental business practices? Do we Americans care at all about the effects we're having on the natural environment that all life must share? Then I saw the only artifact of environmental consciousness in the whole room—a little card that said, 'In order to help the environment, we won't do your linens if you don't ask us to.' Give me a break! After twenty years, all we've accomplished is they won't wash our linens if we don't ask them to!"

"We've all known the frustration and discouragement you were feeling," said Betty Sue. "At least I have. But are you saying that we avoid these issues to avoid the discouragement?"

"Not quite." Peter paused and continued quietly, "I had a difficult meditation this morning. It was very disturbing, as sometimes they are. I seemed to be in touch with an extraordinary fear—just the fear by itself, no thoughts or associations.

"This fear is probably present more than I'm willing to see, except when it suddenly pokes through like it did this morning. The anger I felt at the hotel came from this deeper fear. I've known about the threats to the environment for so long—but the changes we've made are so small, given what's needed and what we're capable of achieving.

"If the future is going to be different, we have to go far beyond these little piecemeal gestures and begin to see the systems in which we're embedded—and I guess I have doubts if we're up for this. The question isn't, 'Do you want your bed linens changed?' It's more like, 'Do you want to change the way you live?' But this question sits on top of an immense fear, and I think that, Betty Sue, is one reason we prefer not to think, or talk, about these things."

Joseph leaned forward. "But isn't that why we're here? Haven't we come together to answer one fundamental question: Why don't we change? What would it take to shift the whole?"

"We don't change because we think we're immortal." Otto's tone was matter-of-fact. "Like teenagers, we might be afraid, but we still think we'll go on forever."

"Perhaps that's true," said Joseph, shaking his head. "I recently read an article that's been circulating in the foundation community written by a man named Jack Miles, a senior adviser to the J. Paul Getty Trust, called 'Global Requiem.'[1] It's a speculation about what would happen if we started to realize that humankind might not overcome these problems, that we might not develop a sustainable society—that the human race might perish. It's an exploration of the unthinkable."

"But don't scenarios like that evoke the very fear Peter is talking about?" Otto asked. "As he showed, this sort of fear is usually met by denial or simply makes us feel hopeless."

"But that doesn't have to happen," Joseph replied. "I've seen many instances where imagining alternative futures, even negative futures, can actually open people up."

"Scenarios can alter people's awareness," Betty Sue agreed. "If they're used artfully, people actually begin to think about a future that they've ignored or denied. The key is to see the different future not as inevitable, but as one of several genuine possibilities.

"Maybe if people really believed we could be headed for extinction, we would do collectively what many people do individually when they know they may actually die—we would suddenly see our lives very clearly."

"If we could actually face our collective mortality—and simply tell the truth about the fear, rather than avoiding it—perhaps something would shift," said Peter.

"Several years ago in one of our leadership workshops, a Jamaican man from the World Bank named Fred told a story that moved people very deeply. A few years earlier he had been diagnosed with a terminal disease. After consulting a number of doctors, who all confirmed the diagnosis, he went through what everyone does in that situation. For weeks he denied it. But gradually, with the help of friends, he came to grips with the fact that he was only going to live a few more months. 'Then something amazing happened,' he said. 'I simply stopped doing everything that wasn't essential, that didn't matter. I started working on projects with kids that I'd always wanted to do. I stopped arguing with my mother. When someone cut me off in traffic or something happened that would have upset me in the past, I didn't get upset. I just didn't have the time to waste on any of that.'

"Near the end of this period, Fred began a wonderful new relationship with a woman who thought that he should get more opinions about his condition. He consulted some doctors in the States and soon after got a phone call saying, 'We have a different diagnosis.' The doctor told him he had a rare form of a very curable disease. And then came the part of the story I'll never forget. Fred said, 'When I heard this over the telephone, I cried like a baby—because I was afraid my life would go back to the way it used to be.'

"It took a scenario that he was going to die for Fred to wake up. It took that kind of shock for his life to be transformed. Maybe that's what needs to happen for all of us, for everyone who lives on Earth. That could be what a requiem scenario offers us."

There was silence for a moment.

"You know," said Joseph quietly, "When all is said and done, the only change that will make a difference is the transformation of the human heart."

2.

Seeing Our Seeing

In the movie *The Truman Show*, actor Jim Carey plays a man whose entire life is a television show, broadcast to millions, unknown to Truman himself. From his point of view, he is just living his life. In the middle of the movie, a group of reporters interview "the director," the Godlike figure played by Ed Harris who literally determines Truman's life—whether it's going to rain or be sunny, the plot for the next week's story, whether or not things will turn out OK for Truman. One interviewer asks the director, "How do you explain that Truman has never figured out that his whole life is just a television show?" The director responds, "We all accept reality as it is presented to us."

Like Truman, our awareness presents itself to us as immediate and unmistakable. A table. A book. A sentence or word. Yet there is always much more than we "see."[1] In the table are also a factory and workers, a tree, a forest, water and soil, and rain clouds. Indeed, a book contains all of these as well. And a simple word or sentence that moves us speaks of a lifetime—of schools and teachers, of questions and dreams, of current problems and possibilities. With just the slightest pause, we can begin to appreciate the symphony of activities and experiences, past and present, that come together in each simple moment of awareness. Yet out of the symphony we typically hear only one or two notes. And these, almost always, are the ones most familiar to us.

The problems that arise from taking our everyday awareness as "given" are anything but "merely philosophical," especially when our world is changing.

In the early 1980s, executives from U.S. auto companies started making regular trips to Japan to find out why the Japanese automakers were outperforming their U.S. counterparts. Speaking with one Detroit executive after such a visit, Peter could see that the executive hadn't been impressed by the competition. "They didn't show us real plants," the Detroit executive said.

"Why do you say that?" Peter asked.

"Because there were no inventories. I've seen plenty of assembly facilities in my life, and these were not real plants. They'd been staged for our tour."

Within a few years, it became painfully obvious how wrong this assessment was. These managers had been exposed to a radically different type of "just-in-time" production system, and they were not prepared to see what they were being exposed to. They were unprepared for an assembly facility that didn't have huge piles of inventory.[2] What they saw was bounded by what they already knew. They hadn't developed the capacity for seeing with fresh eyes.

With hindsight, it's easy to dismiss the "seeing" problem of the Detroit executives as idiosyncratic. But this problem is universal.

Most change initiatives that end up going nowhere don't fail because they lack grand visions and noble intentions. They fail because people can't see the reality they face. Likewise, studies of corporate mortality show that most Fortune 500 companies fail to outlast a few generations of management not because of resource constraints but because they are unable to "see" the threats they face and the imperative to change. "The signals of threat are always abundant and recognized by many," says Arie de Geus. "Yet somehow they fail to penetrate the corporate immune system response to reject the unfamiliar."

The Capacity to Suspend

Seeing freshly starts with stopping our habitual ways of thinking and perceiving. According to cognitive scientist Francisco Varela, developing the capacity for this sort of stopping involves "suspension, removing ourselves from the habitual stream [of thought]." Varela called suspension the first basic "gesture" in enhancing awareness. As the noted physicist David Bohm used to say, "Normally, our thoughts have us rather than we having them."[3] Suspending does not require destroying our existing mental models of reality—which would be impossible even if we tried—or ignoring them. Rather, it entails what Bohm called "hanging our assumptions in front of us."[4] By doing so, we begin to notice our thoughts and mental models as the workings of our own mind. And as we become aware of our thoughts, they begin to have less influence on what we see. Suspension allows us to "see our seeing."

Sometimes it's easier for people to understand suspension physically than conceptually. A very simple physical practice to appreciate suspension starts with sitting on a chair and grabbing its sides. Now hold the sides of the chair more tightly. You might even imagine that there is no gravity and that if you let go, you would float right up out of the chair. Notice how your body feels as you hold tightly to the chair: the tension in your arms, your shoulders and back, stomach and neck. Now release your hold on the chair. Feel all these muscles relax. Often we hold on to our thoughts in much the same way. Suspension starts when we release the hold and simply notice our current thoughts, like noticing the chair you are sitting on. The thoughts may not go away immediately, but we no longer have as much energy tied up in holding on to them.

When we begin to develop a capacity for suspension, we almost immediately encounter the "fear, judgment, and chattering of the mind" that Michael Ray calls the "Voice of Judgment." Ray, creator of highly popular Stanford Business School courses on creativity,[5] starts with three assumptions: (1) that creativity "is essential for health, happiness, and success in all areas of life, including business"; (2) that "creativity is within everyone"; and (3) that even though it's within everyone, it's "covered over by the Voice of Judgement."[6]

When Otto and Joseph interviewed him, Ray recalled a study by Howard Gardner's Project Zero at Harvard that involved developing intelligence tests for babies. The project also tested older subjects. The researchers found that up to age four, almost all the children were at the genius level, in terms of the multiple frames of intelligence that Gardner talks about—spatial, kinesthetic, musical, interpersonal, mathematical, intrapersonal, and linguistic. But by age twenty, the percentage of children at genius level was down to 10 percent, and over twenty, the genius level proportion of the subjects sank to 2 percent.[7]

"Everyone asks, 'Where did it go?' It didn't go anywhere; it's covered over by the Voice of Judgment," said Ray. "What we're trying to do is set up situations where people can attack the Voice of Judgment and access their deeper creativity." Ray believes that we can consistently bring our creativity into our lives by "paying attention to it" and by building the capacity to suspend the judgments that arise in our mind ("That's a stupid idea," "You can't do that") that limit creativity.

In practice, suspension requires patience and a willingness not to impose preestablished frameworks or mental models on what we are seeing. If we can simply observe without forming conclusions as to what our observations mean and allow ourselves to sit with all the seemingly unrelated bits and pieces of information we see, fresh ways to understand a situation can eventually emerge. For example, when the economist Brian Arthur and his colleague, the sociologist Geoffrey McNicoll, were working in Bangladesh in the 1970s, they spent months observing, gathering information, and "doing nothing." This was at a time when it was common for Western economists and institutions such as the World Bank to analyze needs of developing countries such as Bangladesh by simply applying traditional economic models without really questioning them. Eventually, Arthur and McNicoll developed a fresh understanding of how "the goals and structure of the whole" functioned, according to Arthur. They showed how conditions such as landlessness and large families were self-reinforcing over time and how standard "Band-Aid" fixes prescribed by international aid institutions only served to "prop up the status quo." What they saw was new, and the paper they wrote helped shift the focus of these institutions toward addressing fundamental socioeconomic conditions rather than just standard economic indicators of development.[8]

Suspending Together

The Voice of Judgment can stifle creativity for groups as surely as for individuals. It is what we typically call "groupthink," the continual, albeit often subtle, censoring of honesty and authenticity in a team.

This collective Voice of Judgment tells people what they should and shouldn't say, do, and even think. Often, its effects become evident only in retrospect. Alan Webber, who along with Bill Taylor left the *Harvard Business Review* in 1995 to cofound *Fast Company*, experienced this firsthand.

"I remember vividly my sense of liberation when I left *HBR*," he told Joseph and Otto. "All of a sudden I started meeting a whole new group of people. The basis for interaction was completely different: 'What are you working on that is interesting, and who are you, and how does it feel?' I was seeing the world with fresh eyes. I was learning at a rapid clip, going places I'd never been before, and meeting people I would never have met before. It was as though I'd escaped the boundaries of a walled city."

It turned out that Webber's "fresh eyes" saw something that other business publishers had missed, for in less than five years, *Fast Company* reached a circulation comparable to that of *Fortune* magazine.

There is nothing inherently wrong with the collective Voice of Judgment, any more than there is with our individual internal censor or critic. In the jargon of social psychologists, groups are naturally coercive: they need shared norms and shared ways of thinking and seeing to function effectively. But, like our individual internal judge, problems arise when the collective censor goes unrecognized. The difference between a healthy group or organization and an unhealthy one lies in its members' awareness and ability to acknowledge their felt needs to conform. Enhancing awareness doesn't require a search-and-destroy mission against our internal fears or judgments. It only requires recognizing and acknowledging them.

Suspending assumptions, individually or collectively, is easier said than done. The challenges in organizations start with the frenetic pace many people feel compelled to maintain. Often management teams simply don't know how to stop, nor do they know how to integrate suspension into normal ways of working together. But breakthroughs come when people learn how to take the time to stop and examine their assumptions.

William Isaacs, founder of the Dialogue Project at MIT, says that the first opportunity to shift the quality of conversation in a working group often arises when people are confronted with an opinion with which they disagree and find they must choose whether or not to defend their views.[9] In such situations, most of us see only two options: to defend why we think the way we think or to say nothing. Isaacs points out a third possibility: to suspend one's view. But doing this requires knowing how to present one's view and then inquire rather than defend. For example, rather than saying nothing or telling the other person why you think he or she is wrong, you can simply say, "That is not the way I see it. My view is . . . Here is what has led me to see things this way. What has led you to see things differently?" The form of the question doesn't matter. But the sincerity does.

If questions like this are insincere, they will backfire. But often, even one person honestly suspending his or her views in this way can shift a conversation, allowing the collective Voice of Judgment to abate and new possibilities to arise that no one had seen before.[10]

Building a Container

The challenges to suspending and inquiring into established views collectively also arise from the lack of safety and trust in most work settings. Many people recognize the problem of low trust levels, but trust is not something that can be created by fiat. Efforts to get people to trust one another often produce the opposite effect by drawing attention to the lack of trust that currently exists.

In the early 1990s, John Cottrell, president of United Steelworkers of America Local 13 in Kansas City, Missouri, helped establish a project the goal of which was to help the company management team and the elected union leadership to learn to talk together. These people had literally thrown chairs at one another in past meetings and, according to one veteran union official, "had not actually talked with one another for two or three generations." Those who've never been in the middle of union-management relations that have soured have little idea how bad they can be. This was bad.

Within nine months, something almost miraculous had occurred. In separate meetings, Isaacs and colleagues from the MIT Dialogue Project had led each group in mastering the basic practices of dialogue. Then the teams began to meet together—and after only a few meetings, the combined group began to discover the ability to have "real talk" about difficult issues. Eventually, tangible consequences became evident in the plant: dramatic declines in accidents and absenteeism, as well as improvements in productivity. The backlog of grievances fell from 485 to zero. Union and management were starting to work together to address systemic issues that had been neglected for decades.[11]

The effects on the individuals involved were equally dramatic. "For the first time in my life, I'm thinking," said one steelworker. "And I'm listening to my wife," added another. How had this transformation happened?

Cottrell explained it by using the image of molten steel: "We work with energies that can kill you. The essence of our craft lies in containing those energies. If we fail, people can die. The same is true for human beings: we generate energies that can kill one another. The question is, can we hold these energies, or will they destroy us? Just as the cauldron contains the energies of molten steel, dialogue involves creating a container that can hold human energy, so that it can be transformative rather than destructive."[12]

The steelworkers' imagery is strikingly similar to some of the oldest theories of transformation. The ancient alchemists, in their attempts to transform base metals into gold, created a large body of literature on container building, ideas that the Swiss psychoanalyst C. G. Jung claimed were as much about psychological as material transformation. For the alchemists, transformation was a process involving the interaction of elements within a closed, transparent container in relation to a carefully tended fire.

The principle of the container as transformative vessel is present in nature, too. Within the cocoon, just as within the alchemist's container, something "melts" in order to transform itself into something new. The creation of new life often requires a specialized "container" because established systems are naturally hostile to the "other," the "outsider," the "alien." The normal chemistry of an adult human body would be toxic to an embryo, just as the mainstream culture of an organization is often toxic to the innovators it spawns. And when the organizational immune system kicks in, innovators often find themselves ignored, ostracized, or worse.[13]

This same dynamic is at work even in our own learning. When we're learning something new, we can feel awkward, incompetent, and even foolish. It's easy to convince ourselves that it's really not so important after all to incorporate the new—and so we give up. This is our own psychological "immune system" at work. Living systems' natural "prejudice" against otherness helps explain why suspension can be dangerous.

The Courage to See Freshly

The capacity to suspend established ways of seeing is essential for all important scientific discoveries. It is also why the discoverers, like innovators in established organizations, often find that their lives become more difficult as a consequence.

Brian Arthur is well known for his insights into the "network economy" and the dynamics of "positive returns to scale." These insights started to form when he read an essay by the Nobel Laureate chemist Ilya Prigogine on positive feedback. "Prigogine talked about emergent self-organizing structures in everything from the way termites build nests to the phenomenon of languages taking over," Arthur said. "The more people speak English in the world, the more advantageous it becomes to learn English. So what gets ahead tends to get further ahead. I realized that this insight was also important to economics."

Eventually, Arthur saw that small events could lock the economy into different structures. But this meant that the way we organize the economy—whether through capitalism or any other form—does not automatically lead to the best of all possible worlds. And Arthur's ideas got him into trouble.

"It was the middle of the Cold War, the Reagan-Thatcher years, and these ideas threatened the whole edifice that had been built up for two hundred years," he said. "I was saying that you couldn't do economics statically anymore. I was also saying that the outcomes that manifested in the economy—the technologies we end up with, the companies that come to dominate, the legal and banking institutions that develop—are not necessarily the best of all possible worlds. Markets aren't perfect. The economy isn't perfect. Small events can build up and lead you to inferior solutions. When I began to say this, I knew there would be hell to pay. I just didn't realize how much."

Arthur waited more than two years to write up his ideas, and when he did, in 1982, he couldn't get the articles published. It took six years before he could get an article on positive returns into a top economics journal. In the first ten years of his career in economics, he had published many articles and won a faculty chair at Stanford. During the second ten years, he published one article. And in the end, "the hassle that ensued" as a result of that article led him to leave Stanford. Though he eventually became a founding faculty member of the prestigious Santa Fe Institute, a think tank on nonlinear systems and complexity[14] being set up by economics Nobel Laureate Kenneth Arrow and physics Laureates Murray Gell-Mann and Philip W. Anderson, the years of being misunderstood and ignored were part of the price Arthur paid for seeing things differently.

The Inner Work of Suspending

When you consider the risks involved in suspending, you begin to appreciate not only the courage required but also the personal work. By "personal work," we mean cultivating the ability to be more aware of our thoughts, including those—like "I am here and you are there"—that arise so quietly in our awareness that they remain invisible to us as thoughts. A virtually infinite variety of meditative and contemplative methods from Western, Eastern, and native traditions are available to help build our capacity to slow down and gradually become aware of our "thought stream." What matters is not the particular method we choose but our willingness to make our own cultivation a central aspect of our life.

While Brian Arthur was starting to see the economy as an emergent system, he was also beginning to study with a Chinese Taoist teacher. Arthur's study began abruptly, when some of his most unquestioned assumptions were suddenly revealed—and called into question. After attending a weekend workshop, he was invited to join the group, including the teacher, for dinner. "I thought, 'I'm with this high Taoist master, and I should ask him a question,'" said Arthur. "I thought very hard about what I should I ask him because I had a strong instinct that if I asked a real question, I would get a real answer." Trying hard to find the right question, he finally just blurted out, "If I were to take all this up, what would it do for me?"

The master put his chopsticks down, looked directly at Arthur and said, "You would live twenty or thirty years longer. You would be productive twenty or thirty years longer. And you would end up a very nice professor."

Then he paused and added, "If that's all you want."

Arthur was "incensed, insulted, intrigued, and challenged. I'd worked all my life for what he'd just dismissed as 'if that's all you want.'" Soon after, he began training with this master, eventually moving to Hong Kong so that he could work with him daily.

The story of Arthur's initial meeting with the Taoist master shows how opportunities for suspending often start with "stopping," being brought up short or caught off guard. The teacher's comment over dinner startled and shocked him. Reacting from fear or discomfort, he could have ignored the opportunity to ask himself, "Is that all I want?" Instead, in that moment, when his normal thought stream was interrupted, he discerned the beginnings of a journey that eventually would have great meaning for him, the journey of learning to see. Embarking on and continuing this journey requires the willingness to accept many such moments of "profound disorientation," in which our most taken-for-granted ways of seeing and making sense of the world can come unglued.

Integrating Inner Work

Joseph and Otto told this story about Brian Arthur late in the afternoon of the day we had started by talking about the requiem scenario.

"You know, it's amazing that we were the first people Arthur ever told all of this to," said Joseph. "While he was doing his pioneering work in economics, his whole way of seeing the world was changing profoundly. Yet the outside world only saw Brian Arthur the economist. We know from talking with him that over time, the inner work he has done has influenced his evolving understanding of the economy and especially what he thinks business leaders must learn to do. Yet he's written virtually nothing that integrates the personal and professional sides of his journey. In fact, he's only just now beginning to talk about it. That's pretty interesting when you consider that he called meeting the Taoist teacher 'the central event in my life.'"

"Think about it this way," Otto said. "If the tolerance of the economic establishment for radical new ideas like increasing returns was around zero, the tolerance for Arthur's Taoist studies may be minus two hundred. It's off the charts. As Thomas Kuhn found in his study of scientific revolutions, you can't convince the protectors of the old paradigm with better arguments. The reality is that you have to wait until the establishment scholars finally retire from their positions and are replaced by a younger and more open generation of scientists.

"This isn't true only for Brian. A number of scientists we interviewed have very serious spiritual practices that they regard as integral to their science. For me, this connection between inner work and outer work is one of the most important findings from the interviews. But most of them do not feel safe talking about it, even those who have achieved some integration of the two domains."

"It's easy to understand and empathize with their plight," said Betty Sue. "In our present culture we rarely give ourselves permission to talk about connections between the spiritual and the professional. It's tragic. It keeps scientists like Arthur from sharing the full extent of their insights. It obscures the creative process they have lived and limits future generations of students from their own creative work."

"Doesn't this also tell us why suspending is so hard, individually and collectively?" asked Peter. "When we truly suspend taken-for-granted ways of seeing the world, what we start to see can be disorienting and disturbing, and strong emotions like fear and anger arise, which are hard to separate from what we see. To the extent we're trying to avoid these emotions, we'll avoid suspending. To the extent we can't talk about any of this, it limits all of us. We all know that a team that can't tell the truth about its emotional state limits its strategic thinking as well, because the cognitive and emotional are so connected. And this happens on a larger scale as well."

"You didn't say so, Peter, but I imagine that when you spoke at that business and environment conference, you had to struggle not to express how angry the whole situation was making you."

"It seemed impossible to share how I felt," he agreed. "When I spoke that night, I tried to be direct about how far I believe we have to go in developing truly sustainable business practices. But I wasn't direct in communicating my emotions, not even to myself. My emotions were confusing to me. I just knew I was upset. Indeed, it wasn't until a couple of days later that I saw more clearly that the anger arose from the deeper fear."

"But this still leaves one more problem," added Otto. "Peter's experience doesn't seem to have empowered him. He encountered the larger system directly, not through conceptual analysis. But as far as I can see, it didn't shift his sense of possibility in any way. Nor, I think, does suspending in general. I find that in moments of real suspension, like Peter's, people are more likely to feel unsettled than empowered."

"That's true. My immediate experience was more of being a victim, because in the moment I couldn't see any way to influence the system I found myself stuck in. I don't think that's uncommon when people first start to see a larger system at play."

"I think this is because the first awareness of larger forces, or a larger pattern, is just the beginning," said Otto. "It's as if we awake to something that's been going on all around us but that we haven't seen. Maybe we've even subconsciously worked to keep ourselves from seeing it. Then, all of a sudden, we see this larger pattern, and it's a real 'Aha!' By suspending our normal analytic ways of thinking, we allow ourselves to encounter the system directly. But it's still a problem 'out there,' a situation that is separate from ourselves. I think seeing our seeing is just the beginning."

3.

Seeing from the Whole

An empowering awareness of the whole requires a fundamental shift in the relationship between "seer" and "seen."
When the subject-object duality that is basic to our habitual awareness begins to dissolve, we shift from looking "out at the
world" from the viewpoint of a detached observer to looking from
"inside" what is being observed. Learning to see begins when we stop
projecting our habitual assumptions and start to see reality freshly.
It continues when we can see our connection to that reality more
clearly.

Martin Buber evocatively described this as a movement from an "I-
it" to an "I-thou" relationship. In the former, everything we see appears
to us as an "it," an external object separate from us. It actually makes
no difference if the "it" is a table or a person. In the "I-thou" relation-

ship what appears in our awareness is whole and exists in an intimate relationship with us. For example,

> If I face a human being as my *Thou* . . . he is not a thing among things, and does not consist of things.
>
> Thus human being is not *He* or *She*, bounded from every other *He* and *She*, a specific point in space and time within the net of the world; nor is he a nature able to be experienced and described, a loose bundle of names and qualities. But with no neighbor, and whole in himself, he is *Thou* and fills the heavens. . . .
>
> Just as the melody is not made up of notes, nor the verse of words, nor the statue of lines, but they must be tugged and dragged till their unity has been scattered into these many pieces, so with the man to whom I say *Thou*. I can take from him the color of his hair, or of his speech, or of his goodness. I must continually do this. But each time he ceases to be *Thou*.[1]

The key to "seeing from the whole" is developing the capacity not only to suspend our assumptions but to "redirect" our awareness toward the generative process that lies behind what we see.

Redirection: Seeing the Generative Process

When Otto interviewed cognitive scientist Francisco Varela at the Ecole Polytechnique in Paris,[2] Varela referred to redirection as "turning our attention toward the source rather than the object." If suspension is the first "basic gesture" of enhancing awareness, redirection is the second.

"What's funny about suspension is that when many people do it, nothing much happens," said Varela. "That's why most people would say, 'This introspection thing doesn't work. I look, and nothing happens.' Nothing happens at the beginning because the whole point is that after suspension, you have to tolerate that nothing is happening. Staying with it is the key, because suspension then allows for redirection. Suspension leads to seeing emerging events, contents, patterns, whatever. Then, you can actually redirect your attention to them. That's where the new is."

Redirecting attention "toward the source" encompasses empathy but goes further. Dissolving the boundaries between seer and seen leads not only to a deep sense of connection but also to a heightened sense of change. What first appeared as fixed or even rigid begins to appear more dynamic because we're sensing the reality as it is being created, and we sense our part in creating it. This shift is challenging to explain in the abstract but real and powerful when it occurs.

When he was an MIT doctoral student, Daniel Kim spent several years working with a large engineering program, applying systems thinking, mental models, and other tools of organizational learning to improve cost and timing performance in developing a new car.[3] The program had a five-year budget of more than $1 billion and about a thousand full-time equivalent engineers, divided into more than a dozen engineering subspecialty teams, each responsible for an aspect of the product. At one point, a working group made up of several teams created a "causal loop diagram," or systems map,[4] to try to understand what was preventing engineering teams from working together effectively in order to meet critical timing targets.

As they analyzed the systems map they'd drawn, the working team gradually began to see a pattern. When a subspecialty team faced a difficult design issue, they often had a choice: they could apply a quick fix, or they could address the fundamental sources of the problem. Teams could usually implement quick fixes on their own, whereas more fundamental solutions often required collaboration among different teams. Everyone was under intense time pressure, so quick fixes were the norm—unfortunately, often with unrecognized side effects for other teams. For example, when "NVH" (noise, vibration, and harshness) engineers solved a vibration problem by adding some structural reinforcements, they eventually created new problems for the chassis team, who were responsible for overall car weight. Angry with the NVH specialists for creating a weight problem, the chassis specialists solved the weight problem with their own quick fix: taking weight out elsewhere and specifying a higher tire pressure to keep the car stable. When the NVH specialists eventually found out about this, they were furious—because the higher tire pressure meant a new source of harshness. All of this was captured on the system diagram that the group, including NVH and chassis engineers, created.

As the whole group studied the diagram, they realized that this pattern—quick fixes leading to unintended side effects and new problems for others, leading to more quick fixes and more side effects—occurred everywhere among the subspecialty teams and was a primary cause of the antipathy and distrust throughout the whole program. People felt stuck. They didn't have time to collaborate, yet not collaborating meant that they consistently failed to meet their timing goals. But it was also clear that much of the time pressure came from the rework they created for one another.

"At one point, there was a palpable shift in the room," Kim said. "It was as if they suddenly saw what they all knew but didn't know they knew. All the details were very familiar to them—the problems, the reactions, and the strained relationships that characterized their work environment. Now they were actually seeing the systemic pattern that caused this, and they could see that no one individual was to blame. They had created this pattern together. Each team did what made sense to it, but no one saw the larger system their individual reactions created—a system that consistently produced poor technical solutions, stress, and late cars. As the implications of the system began to sink in, one of the group members said, 'My God, look what we're doing to ourselves!'"

The key word in this statement was "we." Up to this point, there had been someone to blame for every problem: the other teams, their bosses, not enough time. When the 'theys' go away and the 'we' shows up, people's awareness and capabilities change. Through many similar moments of awakening, a new attitude gradually developed within the car development program that caused significant changes in how people worked together. Eventually, they finished the car almost a year ahead of schedule and returned $63 million in allocated but unspent overrun costs. When people who are actually creating a system start to see themselves as the source of their problems, they invariably discover a new capacity to create results they truly desire.

Encountering the Authentic Whole

One reason that the shift to seeing from the whole rarely occurs is that it is poorly understood. And as Varela suggests, the capacity for redirection—turning our attention toward the source—builds on the capacity for suspension. Until people can start to see their habitual ways of interpreting a situation, they can't really step into a new awareness. Members of the product development program, for instance, had spent many months practicing suspending and examining their assumptions or "mental models." The group included senior managers in the program, one of whom later said, "We had to stop being bosses. We no longer felt that we had all the answers."

When Otto asked physicist Henri Bortoft what is required to move beyond suspension to develop the capacity for redirection,

Bortoft said, "You have to cultivate a quality of perception that is striving outwards, *from the whole to the part*." He explained that our attention naturally gravitates toward concrete particulars. If we then try to see "the larger system," we usually look at how one part interacts with others and try to infer what the larger pattern of interactions must be—we try to figure out the whole from the parts through an intellectual process of abstracting. Since figuring out the larger system is so hard, we often just give up and go back to concentrating on the parts. But there is another approach: understanding the whole to be found in the parts.

Bortoft illustrated this other approach by explaining how Goethe had studied plants. "It takes time. You have to slow down. You see, and you follow every detail—of a leaf, for example—in your imagination. This process is what Goethe called 'exact sensorial imagination.' You look at a leaf, and you create the shape of the leaf as precisely as possible in your mind. You move around the shape of the leaf in your mind, following every detail until the leaf becomes an image in your mind. You do this with one leaf, with another leaf, and so on, and suddenly you sense a movement, and you begin to see not the individual leaf but the dynamic movement"—the living field of the plant that creates the leaf.

The experience Bortoft describes is similar to what happens when something that was in the background of our perception suddenly shifts to the foreground. The object—the leaf—was in the foreground, and the dynamic living process that generates the leaf was in the background. The living process is usually less evident to us—yet it's the formative field from which the object arises. When they switch and the living process is in the foreground, then we "see from the whole." This shift of the living process to the foreground of our awareness characterizes the essence of redirection.

For the product development group, redirection occurred when

Much of Goethe's scientific study was in botany. He collected samples of plants wherever he traveled. Once, traveling in Italy, he came upon a plant he knew well, the coltsfoot. He had spent many days studying this plant in northern and central Germany and in alpine regions. In his unique way, Goethe's study consisted mainly of simply sitting and pondering the plant, using his active imagination to take in what he saw with his eyes and what he could see in his mind. He had never seen this plant growing by the sea. Here it had spikes, leathery leaves, and a fat stem–features unlike any in Germany. As he contemplated the coltsfoot, he began to "see" the generating whole in a new way, what he called the *urpflanze* or archetypal plant out of which the many manifestations arose. He wrote in his journal, "The One brings the many out of itself."[5]

they slowed down enough to start to connect the "details" of their frustrations and immediate problems to their own actions, and how their actions in turn created problems and frustrations for other teams. Suddenly they saw "the whole"—the vicious cycle of forces they were unwittingly creating and that was undermining their own goals.

Such moments of redirection can be both shocking and instantly empowering: if "we" are creating the problems we have now, then we can also create something different. Bortoft calls this direct understanding of the generative process underlying present reality "encountering the authentic whole." By contrast, when we try to figure out a larger system intellectually, at best we end up with a conceptual understanding, what Bortoft calls the "the counterfeit whole." When we encounter the authentic whole, we encounter life at work, and we are transformed from passive observers to active participants in ways that intellectual understanding can never achieve.

Seeing from Within an Organization

Seeing from the "whole" in an organization may seem difficult, but learning to be more attentive and genuinely curious about the cultures we live in and enact is the first step. Edgar Schein, one of the most respected scholars of organizational culture, says, "If you want to understand an organization's culture, go to a meeting."[6] Who speaks and who does not, who is listened to and who is not, which issues are addressed directly and which are ignored or addressed by innuendo are powerful clues to how an organization actually functions. These clues become still more "real" when we also pay attention to our own reactions. Schein believes that we can always learn much more about organizational culture through careful observation and reflective participation than from reading mission or value statements.

We all internalize the cultures of which we are a part. If that were not so, they would not exist, because cultures exist only as we bring them into being moment by moment. By applying Schein's insight in a disciplined way, we can begin developing the capacity to see from within the whole of the organizations in which we work and live. For instance, if you sit through a typical meeting, participating as you normally would, you can learn to pay attention to the "external" dynamics of the meeting as well as to your own thoughts and feelings. When the meeting is over, look at an incident that engaged you emotionally. Using your imagination, take time to re-create how you felt and what you thought as the incident played out. It can be helpful to talk through your experiences with a colleague or perhaps to write them down.[7]

If you do this carefully for several incidents, you'll learn a lot about yourself and your organization. You'll see where you felt safe and where you felt threatened. You'll see where you were conflicted and where you were aligned with what was happening around you. You'll see where you were distracted and where you were fully present. As you practice this, you'll be able to engage your imagination more actively to "see" the details of your experience.

Then imagine that you were one of the other participants in the meeting. What is similar and different? Try doing this from the point of view of several of the other participants. While your experience in shifting your point of view appears to tell you about the experiences of others, what you're really doing is using your imagination to explore further subtleties of your own experience. Unless they tell you, you have no way of knowing what others actually experience. But you will discover what you were experiencing about others and, empathetically, how the organization's norms and habits are manifested in different people.

As you continue this process of activating your imagination and applying it in different working sessions, you'll start to sense the organization's culture as a living phenomenon. The figure and ground will reverse, just as for Goethe in his study of plants. What was in the background—in this case, the living process of the organization's culture—will start to come into the foreground of your attention. The concrete particulars of the meeting will then become embodiments of this living process. And you will start to see yourself as part of this process, an active agent in enacting the "organizational culture." If you seriously ask, "What am I doing—in my actions, thoughts and feelings—to maintain these patterns as they are?" you will see many ways that you play a part and perhaps a few new options for what you might do differently.

The Inner Work of Redirecting

Like the inner work required for learning to suspend, building the capacity for redirecting attention to seeing from the whole is deeply connected to spiritual practices. In particular, many meditation practices have the common aim of developing the capacity to quiet the mind and to move beyond rigid subject-object separation.

One of the pioneers of meditation and pain reduction research, Dr. Jon Kabat-Zinn,[8] told us that meditation involves "purposefully refining our capacity for paying attention, ultimately to anything and everything that might be relevant to navigating in the world with open eyes and hearts." In his work, he distinguishes between two basic levels of meditation.

The first level is concentration. "When you begin to focus," he said, "two elements come quickly to the fore. One is that the mind has a life of its own and tends to go all over the place. By cultivating paying attention, you can become less reactive and agitated. That's called the *concentration* aspect of meditation.

"Then, if you bring a certain kind of open, moment-to-moment, nonjudgmental awareness to what you're attending to, you'll begin to develop a more penetrative awareness that sees beyond the surface of what's going on in your field of awareness. This is *mindfulness*. Mindfulness makes it possible to see connections that may not have been visible before. But seeing these connections doesn't happen as a result of trying—it simply comes out of the stillness."

Kabat-Zinn's distinction between the concentration and mindfulness levels of meditation corresponds closely to the distinction between suspension and redirection. In particular, mindfulness explores the possibility of dropping "underneath our conventional and highly conditioned way of seeing that separates and reifies a subject and an object." He points out that simply seeing a situation as a "problem" has the effect of allowing us to distance ourselves from it and blocks "observing whatever arises as it actually is."

The power of this nonjudgmental and nondualistic awareness is illustrated in Kabat-Zinn's well-recognized work on pain reduction. "When our patients practice just dwelling in their pain, their relationship to that pain can change dramatically because they are embracing it for a change—not as 'pain' but as bare sensation, allowing it to be met exactly as it is, in awareness, even if it has a strong element of unpleasantness . . . rather than getting caught up in thinking about it and trying to make it go away. Often, without trying to fix anything, over time, the pain can diminish, sometimes quite dramatically.

"In general, if you feel you've got a problem to solve that is 'out there' and you don't necessarily see or want to see any possible relationship between the 'you' who is trying to solve the problem and what the problem actually is, you may wind up not being able to see the problem accurately, in its fullness. You therefore may unwittingly be contributing to maintaining the undesired situation rather than allowing it to evolve and perhaps dissolve."

Kabat-Zinn's comment illustrates what may be the most important consequence of redirection: when people start to see from within the emerging whole, they start to act in ways that can cause problems to "dissolve" over time. In this way, redirection transcends the subject-object dualism of the problem-solving mind-set. By reinforcing the separation of people from their problems, problem solving often functions as a way of maintaining the status quo rather than enabling fundamental change. The problem-solving mind-set can be adequate for technical problems. But it can be woefully inadequate for complex human systems, where problems often arise from unquestioned assumptions and deeply habitual ways of acting. Until people start to see their own handprint on such problems, fundamental change rarely occurs.

This is also why the powerful changes that can result from collective redirection can be difficult to explain, even after the fact. "One of our biggest problems was explaining our success," said the program manager for the car program Kim worked with. "This may seem like an unimportant problem, but it wasn't. Our bosses kept asking, 'What did you do to solve your problems?' and we just said that 'The people started operating differently, and many of the problems just went away.' They found that unconvincing and consequently tended to discount much of what people accomplished. The idea that hundreds of people just started to see things differently and to act more in line with the health of the whole seemed like nonsense to them."

Herein lies the paradox of redirection. Until you do the inner work of learning how to see with "your eyes and your heart open," as Kabat-Zinn puts it, deep problems will persist. Once the capacity for suspension and redirection develops, the types of changes that ensue can be all but impossible to explain to those not involved. Moreover, just as suspension can be threatening, so too can developing the capacity for redirection. Kabat-Zinn speaks of learning to tolerate the "don't know mind," of "just being still, holding the whole in awareness, not having to have to know anything." This is the true inner work of redirection—and almost the opposite of the conditioning of most managers.

4.

Seeing with the Heart

February 2001

More than two months passed before the four of us met again at Maple Avenue. We all knew that Joseph had just returned from a two-week trip to Baja California, Mexico, where he had gone on a wilderness retreat. But we knew nothing about what had happened there nor how important it would turn out to be for the questions we were wrestling with: How can seeing the system in which we're trapped be empowering? How can we learn to see from the whole?

"You know," said Otto, "sometimes seeing the larger pattern does leave people feeling deeply connected and empowered."

"Yes, I've seen that happen too," Peter replied. "But not often—and when I have, the system was 'in the room.' The people who are enacting the current system—as with the product development program that Daniel Kim worked with—are physically together. But how does this understanding apply to issues like the environment or poverty, where having the whole system in the room just can't happen? These issues are so 'big,' people tend to feel powerless just at the thought of them."

"Yes, but I'm not sure that has to do with simply how many people you get together," said Betty Sue. "I think that when it comes to seeing systems like the environment, empowerment starts with the instrument or organ of perception. You can't just analyze such systems from the outside to get to the root causes of things—you have to feel them from within."

"That's right," said Joseph. "Again and again in our interviews, people used the image of the heart when they talked about the shift to seeing from inside the whole. People talked about it in different ways, but the imagery was strikingly consistent."

Otto nodded. "I remember that when Brian Arthur was talking about the 'inner knowing' that comes with innovation, he said 'This inner knowing comes from here' and pointed to his heart. And Eleanor Rosch, the cognitive scientist at Berkeley, talked about the 'deep heart source' as having a unique way of knowing.

"I think the research behind the work of the Institute of HeartMath is some of the most confirming. They've identified three major neuronal networks in the body. The largest, of course, is in the brain. But there are two other major clusters of neurons, in the intestinal track and in the cardial sack. It seems that there is really a physiological basis for 'gut knowing' and 'knowing of the heart.' These are not just metaphors."

"That aligns so clearly with what is called 'perennial knowledge,'" said Peter. "In cultures around the world, when people want to indicate a point that has deep meaning to them, they gesture toward their heart. The association of the heart with meaningfulness and deeper knowing is common to industrial, agricultural, and preagricultural societies. It's even reflected in some of our oldest language systems: the oldest Chinese symbol for 'mind' is a drawing of the heart. It may well be that 'seeing with the heart' not only is more than a metaphor but is exactly what lies behind the extension of awareness that characterizes seeing from the whole."

"I think that was the essence of what I discovered on my trip to Baja," said Joseph. "We have to learn how to see with our heart first, before we can see from the whole. I don't think I ever experienced the truth of this so powerfully before."

"This was the wilderness retreat you just did with John Milton?"

"Yes. As soon as Brian Arthur told me about John and invited me to come, I just knew I had to go. I simply cleared my calendar and said, 'I'm doing this.' John's a remarkable person. He's an explorer—I think he's done something like twelve first ascents of peaks in Alaska, Canada, and Nepal. He's a professor of environmental studies who has written books on ecology and environmental conservation. As a Woodrow Wilson fellow in Washington in the early 1960s, he was actually one of the initiators of the environmental movement in the U.S., developing some of the first land preservation legislation."

"I remember you said that you felt like you were going to work with Brian in the future, and then Brian telling you about John. What was it like? What happened when you were there?" asked Otto.

"Well, when I first arrived, John and I spent several hours talking, and almost immediately, I felt as if I had known him for years. He began doing wilderness solo journeys and vision quests, with the encouragement of his grandfather and parents, at the age of seven. He told his parents he wanted to go to the mountains 'to be in the real church.' For the next five years, he did one or more wilderness quests each year where he grew up, in northern New Hampshire and Maine. When he was fifteen, he did his first month-long solo in the Olympic Mountains of Washington State. Starting at age sixteen, he went on numerous expeditions in remote areas seldom explored by Westerners. Since those early days, he said his main teacher had been 'wild Nature and the Great Spirit.'

"In the 1950s, John began deepening his knowledge by studying with teachers in many traditions including Mayan shamanism, Taoism, Buddhism, and Tai Chi. Thirty years later, he began teaching these traditions as a preparation for wilderness solos, and this established what he calls "Sacred Passages." The Passages—like the ones Brian had experienced and that I was about to begin—are part of a deep ecology training aimed at opening people to experience nature as a guide.

"I told John about the conversations we four had been having, and I raised with him the central questions I was living with: How can we shift the whole? Is the requiem scenario a real possibility? If so, how can we best work to avert this future?

"After reflecting a moment, he said he's become convinced that political, legal, and economic approaches don't go deep enough. By themselves they won't bring about the penetrating changes in human culture that we need for people to live in true harmony and balance with one another and the earth. He told me that he is convinced that the next great opening of an ecological worldview will have to be an internal one, and then he said, 'I believe the experience you'll have over the next few days will deepen your understanding of what this means.'

"By the time we'd finished talking, I had the same inner knowing that we would work together that I had felt in talking with Brian Arthur.

"I spent fourteen days there in all—seven alone by the ocean and seven days in the base camp before and after the solo with the other participants. John led the four days of pretraining around a beautifully carved log table under a large palm hut *palapa* he built for a meeting space. Even in the heat of the day, the breeze kept us comfortably cool, and at night, when the temperature fell, we needed caps and warm jackets. The faint roar of the ocean about half a mile away could always be heard in the background.

"Each day we went to the garden just by the *palapa* to learn the ancient Chinese practice of qigong. *Qi*, in Chinese medical theory, is the life force that animates all living beings. John said that practicing these basic qigong exercises helps people quiet themselves and align their energies, and, most importantly, become more open physically and mentally to the larger life force available on their solos. After qigong we'd return to the log table and work until lunch. Then, after an hour or so break for exercise or a siesta, we'd resume again, finishing at seven or eight in the evening with a talk by John.

"I found myself completely absorbed in John's teaching, hanging on every word. He was so interesting and compelling to me—in some ways new but in other ways deeply familiar, in the sense of a faint reminiscence or remembrance from long ago. We learned basic wilderness skills: the principles and practices John had distilled from his own wilderness expeditions and solos together with insights provided by the world's classical traditions—and all focused on the realization of inner nature and harmony with outer nature.

"On the final day of training, before we began our solos, John drew a map of the coastline, describing the features of each remote site. I selected the one furthest from the base camp. Since the solo was intended as a time to be alone with nature, John told us to leave all means of distraction behind, including watches, reading material, cameras, radios, and even writing journals. 'The less you pack, the more awaits you,' he said.

"Before we left, John taught us a ceremony derived from various Celtic, Native American, and Tibetan ceremonial processes as well as the inspiration he had received during many of his own wilderness experiences. The ceremony was specifically designed so we could personalize it and make it our own. 'The most important aspect of ceremony,' he said, 'is that it comes from your heart—that it expresses the truth of your heart's natural love, and that it comes from the depth of your being.' He then proceeded to describe the 'eleven directions ceremony.' The eleven directions refer to the four cardinal directions (North, South, East, and West) plus the four intermediate diagonal directions (Northeast, Southeast, Southwest, and Northwest). The final three are 'below,' 'above,' and the 'infinite within.' As we addressed the directions, we always turned clockwise, radiating love and appreciation and making an offering of sage, cedar, or rice to that direction. The real offering, John said, is love itself. Brian, who had already had twelve solo experiences, told us the ceremony is 'extremely powerful—you establish a relationship with the directions and they teach you.'

"After an early lunch, we gathered our gear for the trip out to the trailhead where John would drop us off. As I was loading my backpack in to the car, John pulled me aside and said, 'Joseph, don't forget. If you pay your deepest appreciation to nature, you'll be amazed at what she will teach you.'

"We drove for almost an hour before dropping Brian at his site. Then we drove south for about ten miles before we stopped near a vast, unsettled coastline. John left me at the trailhead with a week's supply of water. I backpacked for a couple of hours, and then, as I approached my designated area, I stopped, took off my pack, and sat down to take in what I saw. I picked a site up on a cliff about fifty feet above the ocean. Down below was an exquisite light sandy beach where Baja's western shores joined the Pacific. The humidity that day was extremely low, which allowed me clear views out across an apparently infinite, deep blue-green ocean. The beach was about two hundred yards long. It was flanked on either side, north and south, by formations of black boulders. On the south side to my left as I faced the ocean, the boulders formed a huge cliff—maybe a hundred and fifty feet high. On the north side, the boulders were not as large—they varied from just a few feet high up to perhaps thirty feet high. This north side, in fact, was a lovely rock garden molded by the incessant pounding of the sea.

"I decided to pitch my tent on the cliff overlooking the beach, next to a rock that looked like a perfect bench. I sat down for a moment and looked around me. I was in the Sonoran Desert—the terrain was sandy, rocky, and full of many species and all sizes of beautiful cacti. Among the cacti was the occasional indigenous grass and mesquite. Off in the distance behind me lay the foothills of the Sierra de la Laguna range, named for the large lagoon that had existed at the top of the seven-thousand-foot mountains. It was all stunningly beautiful to behold. But by the time I hiked back to the trailhead, carried in my water, and made camp, it was dark, and I was too exhausted to explore.

"The next day I scouted the entire beachfront, including the rocks on either end. I hiked over to my checkpoint—leaving a sign to let others know I was OK—and back, and late in the afternoon I performed my eleven directions ceremony. I marked the center spot on the beach near a large flat rock protruding from the sand. Then I marked off 108 paces from the center in each of the four primary directions, according to John's instructions, and marked four ceremonial spots in each of them.

"I began the ceremony by facing the East—the direction of spiritual birth and awakening. I was facing the desert and the mountain range, looking at the huge cacti in the distance and the deep blue sky above. Being in this vast and beautiful coastal wilderness all alone was a compelling experience. My heart was full of love and gratitude for all I was experiencing as I knelt to the ground, silently saying, 'Thank you, thank you, thank you.'

"I turned clockwise and went to the point on the pinwheel facing South and the rock cliff made up of house-sized boulders. South represents life force, vitality, and unconditional love. I began to make my offering of appreciation, and the same thing happened. I silently spoke through my tears of heartfelt appreciation. I went to the westerly point representing transformation and death, facing the ocean and the now setting sun; then clockwise to the North—the direction of universal wisdom and purification. Each of these directions spoke directly to me of events of my life—of people who were important to me and of the unfolding path that lay in front of me.

"When I finished, I sat on the large rock at the center of the pinwheel. By this time, the whole sky was ablaze with the orange and red of the setting sun, and two beautiful pelicans flew past, directly in front of me. Immediately afterward, just off the shore, two large gray whales showed up. I hadn't seen any whales at all before this. First I noticed their sprays of water, and then I saw them rolling in the ocean like porpoises. I sat there alone on the rock watching the sunset, aware of the ringing in my ears and the incredible lightness of being—I felt the walls of my mind had fallen away. The boundary between nature and me had collapsed. I stayed on the rock until dark and then made my way to camp.

"Two days later, I started a three-day fast and, following John's instructions, drank only a mixture of water, lime juice, and maple syrup, which proved completely sufficient to maintain my strength. I spent the time meditating, exploring, and experiencing all that was before me. I found myself profoundly relaxed and present.

"The north side of the beach was full of black rocks that had been sculpted by the ocean over centuries. There were thousands of these rock 'sculptures,' ranging from the size of my hand to thirty feet high, but each was a masterpiece, something that would fit in the finest museum. It was stunning just to be in the midst of them. I sat among the rocks for what seemed hours, watching the surf crash up on them, the water coursing up through the rocks to within a few feet of where I was sitting. Then, as the water receded, the remaining pools dissolved into the most intricate patterns. Each wave created a new dynamic and a new pattern, as if formed by a great artist. As I watched, I thought of the first principle John had taught us: 'All forms are in constant change, all interconnected, all in a continuous state of manifestation and dissolving into Source.'

"There was so much to observe and so much to learn. I found a piece of driftwood almost five feet long, three inches thick, and perfectly round, which made a great walking staff. I used it to help me as I explored the desert and the rocky areas on either side of the beach. Every afternoon just before sundown, I performed my version of the eleven directions ceremony, offering deep love and appreciation to nature for all I was experiencing. And without fail, every day, she would respond within a short time. One day it was two whales for perhaps an hour; then pelicans and a formation of frigate birds—very large beautiful black-and-white seabirds. On another, it was three whales for a short period; on another it was a stirring sight of twenty-one pelicans in formation just in front of me. But the most spectacular show I watched came in the middle of the last day of my fast. At noon on the preceding day, I had started a twenty-four-hour version of the traditional vision quest. That morning it became very overcast, and a high wind out of the north began to blow. The temperature dropped precipitously. By midday, when my vision quest started, the winds had grown very strong.

"John had instructed me to draw an eight-foot circle and to stay within that area the entire time. I was to do my best to stay awake. I was even holding the water mixture to a minimum. Also, I was to stand as much of the time as I could, using a standing meditation John had taught us.

"I drew my circle on the sand near a large black rock on the north end of the beach. Since the winds were increasing, I took a blanket and a jacket into the circle as well as my sleeping bag to wrap around me to help break the force of the wind. After sunset, the winds became gale force, gusting forty to fifty miles per hour, as I later learned. The waves began crashing against the rocks, covering me with fine ocean spray all through the night. Frankly, I was miserable standing in the face of the wind and the ocean spray, and it took all of my strength just to remain in the circle. I was unable to sustain any deep meditation, and since the moon and the stars were covered by clouds, I felt unable to draw energy from them. It was all I could do to stay awake.

"Just before first light, I began the series of qigong practices John had taught us. I really concentrated on them and 'doubled up' on the entire series, taking about an hour and a half to do them. In the midst of the practice, I became much more alert and energized. But in spite of this unexpected energy, I was disappointed that I had achieved no revelation or insight as a result of the vision quest. I wondered if I had failed to hold the proper intention or had done something else to dampen the experience.

"The morning broke cool and extremely clear, not a cloud in the sky. It was as if you could see forever over the deep blue-green water. When I finally left the circle at noon, I hiked out of camp to my check-point, and on the way back, I went over to a beautiful high rock bluff overlooking the ocean where there was an enormous rock sculpture. The bluff was so high, it was hard for me to imagine how the seas under any circumstances could reach this area and how many hundreds of years it had taken to create this sculpture.

"I made my way out to the very end of the bluff and sat down just to take it all in. I prayed and gave thanks to God and all of Nature for the opportunity to be there at that moment. As I began to meditate, I looked to my left and saw two huge whales spouting water simultaneously. Then the whales put on the most unbelievable show. I counted them rising into the air seventeen times, their bodies arcing completely out of the water like porpoises and diving back into the water headfirst. It was magnificent. My heart was pounding, and I sat there in awe. Then all was quiet for a few moments. Suddenly, from the depth of the ocean, like missiles going straight up into the air, the whales shot up out of the water. Their tails cleared the water, and they hung in the air momentarily and then slipped back straight into the water, seemingly without a ripple. They did this three times.

"When they finished, I knelt there on the bluff just sobbing, 'Oh God, what if we harm these whales? What if we did that, oh God, what if we harm this coast? What if we did that?' Then directly in front of me, about a hundred yards out, a lone whale gave me four spouts. Silence. A minute afterwards, off to my left, a whale rolled over in the ocean four times. And then there was nothing. I knelt there for the longest time. I felt as if I was bleeding from an open wound. I felt my heart was completely open and had merged with those of the whales. There was no separation between us. I remained in that open state of intense compassion for a long time, feeling as if I were on holy ground, as if I were in a great cathedral. I knew that I would never be the same again.

"I concluded my fast the next day in the morning and spent my last full day visiting my old haunts: hiking to the end of the bluff where I had seen the whales the day before, spending time with the beautiful rock sculptures, and finally, late in the afternoon, I made my way to the beach, where I offered my final eleven directions ceremony. Through the ceremony I offered my deepest love and appreciation for all I had learned. It was a powerful experience, and at the end I sat on the big rock in the center of my ceremony site. I saw no whales and smiled inwardly, thinking that the events of the preceding day were enough to last a lifetime.

"Just before sunset, I walked to the south end of the beach, to the base of the high cliff made up of the gigantic boulders. I stood in the sand, looking at one of them, thinking about how to describe its immense size and presence to my friends back home. As I was focusing on the boulder, I became aware of another presence and glanced to my left, where, just fifteen feet away on another of the boulders, was a female sea lion. I was startled and exclaimed, 'Oh!' She didn't move, just looked at me peacefully with huge, soft brown eyes. We stayed there, relaxing in each other's presence for several minutes.

"Then she began to move, and I thought she was leaving—but I was wrong. She climbed off the rock and came toward me, stopping only eight or ten feet away. She rested her head between two rocks that formed a V-shape, as if to mimic my chin resting on my staff. She rubbed her cheeks against one rock and then the other. Finally she gave a big yawn and then just sat there looking into my eyes. Her eyes were beautiful, kind—and sorrowful, I thought. She stayed maybe ten minutes with me and then very gently moved away from the rocks and made her way back to the ocean. At that very moment, the entire sky turned red—not just the western sky but the entire sky, all of it, from east to west. I don't think I've ever seen this happen before, and I just stood there overcome, moved to the depths of my whole being.

"That night, under the moon, I sat on my rock bench and reflected on the gifts that had been given to me, my experience in nature, and particularly the gift of the whales and the sea lion. I thought about the words John had spoken the day after I arrived, which now seemed a lifetime ago: 'The next great opening of an ecological worldview will have to be an *internal one*. The experience you'll have over the next few days will deepen your understanding of what this means.' I knew then that nature had become my teacher. She had helped me access who I am and what my work really is.

"The next day I hiked out to the trailhead to wait for a ride back to base camp. When they picked me up, I spoke little. I couldn't put my experience into words just yet, so I held it in. That night we all gathered around the log table to share our stories. At the beginning, John acknowledged that what each one of us had experienced were learnings from 'deep Source' and that the seeds liberated from the process might take weeks, months, or even years to germinate. He suggested we make some spiritual and psychic space when we returned home to help nurture the process.

"We went around the table, sharing our stories. John then reflected on each one, much as in Native American tradition, where a shaman interprets the learners' stories. When it was my turn, I didn't want to speak. I wasn't sure I could convey to the others the depth of my experience. But as I began speaking, the words emerged as if spoken from another place and time. The experience was real in me again, and I felt it become real for the others as well. The gift I was given became a gift I could share with all of my friends gathered around the table. As I ended my story, there was complete silence. Finally John spoke, saying this experience was a window into a fundamental truth.

" 'When it's time for us, fundamental truth manifests,' he said. 'This passage is a doorway for you—keep it alive and keep it vital with meaning. Remember, you can revisit it anytime through that doorway. Time is a matrix, not a linear band. You can evoke the past through that doorway.'

"Several days later, before returning home, I again raised the central questions I'd shared with John when we first talked: Was the requiem scenario a real possibility? And if so, how could we best work to avert this future? What would it take to shift the whole?

"John said the problem we face is 'fundamentally because of lack of relationship, not just with each other but with all of nature. We are out of relationship with all of nature because we've moved into a reductive kind of awareness that is based on alienation and separation. We have to change that relationship to one of cocreation. The fate of the human species is still very much in our hands. Certain things have been set in motion that will be difficult to reverse. But we have two openings that are immensely helpful. First, there is a higher ecological awareness emerging, a coming into personal awareness of our interdependence with other life and our mutual responsibility. And second, there is an earth-based spirituality building at a very rapid pace. Those two factors provide the opening for us to eliminate the need for a physical cleansing of the earth. In that opening, there must be a profound transformation of our spirit and our mind—and of our relationships to each other and to the earth.

"'If we change our attitude from thinking that the earth is there for us to an understanding that we're really cohabitants of the earth with many other species, that we're not privileged as a species more than any other, then I believe we could go on for quite a long time. Nothing is fixed yet. The transformation we're talking about has to occur in time—but time is running out.'

"When I told John that I believe that business is the most powerful institution in the world today and can play a key role here, he agreed and said, 'The transformation must occur in business if the requiem scenario is to be averted.'"

Joseph paused. "I've been waiting to tell you this story since I returned, because it's such a part of what we've been talking about. I knew that you would understand how this relates to learning to see and to the shift we all need to go through. It's like what we said a few months ago: the only change that will make a difference is the transformation of the human heart. For me, it's almost like learning to see with the heart."

We sat quietly for a while, and then Betty Sue said, "Joseph, I love your story, but it makes me feel a little wistful. Do we all need to go out to Baja and learn these rituals from a master like John Milton in order to have the kind of experience you're describing?"

"I don't think so," Peter said, "but maybe that depends on what experience we think Joseph had."

"Joseph's experience with nature and the whales was very different from our usual experience with animals," Betty Sue explained. "You know, you go to a zoo, and you look at the animals—and maybe they look back at you. But you're clearly on two sides of a boundary, literally and psychically. It's not simply a matter of the bars between you. There's just a huge gap between other species and us and, most of the time, even between the other members of our own species and us."

"Joseph's experience broke through that boundary into another way of being," said Otto, "which allowed him to see that what happens to these animals happens to us as well. And this seeing was like a birth into a larger world. I think part of what allowed it to happen was that Joseph was totally present out there. He was open to the world, not in a little cocoon of himself. He was just completely present."

"That kind of openness is so rare in adults," said Betty Sue. "The only people I know like that are artists and other creative people."

"But you know, I don't want to leave you with the impression that this is just about animals or the environment or some kind of mystical experience that feels nice at the time and then is just a memory." Joseph spoke with quiet intensity. "I saw something there that changed my life and changed what I'm going to do with the rest of it, as far as I can see now. The experience was profoundly affirming of what I'd been thinking about for a long time and absolutely essential to what we're talking about here.

"It was an experience of being 'called forth,' to be used as an instrument. I've had similar experiences before, but in Baja I discovered that what keeps this awareness from developing on a larger scale is our profound sense of separation. I experienced boundaries breaking down that I didn't even know existed."

"And these boundaries form the architecture of our everyday reality," said Otto. "This architecture seems 'more real' than the 'miracles' that Joseph experienced in Baja—until the boundary breaks."

"I remember one conversation we worked on in *The Power of Myth* when Joseph Campbell was talking about what leads people to risk their lives for strangers," Betty Sue added. "And he said it involved the breakthrough to a metaphysical realization that you and the other are two forms of the same life. Under conditions of extreme crisis, this metaphysical truth can break through spontaneously."[1]

"But, Joseph, what's really remarkable about your experience is that this breakthrough of oneness crossed a species boundary," Peter interjected. "You felt at one with the whales and with nature."

"I did, but I keep struggling to find words that really describe the connection I felt," said Joseph.

"Your words touched me nonetheless," said Peter. "When you told us how you cried in front of the whales, tears rose in my eyes as well. Something in your story evoked an unfathomable sadness in me. I don't know where it comes from."

Otto looked up. "It's the sadness of separation," he said.

Part 2

Into the Silence

5

The Generative Moment

April 2001

Over the next few months we stayed in touch by telephone, sometimes talking for hours at a time. By the time we met again in person at Otto's home, it was midspring, and as we talked about our diverse projects, the conversation continually led back to the question now alive among us.

~

"The scenario-planning work I've been doing at Shell has reminded me how important stories are in helping people make sense of a complex reality," said Betty Sue. "Using scenarios to think about alternative stories of the future is only one of the ways that organizations can become more aware of the assumptions that lie behind their strategies. But without some discipline or practice like this, we tend to get stuck in a single story that we accept without thinking. And it seems to me that's exactly our larger predicament in the world today: we're stuck in a story of who we are on this earth as human beings, and something in us wants to break free of it."

"I think you're right," said Joseph. "It's as if the perceived separation of humans from one another, and from other forms of life, is the glue that holds our current story together. We've got to find out what it will take to break free of this tragic story."

"Dr. Deming, the quality management pioneer, used to speak of 'losses unknown and unknowable,'" said Peter. "We have no idea the cost we pay for living this story of separation. I'm beginning to see that a cornerstone of our work has been simply creating ways to help people connect more deeply with one another, and with their common concerns and sense of purpose.

"I was in Egypt recently, visiting the new library of Alexandria. The old library was a powerful symbol for the gathering and sharing of human wisdom, and the Egyptian government hopes the new library will re-create that purpose. Since no one knows for sure what the original library looked like, they didn't even attempt to replicate it. The new building is shaped like a huge disk, and when you see it from the Mediterranean, the glass and metal surface looks like the sun rising on the horizon. But what most moved me was what you see up close. All along the concrete façade, the creation stories from ancient traditions around the world are engraved in their own script. Betty Sue is so right that our willingness to hold and consider different stories can free us from being isolated in our own. Being in Egypt was a powerful reminder of how far we all have to go in realizing that freedom."

"But we may know more than we realize about how to transcend our story of separation," said Joseph. "I've been thinking about those magic moments where something shifts in a group. We've all seen it happen. In a way, we've been learning about how to transform the heart for years. We've just never thought about it that way.

"We've even seen it happen occasionally on a large scale. Do you all know about the Mont Fleur scenarios that Adam Kahane worked on in South Africa in 1991 and 1992? The scenario team included people from the formerly banned political organizations like the ANC—the African National Congress—and the Communist Party of South Africa that weren't even legal until 1990. There were also academics, activists, trade unionists, and members of the white establishment— top businessmen, entrepreneurs, economists, and representatives from the Chamber of Mines, the premier establishment industry. At the most important meetings, representatives from what were then strictly white political parties also attended: the ruling National Party, the right-wing Conservative Party, and the liberal Democratic Party. It was almost unprecedented.

"In fact, the whole history of change in South Africa is a remarkable example of people creating a different future together. Who could have predicted in 1985 that only ten years later, South Africa would have gone through a transition to a multiracial democracy without armed conflict and major bloodshed?"

"Well, I know that there was actually an earlier scenario-building exercise in the mid-1980s," said Peter. "That one was conducted by Anglo American Corporation, the powerful South African mining conglomerate, and involved almost no inputs from blacks. But it had a lot to do with opening people's minds—just like we're saying. I saw a videotape presentation of the scenarios around 1987, based on TV broadcasts shown widely in the country. Two scenarios were presented, called the 'low road' and the 'high road.' The 'low road' scenario described a likely future if the official apartheid policies continued and the country became increasingly isolated from the larger world; the 'high road' scenario described the reintegration of South Africa into the world community if apartheid was ended. Not only did public conversation about these two possible futures cause many whites to think about the implications of continuing with the present policies, it also reinforced the idea that the country did have a choice about its future."

Joseph nodded. "Probably in part because of the success of that earlier exercise, when President de Klerk officially started the process of ending apartheid in 1990, there was openness to a new round of scenario building, which Shell helped to fund and Adam Kahane, who worked for me at that time, facilitated. The idea was to involve people who would be part of creating the country's first multiracial government in thinking together about alternative futures. When done well, scenario work allows people to raise difficult issues while at the same time avoiding the kind of rhetorical positioning and arguments that usually accompany a political debate about the future.

"The team eventually came up with four scenarios, each with a playful, nonthreatening name. 'Ostrich' was one in which the current white South African government put its head in the sand, avoiding facing problems. In 'Lame Duck,' the powers of the new black government were so strictly limited by the constitutional settlement that its power to act was completely crippled. In 'Icarus,' the new government instituted radical economic reforms that increased state ownership of land and enterprises—and, like Icarus flying too close to the sun, lost its ability to 'fly,' bringing the economic system down with it.

"The scenario called 'Flamingo' was one that no one particularly liked initially because flamingos take off very slowly. But they also take off together. As the group thought through these different stories, they came to the conviction that the only viable way forward was 'Flamingo.'

"When you look back at it, there clearly was an opening of people's minds and hearts. Otherwise, they couldn't have converged on the scenario that they must move forward together. Such a view could never have happened had one member of the group tried to persuade the others. Of course, I don't think anyone could ever say how much these scenarios actually influenced the course of change in South Africa. But I believe they had a major impact in shaping the thinking that has allowed the new South African government to hold together the diverse constituencies in the country.

"There have been many scenario exercises over the years that don't seem to have had as strong an impact. I've often wondered what made this one different."

"I have, too," said Betty Sue. "Scenario planning is certainly not a new tool. Yet this one was different, in degree if not in kind. If we could better understand why, we might gain some real insight into what is involved in seeing with the heart collectively. In particular, we could see what happens when that 'magic' occurs in a group and how one group can become a microcosm for shifting a larger whole."

Otto looked thoughtful. "I think a group becomes a generative microcosm when it connects deeply with its real purpose. Adam gave a presentation on a more recent civic scenario project at a conference a few months ago that holds a clue to how this happens."

"Which project was that?" Joseph asked.

"Guatemala. Adam started working there in 1998. A small group of local businesspeople, government officials, and human rights activists who knew of his work in South Africa asked for his help. They decided to convene a team of forty-five leaders drawn from every sector of Guatemala—government ministers, former guerrilla and military officers, business owners, university presidents, church leaders, journalists, mayors, students, and community organizers. They wanted a group that could think and act together, to begin to revision and revitalize the country. Guatemala had thirty-six years of civil war, which ended only in 1996. More than two hundred thousand people, out of a population of only eight million, had been killed or 'disappeared.' Despite the formal peace treaty, you can imagine how torn the social, political, and economic fabric of the country was.

"The team, which called itself 'Vision Guatemala,' started by developing a set of scenarios as to how things could unfold in Guatemala over the next ten years. The scenarios were clear and simple and illuminated some of the key national dynamics, like whether or not the reforms called for in the peace treaty could be sustained and the need to recognize Guatemala's diverse cultures. Fifty percent of the people in the country, for instance, are Mayan Indians.

"The group began to use these stories to engage the nation as a whole through formal presentations and informal conversations. The scenarios summarized their understanding of the emerging reality of their country, what they had to do, and what they couldn't afford not to do. Over the past three years, the impact of this group seems to have been considerable. Vision Guatemala team members have played important roles as elected leaders; in educational, constitutional, and government finance reform; and in many local development projects. They've replicated the team's dialogue process with hundreds of diverse organizations, as one strategy to reknit the country's social fabric. A UN official said in a recent study that things are still very difficult in Guatemala but that without Vision Guatemala, 'I think we would have already seen a coup d'etat.'[1]

"But what was especially interesting for me in Adam's account was one event that happened early in the project. Everyone seems to agree that the Vision Guatemala process produced a remarkable network of trusting relationships and shared commitment among influential national leaders. Many of these people had been strangers before the project; others had even been enemies. Adam traced this deep shared sense of commitment to a single five-minute episode during the first workshop. This was what I was remembering when you were wondering what makes the 'magic' happen.

"On the second evening of this meeting, the team gathered in a circle after dinner to tell stories about what had happened to them during the war years. In other words, each opened a personal 'window' onto the dynamics that the scenarios were intended to illuminate. For example, one businesswoman, who was a prominent fighter against judicial impunity, told the story of the day her sister had been assassinated by the military and how she went from office to office trying to find out what had happened. Telling her story took a great deal of courage and honesty: the first military official she had spoken with, who had denied everything, was the man sitting next to her in the circle that evening.

"The next morning, soon after they had gathered again, a man who had not spoken the night before said that he wanted to tell a story. His name was Ronalth Ochaeta, and he is now Guatemala's ambassador to the Organization of American States in Washington. At the time, he was the executive director of the Catholic Church's human rights office. He spoke about what had happened when he went to a rural Mayan village to observe the exhumation of the graves from a massacre. Many such massacres occurred during the civil war. During the exhumation, he had seen small bones and asked one of the forensics people whether people had had their bones broken. The man said,

'No. These are the bones of the unborn children of murdered pregnant women.'

"Now, to appreciate this story you need to remember that Adam is a very pragmatic craftsman. Joseph, you know Adam best, but I think one could say that he's quite reluctant even to talk about things like 'magic moments.'"

"Yes, he sure is," Joseph agreed.

"So here is what Adam said next. 'After Ronalth finished talking, everyone in the room was completely silent, for maybe five minutes. Something happened during that silence. One team member said later that there had been a spirit in the room. Another said that this had been a moment of communion. I don't consider myself very sensitive to these extraordinary phenomena. But if you turn up the volume enough, even I can hear. I heard something then.'

Otto paused. "Adam said that he believes that the later success of the Vision Guatemala team in doing the hard work of agreeing on the scenarios and vision, then acting in alignment over the subsequent years, can be traced to that episode. That was the moment where, as he said, 'the shared will and shared commitment of the group became clear to the group, when everyone knew why they were there and what they had to do. It was as if we saw deeply into the reality of our situation, from the inside of that reality. And in that seeing, we knew who we were and why we had come together.'

"Guatemala has the highest percentage of indigenous people in the Americas. The sacred book of the Mayans is called the Popol Vuh, and there's a line in it that says, 'We did not put our ideas together. We put our purposes together. And we agreed. Then we decided.' Adam says, 'This is what happened in Vision Guatemala.'"

There was silence for a moment—not the absence of words but the presence of understanding.

Finally Peter spoke. "Adam said that the volume needs to be turned up in order for him to hear. Maybe he's not so different from the rest of us—we all must spend our lives learning to 'hear the silence.' The Indian teacher Krishnamurti said that this is why real communication is so rare: 'Real communication can take place only where there is silence.' But there is also something more in this silence that goes beyond opening the heart and seeing 'from inside.'"

"They had a glimpse of their purpose, as I did in Baja," said Joseph. "In that special silence, you can hear, or see, or get a sense of something that wants to happen that you wouldn't have been aware of otherwise."

"That's true," said Otto, "though I would put it a little differently. My personal experience is that in moments like those Adam described, this larger reality we connect with is not just sitting there. It's unfolding or emerging, and we're part of that emergence. There's an emerging future that depends upon us."

"I'm not sure I understand what you mean," said Betty Sue. "What does that feel like? How is it different?"

"It's not as passive—I think there's a greater element of active participation. It's more like you and this emerging future are connected—or, at least, there is a potential for connection if you choose to access that potential."

"I think I recognize what you mean, but it would help if you could ground it with a concrete example," said Peter.

"Well, the first time I experienced this feeling, I was sixteen years old. I left for school one morning, and by the time I got home, everything had changed."

"What happened?" asked Peter.

"About halfway through the day, the principal called me out of my class and told me to go home. She didn't tell me why, but I noticed that her eyes were slightly red, as if she had been crying. I walked as quickly as I could to the train station, and from there I called home, but no one answered—the line was dead. I had no idea what might have happened, but by then I knew that it probably wasn't good. I boarded the train, and after the usual forty-five minute ride, I took a cab rather than wait for the bus to take me the last few miles home. It was the first time I'd ever taken a cab.

"Long before we arrived, I saw it. Huge gray-black clouds of smoke were rising into the air. The long chestnut-lined driveway that led to the farm was choked with hundreds of neighbors, firefighters, policemen, and gawkers. I jumped from the cab and ran the last half mile.

"When I reached the courtyard, I couldn't believe my eyes. The huge 350-year-old farmhouse, where my family had lived for the past two hundred years and where I'd lived all my life, was gone. As we stood there, I saw that there was nothing—absolutely nothing—left but the smoldering ruins. As the reality of what was before my eyes sank in, I felt as if somebody had removed the ground from under my feet. The place of my birth, childhood, and youth was gone. Everything that I had was gone.

"But then, as my gaze sank deeper into the flames, the flames also seemed to sink into me. I felt time slowing down. Only in that moment did I realize how attached I had been to all the things destroyed by the fire. Everything I was and had been intimately connected to had dissolved into nothing. But no—I realized not everything was gone: there was still a tiny little element of myself that wasn't gone with the fire. I was still there watching—I, the seer. I suddenly realized that there was another whole dimension of my self that I hadn't been aware of, a dimension that didn't relate to my past, to the world that had just dissolved.

"At that moment, time slowed to complete stillness and I felt drawn in a direction above my physical body and began watching the whole scene from that other place. I felt my mind expanding to a moment of unparalleled clarity of awareness. I realized that I was not the person I thought I was. My real self was not attached to the tons of stuff now smoldering inside the ruins. I suddenly knew that I, my true Self, was still alive—more alive, more awake, more acutely present than ever before. I now realized how much all the material things that I'd become attached to over the years, without ever noticing it, had weighed me down. At that moment, with everything gone, I suddenly felt released and free to encounter that other part of my self, the part that drew me into the future—into my future—and into a world that I might bring into reality with my life.

"The next day my grandfather arrived. He was eighty-seven years old and had lived on the farm all his life. He had left the house a week before to go to the hospital for medical treatments.

"Summoning all the energy he had left, my grandfather got out of the car and walked straight to where my father was still working on the cleanup. He didn't even turn his head toward the smoking ruins of the place where he'd spent his entire life. He simply went straight up to my father, took his hand, and said, 'Keep your head up, my boy. Look forward.' (*Kopf hoch, mein Junge. Blick nach vorn.*)

"Turning around, he walked directly back to the waiting car and left. A few days later, he died quietly."

There were tears in Otto's eyes as he finished his story.

"You can see that even after all these years, this moves me still—that little scene of my grandfather walking by, ignoring the ruins of his home, and focusing all his remaining life energy on shifting my father's attention from reacting to the past to opening up to what might emerge from the future.

"It also evoked a question in me that still remains: What does it take to connect to that other stream of time, the one that gently pulls me toward my future possibility? It was that question that eventually prompted me to leave Germany to do my postdoctoral research at MIT several years ago and that later drew me to working with Joseph."

"And that is the question that draws you still, right to this very moment," Betty Sue affirmed quietly.

6.

An Emerging Understanding: The Theory of the U

As we continued to talk about Adam's experiences in Guatemala and Otto's fire story, we gradually realized that an understanding that had been incubating for many years was becoming clearer. This understanding had been embedded in the work Joseph and Otto had been engaged in for several years, and in experiences each of us had had when we encountered "an emerging future that depended upon us." Insights from Joseph and Otto's interviews now started to combine with our direct experience to reveal the process at work in these extraordinary moments. Many of the people Joseph and Otto interviewed had illuminated different aspects of this process, and one, the economist Brian Arthur, had laid out a complete picture.

The Seeds of a Theory

In 1999, when Otto and Joseph first interviewed him, Arthur talked about the need to "sense an emerging future" in order to meet the challenges of managing in an increasingly technology-based economy.[1] As the pace of technological development quickens, so does the rate of what the economist Joseph Schumpeter called "creative destruction"[2]—of products, companies, and even entire industries. This leads, said Arthur, to the continual "forming, configuring, locking in, and decaying of structures."[3] Little is predictable or repetitive. Problems are not well defined. The rules of the game as well as the other players change rapidly as the stakes get increasingly higher. Overall, business operates less and less like "the halls of production of the old, repetitive manufacturing industry" and more and more like a kind of "casino of technology." In this kind of business environment, making decisions based on the habits of past experience is no longer optimal—or wise. As Arthur pointed out, business leaders such as Bill Gates, Steve Jobs, and Sam Walton have succeeded in the new business environment because they know "how to distance themselves from the 'problem' and to avoid knee-jerk reactions." They have developed the capacity to avoid imposing old frameworks on new realities.

Arthur's view encompassed suspension and redirection, but it also linked these to a different way in which action arises, through a process he called a "different sort of knowing." "You observe and observe and let this experience well up into something appropriate. In a sense, there's no decisionmaking," he said. "What to do just becomes obvious. You can't rush it. Much of it depends on where you're coming from and who you are as a person. All you can do is position yourself according to your unfolding vision of what is coming. A totally different set of rules applies. You need to 'feel out' what to do. You hang back, you observe. You're more like a surfer or a really good race car driver. You don't act out of deduction, you act out of an inner feel, making sense as you go. You're not even thinking. You're at one with the situation.

"Traditionally, Chinese and Japanese artists sit and look at a landscape. They might sit on a ledge for a whole week just looking at the landscape and then suddenly move to paint something very quickly. It's the same with martial arts: if you have to think in martial arts, you're dead. The twenty or thirty years of training you've had mean that you've internalized lots of possible patterns and can direct all your attention to what is happening right now."

He pointed out parallels in science as well, saying that "most scientists take existing frameworks and overlay them onto some situation," while "first-rate ones sit back and study the situation from many, many angles and then ask, 'What's fundamentally going on here?' My observation is that these outstanding people have no more intelligence than the 'good' scientists do, but they do have this other ability, and that makes all the difference.

"There are many types of understanding. The simplest is a sort of knee-jerk understanding where you just say, 'Oh, they've got an inventory problem here.' Then there's the deeper kind of understanding that asks, 'What really is the problem here?' The first type of understanding tends to be the standard cognitive kind that you can work with in your conscious mind. But there's a deeper level that's more fundamental—and more rewarding. Instead of calling it 'understanding,' I would call this deeper level 'knowing.'"

When Otto asked about this "knowing" and how it arises, Arthur responded, "This inner knowing comes from here," pointing to his heart. "Every one of us has experienced this in different ways, consciously or unconsciously."

In response to Joseph asking how this would work for managers and leaders who are under enormous pressure to act fast, Arthur replied that the kind of observation he was referring to "might take days or hours or fractions of a second in martial arts, or in sports. My point is that if you do the knee-jerk thing, you're overlaying a stock solution on a new situation. In this country, managers think that a fast decision is what counts. If the situation is new, slowing down is necessary. Slow down. Observe. Position yourself. Then act fast and with a natural flow that comes from the inner knowing. You have to slow down long enough to really see what's needed. With a freshness of vision, you have the possibility of a freshness of action, and the overall response on a collective level can be much quicker than trying to implement hasty decisions that aren't compelling to people."

A Second Type of Learning

Eventually, with the help of stories like those of Vision Guatemala and Otto's experience with the fire, we began to see that Arthur was talking about a "second type" of learning, in which the future becomes more active. From John Dewey on, theorists have argued that we learn from the past through cycles of action and reflection that lead to new actions. But Arthur was pointing to a different type of learning process where we learn instead from a future that has not yet happened and from continually discovering our part in bringing that future to pass. Learning based on the past suffices when the past is a good guide to the future. But it leaves us blind to profound shifts when whole new forces shaping change arise.

Dewey's original articulation of the learning cycle involved four stages: "observe," "discover," invent" (new actions), and "produce" (those actions). Since then, academics and consultants have developed many versions of the Dewey learning cycle. While these versions differ in terminology and particular details from Dewey's original, they remain true to Dewey's original intent of characterizing what happens in learning from past experience—as do virtually all models of sustaining learning based on past experience in working teams and in larger organizational units.[4] The same is true for common models of organizational change. For example, models of "planned change" typically involve three stages: gather information, following due diligence procedures; decide what you want to do, making decisions and enrolling people in the decision; and follow through, monitoring and adjusting as you go.[5]

But as Adam Kahane says, most change processes are superficial because they don't generate the depth of understanding and commitment that is required for sustaining change in truly demanding circumstances. Planning, deciding, and monitoring and controlling the ensuing process may be all that are needed in situations where change is essentially about reacting to new circumstances but, says Kahane, "when you're facing very difficult issues or dilemmas, when very different people need to align in very complex settings, and when the future might really be very different from the past, a different process is required."

For several years, Joseph had talked about this different process as "sensing and actualizing new realities prior to their emerging."[6] At the same time, Otto had been developing a theory of different levels of perception and change, using the image of a "U" to distinguish different depths of perceiving reality and different levels of action that follow from that.[7] In Arthur's terms, the process entails three major stages or elements: "Observe, observe, observe"—become one with the world; "retreat and reflect"—allow the inner knowing to emerge; "act swiftly, with a natural flow." We have come to call these sensing, presencing, and realizing.

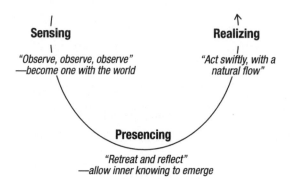

Sensing

The three basic aspects of this U movement are extensions of what happens in all learning processes. That's why they bear a superficial similarity to standard models of planned change. In a sense, more superficial learning and change processes are abbreviated versions of the U movement. Most change efforts, for example, don't move very far "down the U" because little deeper sensing occurs. Gathering information doesn't necessarily imply either suspending habitual ways of seeing or redirecting our attention to sense what is happening from within a situation or phenomenon, rather than from outside. It's quite possible to simply gather information that confirms our preexisting assumptions—indeed it's common.[8] We "download our mental models," as Otto says, and see what we're prepared to see. In a sense, what we're seeing is our past, in the form of our mental models reflecting past experience. Even when we do suspend and see freshly, there's no guarantee that we will see our own connection to what exists already. By contrast, Arthur talked about not imposing preestablished frameworks, even tacitly, and immersing yourself in the reality of the situation until ultimately you become "one with the situation."

Presencing

Likewise, the depth of what happens in "sensing," moving down the U, shapes what happens thereafter. Standard theories of change revolve around making decisions, determining "the vision," and very often acting through a charismatic figure who can command people's "commitment to the vision." But Arthur spoke of reaching a state of clarity about and connection to what is emerging, to an "inner knowing" where, "in a sense, there is no decision making. What to do just becomes obvious," and what is achieved "depends on where you're coming from and who you are as a person." The rational calculus model of decision making and following through pays little attention to the inner state of the decision maker.

The state at the bottom of the U is *presencing*—seeing from the deepest source and becoming a vehicle for that source. When we suspend and redirect our attention, perception starts to arise from within the living process of the whole. When we are presencing, it moves further, to arise from the highest future possibility that connects self and whole. The real challenge in understanding presencing lies not in its abstractness but in the subtlety of the experience.

For example, as Otto stood in front of his burning home, all his habitual thoughts stunned into suspension, he experienced a subtle progression. When he realized that virtually everything that had defined him was gone, his habitual sense of identity started to shift. Yet he knew he was still there. Then, "as my gaze sank deeper into the flames, the flames also seemed to sink into me." This is redirecting—moving from seeing the details to accessing the imaginative capacity to see the living whole of the fire and the self.

At that point he felt himself dropping to a still deeper level: "At that moment, time slowed to complete stillness and I felt drawn in a direction above my physical body and began watching the whole scene from that other place. I felt my mind expanding to a moment of unparalleled clarity of awareness. I realized that I was not the person I thought I was." Otto realized that he was not attached to "the tons of stuff now smoldering inside the ruins" and that "I, my true Self, was still alive—more alive, more awake, more acutely present than ever before."

Then, he added, "At that moment, with everything gone, I suddenly felt released and free to encounter that other part of myself, the part that drew me into the future—into my future—and into a world that I might bring into reality with my life."

For Otto, this was the experience of presencing in that particular moment. For others, it may be different. Peter speaks of "totally forgetting myself" sometimes when speaking with groups. "I am the audience, and they are me. When this happens, I know with certainty that whatever arises is exactly what needs to arise at that moment." Reflecting on the profound silence that followed Ronalth Ochaeta's story of the bones of the unborn children, the Vision Guatemala team members said that it was as if there were "a spirit in the room" or "a moment of communion," which led to their later success. Joseph felt a "heightened sense of awareness and a panoramic sense of knowing" in Baja when "boundaries between animals and me, and seemingly all the larger world, were collapsing. Out of this profound opening of the heart, all my past commitments were released. I was about to discover what I would be doing in the next phase of my life."

In effect, presencing constitutes a third type of seeing, beyond seeing external reality and beyond even seeing from within the living whole. It is seeing from within the source from which the future whole is emerging, peering back at the present from the future. In these moments, we can feel linked to our highest future possibility and destiny. The source of intention shifts from our past to a future that depends on us, as Otto says, "from your historical self, your desires and needs, to your Self with a capital 'S' as your highest future possibility." The bottom of the U is where, in Joseph's words, you discover "who you really are as a servant or steward for what's needed in the world. This is the 'inner knowing' Arthur is talking about. Then, once you see what's needed of you, you act spontaneously."

We chose the term "presencing" to describe this state because it is about becoming totally present—to the larger space or field around us, to an expanded sense of self, and, ultimately, to what is emerging through us.

Realizing

Moving up the U involves bringing something new into reality, just as in the standard model of learning—but this action comes from a source that's deeper than the rational mind. Arthur's analogy to martial arts ("If you have to think in the martial arts, you're dead") emphasizes the importance of the ability to act in a natural flow. As one interviewee put it, "It's almost as if I'm watching myself in action. I'm both engaged and simultaneously detached. When that happens, I know there will be magic."

In part, the magic comes from the capacity to sense something new and act instantaneously in accordance with what that felt knowledge dictates. By contrast, the chronic shortcoming of many planned change efforts is blind adherence to "the plan."[9] The magic also arises because our awareness is expanded and the source of our intention has shifted. Just as moving down the U requires refraining from imposing preestablished frameworks, moving up from the bottom of the U involves not imposing our will. As Joseph puts it, "Operating from this larger intention brings into play forces one could never tap from just trying to impose our will on a situation."

We also realized that people moving up the U do not feel alone. They feel connected to one another and to the world. The most basic distinction between the theory of the U and the way we usually try to produce change lies, as Otto put it, in "the relationship between us, as observers and as actors, and the world in which we operate." At its essence, the theory of the U poses a question: "What does it mean to act in the world and not on the world?" In the standard model, the change leader or leaders are separate from what they're seeking to change. For example, executives seek to "change their organization," as if it were an entity separate from themselves. They then find themselves frustrated when others resist the planned changes, again externalizing the difficulty. Indeed, the very terms "change program" or "rolling out the change initiative" imply the imposition of human will on a presumed external reality.

But the U theory suggests a different stance of "cocreation" between the individual or collective and the larger world. The self and the world are inescapably interconnected. The self doesn't react to a reality outside, nor does it create something new in isolation—rather, like the seed of a tree, it becomes the gateway for the coming into being of a new world. Ultimately, it becomes impossible to say, "I'm doing this" or "We're doing this" because the experience is one of unbroken awareness and action. This sensibility was beautifully expressed more than two thousand years ago in the *Bhagavad Gita*: "All actions are wrought by the qualities of nature only. The self, deluded by egoism, thinketh: 'I am the doer.'"[10]

7.

The Eye of the Needle:
Letting Go and Letting Come

In ancient Jerusalem, there was a gate called "the needle" which was so narrow that when a fully loaded camel approached it, the camel driver had to take off all the bundles before the camel could pass through. Referring obliquely to this well-known image of his day, Jesus said, "It is easier for a camel to go through the eye of a needle than for a rich man to enter the kingdom of God."[1]

At the bottom of the U lies a sort of inner gate, which likewise requires us to drop the baggage we've acquired on our journey. As we move through it, we begin to see from within the source of what is emerging, letting it come into being through us. Some of our interviewees described this inner gate as a "membrane" or a "threshold." Some even saw it as a type of death-and-rebirth cycle: letting go and surrendering belong to the death part of this cycle, while the coming into presence of a different sense of self seems to belong to the early stages of a new birth. When this "threshold" is crossed collectively, people offer many different accounts of the experience. Some talk about extraordinary creativity, some about almost boundless energy, yet others about a dialogue where people forget who is saying what as the flow of discovery seems to gather everyone together. Many simply say that what happens cannot be understood rationally because something that appears impossible has occurred—like a camel passing through the eye of the needle.

A Question from the Heart

In 1998, two of the largest companies in the world had just completed a massive merger of two key operating units. Now the new company, made up of two former competitors, had to compete against others, and there were many reasons to doubt its success. The seriousness of the challenges facing them led the CEO to appoint a team made up of managers from all the key business units, along with Joseph and Otto as external participants. Their task was to design a process that would develop leaders who could enable the existing businesses to compete effectively as well as create new businesses.

The team worked together for four months. Still, on the last day of the last scheduled meeting, the design for the leadership development process had yet to be completed. The chief learning officer and formal leader of the team was scheduled to present the design to the CEO the next day and request the necessary funding for implementation. The design had to be ready to go by the end of the day—which at that point was just three hours away. Despite the importance of the task, there was a total lack of creativity among the participants, even though everyone knew that creativity was exactly what was needed. If the meeting ended with no compelling design, the whole project would be seen as a failure.

As the anxiety grew, the atmosphere became increasingly tense. Then a normally quiet and reserved deputy head of one of the major business units named Dave stood up and faced the group. The passion and vulnerability in his voice made it clear that what he had to say took courage. Looking at the charts on the wall that summarized the group's work, he said, "I'm really struggling here. I think I truly understand the pieces, but I just can't complete the whole picture." Turning to Otto, he asked, "Can you help me? Can you explain this to me? If we can just see that whole, we'll have the breakthrough we need."

Otto didn't respond, in part because he didn't have an immediate answer to Dave's question and in part because he did not want to disturb the deepening silence. For a moment everyone was still. No one in the group had ever asked for help quite like this before. Then Joseph looked at the people sitting around the room and said, "You know, I think what's been missing is our willingness to speak and listen from the heart." After a pause, another team member said, "I think we could create any change we wanted to if the sort of personal courage Dave just demonstrated guided our everyday actions." During the ensuing hour, "everyone in the room seemed to begin speaking from a deeper source," said Joseph. "The design for the entire program became clear, seemingly without effort. What had seemed impossible just before took shape as if in an instant."

Although many in the group didn't know what to make of what had happened, the experience was powerful. "It was as if the pattern underlying the design had been there all along but we were so caught up in the details we just couldn't see it," said one participant later. "It was one of the most productive hours of collaborative work I've ever experienced," said another. In the ensuing months, the new leadership development process, dubbed "the Leadership Lab," inspired a major change in two key business units that were starting to show promising results. Two years later, each of them went from "worst to first" in performance ratings. And just as important, Dave and several others had discovered, as he said, "the energy and excitement that came from being able to go to this different place in ourselves. It allowed us to know where we needed to go—and to get there."

Surrendering Control

Getting to the "different place" that allows presencing to occur begins as we develop a capacity to let go and surrender our perceived need to control. Varela identified letting go as the third "basic gesture," after suspending and redirecting, in enhancing awareness: "Usually it's life that makes you let go. Sickness, danger, the disappointment of love— something extreme forces you into that gesture of letting it go, letting it be." But he also believed that letting go was a capacity that could be developed.

Suspension allows us to be more aware of what our habitual thoughts are, as we simply step back and notice them. Redirection opens up new levels of awareness by moving beyond the subject-object duality that normally separates us from our reality. But it is easy to become attached to that new awareness: perhaps because it is pleasant, perhaps because it's unpleasant, perhaps because it's novel, or simply because it feels "right." Regardless of the causes, the attachment takes us out of the present moment. Continually letting go keeps bringing us back to the here and now.

Developing the capacity to let go allows us to be open to what is emerging and to practice what Buddhism and other meditative traditions call "nonattachment." In Buddhist theory, two Sanskrit terms, *vitarka* and *vicara*, are used to describe the subtle attachments of mind. *Vitarka* characterizes the state of "seeking," when our attention is attached to what we're trying to make happen. *Vicara* characterizes the state of "watching," when, even though we're not trying to force something to happen, we're still attached to an outcome we are waiting for. With either, our mental attachment makes us blind or resistant to other aspects of what is happening right now. Overcoming the traps of *vitarka* and *vicara* requires continual letting go.

When Dave asked the simple, honest question—"Can you help me see the whole?"—he let go of his attachment to whatever expectations he had had of what their company's leadership development program should look like. He also let go of any attachment he had to his image in the group as someone who didn't need help. In a sense, he spoke for the larger group and enabled many others to let go of the preconceived notions they held. By letting go, they could allow something truly new to emerge.

Primary Knowing

Letting go extends the dissolution of subject-object awareness that starts with redirecting, opening the way for a larger awareness, including, ultimately, a sense of what is emerging. Philosophers have explored letting go for thousands of years, but several among our interviewees brought modern scientific perspectives to bear in understanding this shift—people such as Francisco Varela and Eleanor Rosch, professor of cognitive psychology at the University of California at Berkeley.

Rosch is well-known for her work on color perception and categories, which demonstrates the limitation of traditional notions of formal, independent categories in a world where "nothing is independent." But in the midst of a very successful academic career, she began "unhappily poking around, asking myself, 'Is there any other way to do psychology?'" Eventually this exploration led her to Buddhism, Taoism, meditation, and, some twenty years ago, to a feeling that she was pursuing something that could "remake psychology."

In their interview, Otto asked her to elaborate on her comment that science needs to be performed with the "mind of wisdom." Rosch responded that this need wasn't limited to scientists. "What executives do is not that fundamentally different from what artists do. Great artists naturally operate from this other level and always have." This "other level" entails a different sort of knowing, what is called in Tibetan Buddhism "wisdom awareness." Such knowing, said Rosch, is based on the view that "mind and world are not separate." Buddhism, she explained, "has no self built into it. You don't have independently existing selves or objects. They're codependent."

But the Buddhist theory of the unity of mind and world is alien to Western thought, and developing the ability to talk about it took Rosch a long time. Eventually she concluded that saying "mind and world are not separate" was not enough. Today she starts by distinguishing two types of knowing: "analytic knowing" and "primary knowing."

In the "analytic picture offered by the cognitive sciences, the world consists of separate objects and states of affairs, the human mind is a determinate machine which, in order to know, isolates and identifies those objects and events, finds the simplest possible predictive contingencies between them, stores the results through time in memory, relates the items in memory to each other such that they form a coherent but indirect representation of the world and oneself, and retrieves those representations in order to fulfill the only originating value, which is to survive and reproduce in an evolutionarily successful manner."[2]

By contrast, "primary knowing" arises by means of "interconnected wholes, rather than isolated contingent parts and by means of time-less, direct, presentation" rather than through stored "re-presentation." "Such knowing is open rather than determinate, and a sense of uncon-ditional value, rather than conditional usefulness, is an inherent part of the act of knowing itself," said Rosch. Acting from such awareness is "spontaneous, rather than the result of decision making," and it is "compassionate . . . since it is based on wholes larger than the self." [3]

As Rosch told Otto, all these attributes—timeless, direct, sponta-neous, open, unconditional value, and compassionate—go together as one thing. That one thing is what some in Tibetan Buddhism call "the natural state" and what Taoism calls "the Source."[4]

"It's what is 'at the heart of the heart of the heart.' When we're con-nected to that source, things become more and more integrated as a path—with intention, body, and mind coming together rather than being all over the place," she said.

According to Rosch's theory, primary knowing is possible because mind and world are aspects of the same underlying field. When we begin to connect to the source, perception arises "from the whole field. The notion of 'field' was the closest thing I could come up with-in our current sciences to describe this phenomenon.

"Think of everything happening as moment-by-moment presenta-tions from this deep heart source that has a knowing dimension to it. Tibetan Buddhism talks about emptiness, luminosity, and the knowing capacity as inseparable. That knowing capacity actually is the field knowing itself, in a sense, or this larger context knowing itself."

The problem is that most of us have spent our lives immersed in analytic knowing, with its dualistic separation of subject ("I") and object ("it"). There's nothing wrong with analytic knowing. It's useful and appropriate for many activities—for example, for interacting with machines. But if it's our only way of knowing, we'll tend to apply it in all situations.

When we interact with a living system from the analytic stance, problems inevitably arise because the living field "doesn't know itself." "A field that doesn't know itself collapses into this little unidimensional subject-object consciousness, which is how we go galloping about the world." The consequence is action uninformed by the whole. Rosch believes that lacking that connection to the source, "or being ignorant of it, we just make terrible messes, as individuals, and as nations and cultures."

The Alien Self

As a living field, in Rosch's terms, comes to "know itself," our identification with the "localized self" diminishes, and a broader and more generative sense of self begins to arise. It's not that personal awareness ceases, nor does does this loss of identification with the localized self mean a loss of personal responsibility. But there is a shift in the locus of awareness. This is what Dave called "going to this different place in ourselves."

Our interviewees had different ways of characterizing this expansion or "decentering" of the experience of self. Varela spoke of the "virtual" or "fragile self" as a way of helping us "get closer to understanding what it means to be a subject," to experience our personal, subjective point of view. A subject "is not a stable, solid entity," he said. In coping with continually changing circumstances, the self is constantly "updating itself or renewing itself. . . . So virtuality is not just an absence of a central self; it also has that kind of *fragile flotation* of coming and going."

This process, explained Varela, is like a constant reframing of yourself into what seems to be more real in each emerging moment. "You know, the paradox of being more real means to be much more virtual and therefore less substantial and less determined."

He added, "A life of wisdom consists of being constantly engaged in that letting go, and letting the virtuality or the fragility of the self manifest itself. When you are with somebody who really has that capacity to a full-blown level, it affects you. When you meet those kinds of people, you enter into a kind of resonance with them. You relax—there's something very enjoyable about that way of being. There's a joy in that kind of life.

"A fully developed human being is presencing constantly. . . . It's to be there where things happen. But it's something that clearly cannot be done if there's a little me there that's saying, 'Oh, I'm manifesting presencing.'"

Ryosoke Ohashi, a scholar of Japan's leading twentieth-century Zen philosopher, Kitaro Nishida,[5] used the word "alien self" to describe what arises when the localized sense of self fades: "Something which is quite alien to me enables my existence." Eastern traditions often label this "nothingness": "This nothingness enables my existence and also my relation with all." But "in traditional Christian terminology, this absolute alienness could be said to be God. God is in me— although Nishida doesn't directly say 'God.' But something that is quite alien to me is in my own self."

Stanford's Michael Ray considers the shift in sense of self central to creativity. He believes that the key to helping students access their deeper sources of creativity can be found in two questions: "Who is my Self?" and "What is my Work?" When we talk about "Self," said Ray, "we're talking about your higher self, your divinity, your highest future potential. And by asking 'What is my Work?,' we're asking what is the purpose of your existence or what are you meant to be."

Varela added that the decentered self spontaneously transforms one's relations with others. "The more the fragile self-subject deploys itself, the more compassion deploys itself. . . . there's the opening of space to accommodate or to take care of the other." In the decenteredness, "the other appears closer. Solidarity, compassion, care, love—all of the different modes of being together—appear when the self is decentered. Now that, to me, is a great gift of the universe. Since we're not solid and private and centered, the more we're who we are . . . [there are] both you and I. Not just me, but the 'usness' in us."

The birth of the decentered self is not without its problems. Since the normal localized self is our vehicle for making sense of most of our experience, transcending this self can be profoundly disorienting, and when it happens, people often have great difficulty describing the experience. The localized self can find the decentered, fragile self impossible to grasp and will try to reduce it to its own terms. Even for those who try, describing this experience can be difficult. Talking to Joseph long after the original leadership development design workshop, Dave said, "I've talked to many people about what it feels like to be in this different state—the body feelings, where your ears are ringing, and you have a heightened sense of awareness, and everything around you seems to slow down. You're literally reading people's thoughts as they talk to you. It's as if people are one as they're talking.

"When I describe this to people, you can almost see a jolt in their body. Because they're remembering, and they're saying, 'Yes! I've had that experience!' So why did they turn it off? Because they don't know how to express it. Or they're afraid to express it because that's 'hocus-pocus stuff.' But it's so much a part of us. We're just afraid to turn it on because of what people might say about it."

Surrendering into Commitment

As the localized self's grip on our awareness releases, there's a "change in the quality of attention," in Varela's words, "from 'looking for' to 'letting come.'" Here, "surrendering control" evolves into what Joseph calls "surrendering into commitment," the gateway to operating from one's deepest purpose, in concert with a larger whole.

When Joseph and Otto interviewed entrepreneurs and asked them to describe the deeper aspects of their creation journeys and especially why, in spite of all the adversities, they kept going, they all answered that they felt compelled to continue, that they couldn't "not do it." This response points to a type of commitment that's different from an act of willpower in the normal sense.

One way to understand this passage through the eye of the needle is as a continuation of the transformation of the relationship between self and world that begins with sensing. When we start down the left-hand side of the U, we experience the world as something given, something "out there." Gradually, we shift our perception to seeing from inside the living process underlying reality. Then, as we move up the right-hand side of the U, we start to experience the world as unfolding through us. On the left-hand side of the U, the world is "as it is" and later "as it emerges"; on the right-hand side the world is "coming into being through us." Starting down the left-hand side, the self is an observer of this exterior world, which is a creation of the past. Starting up the right-hand side, the self turns into a source through which the future begins to emerge.

The shift involved in moving from one state to another is the mystery that happens at the bottom of the U. This inversion of the relational web of self and world cannot be reduced to words, and people experience it in different ways. This was Otto's shift in awareness at the fire, leading to feeling "released and free." It is Peter's experience that "I am the audience and they are me" and that "something precious is about to be given to us." It is Betty Sue's sense of the emergence of an "already existing yet still-to-be-created design that you are somehow part of." And it is Joseph's "profound opening of the heart."

All these are examples of the third aspect of presencing—the sense of being present to, as Otto puts it, "what is seeking to emerge through me." The intentionality of what is emerging implied in this statement mirrors another observation of Rosch's. Speaking of her experiences as a longtime meditator and student of Buddhism and Taoism, Rosch observed, "If you follow your nature enough, if you follow your nature as it moves, if you follow so far that you really let go, then you find that you're actually the original being, the original way of being. . . . The original being knows things and acts, does things in its own way. It actually has a great intention to be itself, and it will do so if you just let it."

Referring to the Taoist notion of Source, Rosch said, "There's this awareness, this little spark, which is completely independent of all the things that we think are so important—achievement or nonachievement, even being alive or dead, or awake or asleep. This supposed world actually radiates from that. This is the way things happen, and in the light of that, action becomes action that supports the whole, action that includes everything and does everything that's needed."

Action that originates from this connection with Source appears "without conscious control—even without the sense of 'me' doing it—a spontaneous product of the whole." And such action, said Rosch, "can be shockingly effective."[6]

8.

The Wedding

May 2001

Whenever we had the opportunity in the following weeks, we talked about experiences of the mysterious reversal at the bottom of the U, especially when it happened collectively.

During one meeting on Maple Avenue, Otto told us a story about a health care project he'd been working on for several years with his colleague Ursula Versteegen in the Main region north of Frankfurt, Germany. This area, with a population of about 300,000 people, is served by a variety of private health care systems overseen by the German government's Gesundheitsministerium, or health care ministry. Ursula and Otto had been working with a network of physicians who wanted to innovate and improve emergency care service. As with health care professionals around the world, this group was under enormous stress to manage costs and quality, but behind these problems were deeper questions. What really was their purpose? Were they there to just "patch people up"? Or were they truly committed to physical, mental, and emotional health? And is this even possible in today's hectic and stressful world?

"We began the project by conducting more than one hundred and thirty interviews over several months with both patients and physicians, focused mainly on the doctor-patient relationship," Otto related. "Then we invited the people we'd interviewed to come to a weekend meeting to look at the results. The meeting was held in an old school in the regional capital. Almost one hundred people showed up.

"We had organized our findings from the interviews around four different levels at which doctors and patients can, potentially, relate.

"The first level of the doctor-patient relationship is simply transactional. If I'm a patient with a broken part, the doctor is like a mechanic, there to fix my broken part. So, for example, one of the interviewees said, 'I'm coming with a problem, and he must solve my problem. My role is that I need help. The role of my doctor is that he provides that help.'

"The second level involves a different kind of relationship in which the focus is not just on the broken part but also on how that brokenness is related to behavior. At this level, the physician relates differently to me as a patient, in that I must change my behavior. For example, the doctor gives me a certain diet or a list of 'do's' and 'don'ts.' One patient said, 'Does it always have to be a pharmaceutical treatment? No, not for me. I want to be told, 'It's your attitude—you must change your behavior. You must do more for yourself.'

"Then, on a deeper level, the doctor might help patients reflect on why they are behaving as they are. On that level, the doctor is a coach who creates an environment that helps patients to reflect on the assumptions that might lie behind their behavior. Another patient told us, 'When you don't consider life as a gift, than you become sick—and are forced to think.' Many told us, 'Oh, I didn't realize how important life is. You take it for granted.'

"But in a few cases, we also found that there was a fourth level of relationship, which we weren't quite sure how to describe initially. It seems to be related to 'who I, the patient, am—my uniqueness as a person.' At this level, the real changes might require letting go of an old identity and entering into a new identity. At that level, the doctor and patient enter a relationship of mutual influence and vulnerability, each open to discovering themselves. For example, one patient told us, 'I'm somebody who never got sick. And then all of a sudden I had cancer. I used to be the entertainer everywhere, I worked hard, I was a member of various committees, and I just neglected the fact that I was sick. I only learned at the age of fifty-eight to say "No." Before, I was always ready to go. I always functioned. I didn't even realize that I'd lost my identity on the way down. I'm not concerned about my future anymore. Today is what is important to me. Now.' 'There are times when I really feel like I'm making a difference,' said one doctor. 'These aren't the times when I just prescribe something or repair something, but when there's a quality of conversation in which both the patient and I see something truly new, something that really proves to have a healing quality.'

"At the weekend meeting, we organized the participants into small groups to discuss what these levels meant to them. Then we gave them little sticky dots and asked them to put a red dot on the level of doctor-patient relationship that represented their personal experience of the current system and a green dot on the one that they wanted the reality to be. When the voting was over, more than ninety-five percent of all the red dots were at level one and two, and ninety-five percent of the green dots were at three and four. When that picture became obvious, the room grew very, very quiet.

"We pointed out that as patients and physicians, almost everyone seemed to want the same thing—to operate on level three or four—but that what they collectively produced was levels one and two. 'But,' we told them 'the system isn't something out there—you're the system. The system is what you enact.'

"Then a guy in the middle of the room got up. It turned out that he was the mayor. He said that he was encountering the same thing in his administration—all they were doing was reacting and fixing broken parts on levels one and two, and they were unable to move politics into levels three and four.

"When the mayor sat down, a woman stood up and said that she was a teacher at the school—and there it was exactly the same story. She said that all they did was to organize the learning process around level one or level two, 'pouring dead bodies of knowledge into empty barrels'—they weren't really able to get to these deeper levels of knowing that release people's awareness of who they are. True education on these deeper levels means not to fill a barrel but to 'light a flame.'

"Then a farmer stood up and said that it was the same in farming. 'All we do is fix the soil with our fertilizers, repairing what we think is broken in order to get the production we want.' He talked about how the whole conventional farming mentality arises from treating the land with an industrial age, mechanical input-output view of production. 'There's no deep appreciation of the earth or of the need to work with it, to enhance the quality of the soil. But the earth is something alive—it has its own life.' He talked about how it's possible for people and the land to cocreate the food that we need but how that doesn't happen today. 'We don't conceive of a farm as a living whole, as an ecology. We see it as a level one or two mechanical thing,' he said.

"That was the way the whole morning conversation went. One person after another talked, and gradually there was a huge, collective reframing—not just for individual people, but for the community as a whole."

Otto paused.

"Otto," Peter said, "I could almost feel what was about to happen in your story when you described the group looking at all the red and green dots. What felt most familiar was the quiet you described. Then, when people took turns speaking, I could almost feel a sort of field coming into existence, something that gathered up everyone and all of those problems and which gradually revealed itself as the deeper generative source."

"I like the way you put that," Otto replied, "that in these situations you feel a field that gathers everyone up. That is precisely what Eleanor Rosch was talking about when she described the 'field knowing itself' and 'developing according to its own nature.' Clearly, something had shifted in that room. It's very hard to say what it was, exactly—after all, there were only a hundred people in this meeting—yet you could feel the presence of a much larger system."

Peter nodded. "And that larger system included much of human history. It was remarkable how inclusive that new awareness became. It went way beyond the health care system. When people stood and spoke, they basically recapitulated, in reverse order, the history of social systems. First they spoke about the health care system, which is relatively recent. Then they worked back to the older systems of governing and educating and, finally, to the very earliest system humans invented, our system of food production. Not only did the deep pattern of operating at level one or two in all facets of the current health care system show up, but the same pattern showed up in most aspects of our current way of living. It amazes me how 'the whole of things' can emerge, almost magically, in the midst of something very concrete and immediate, like the problem of how a particular group of doctors and patients can relate better. This is surely Goethe's whole 'presencing itself in the parts,' with deeper patterns revealing themselves through 'the concrete particulars.'"

"For me, this was an indication of just how deeply that community was listening," said Betty Sue. "The more clearly we 'see' the specific system and our part in creating it, the more clearly we also see how the specific system mirrors the deeper systems as well.

"But Otto, this story raises a question I've been struggling with. What really happens at the bottom of the U? Moving down the U is about slowing and quieting so that we can truly sense or take in what is happening around us. Moving up the U is all about bringing the new into being, about realizing and cocreating. Obviously, there's a major shift between these two that somehow occurs at the bottom of the U, and I don't yet see it in your story. Doing the interviews and then bringing all these health care workers together helped everyone sense what was happening. They started to see the whole of the system, the sickness that's so embedded everywhere. And they started to see their part in creating the system as it is.

"Still, at this point, you don't see the future that 'wants to emerge' but only the whole system as it is now, which is all based on the past. So isn't it true that at this point, in a sense, everyone was still looking at the past?"

"Yes, that's true," said Otto. "But your question reminds me of something else that happened. When all the participants in the project saw that they were operating on levels one and two and not on three and four—and not just in the health care system but everywhere—a woman leaned forward and addressed the doctor who'd spoken just before her, saying 'I feel I have to shelter my doctor so that he doesn't get killed in this system.'

"Now, if you know anything about the psychology of doctors in Germany, you know that they have a high aspiration to alleviate suffering, but they operate in a system that makes it difficult for them to do this. They suffer because what they do is so far from their intent—and the patients also suffer because the doctors often treat them poorly. This woman was enacting the doctors' highest aspirations for how they wanted to act in relation to patients. It was such a simple, heartfelt statement that it opened a space in the conversation. Looking back at it now, I think that it offered a glimpse of how this whole system could operate in the future. It was a moment where the collective field shifted from enacting the patterns of the current whole to uncovering an emerging possibility."

"So she, or her statement, was the 'part' of a whole new possible future showing up," said Betty Sue. "In other words, at the bottom of the U, the essence of what might be starts to become real in how we are with one another right now."

"Yes, at the bottom of the U, you start to see the future that wants to emerge as people spontaneously enact new ways of being in the moment. We all have our own experiences of this. For me, when I'm part of a social field that crosses the threshold at the bottom of the U, it feels as if I'm participating in the birth of a new world. It's a profound, quieting experience in that I feel as if I've been touched by eternal beauty. There's a deep opening of my higher Self. The movement 'upwards' is caused by what begins to come into being through that opening."

"And this newness starts to be evident by what is happening in that moment," added Betty Sue.

"Yes," Otto replied. "And at this point, crystallizing this larger intent into concrete visions for action can really be quite simple.

The visions don't have to be perfect. They just need to be enough to get started.

"For example, later on that same day we said, 'Okay, everybody can see that we're producing levels one and two. So what initiatives could we undertake that would bring us from one and two to three and four? If there aren't any, we'll just close the session here.'

"Before long people began to suggest ideas, and by the end of the afternoon, several groups had committed to working together. The projects they formed—including a highly innovative emergency care system—have contributed significantly to the ongoing health development of this region over the four years since the original weekend forum. I recently asked one of the senior health care executives in the region, who was not involved in the original group, why an idea that many experts had regarded as good, but unlikely to succeed, had, in fact, succeeded. He said that there is a highly committed core group of a hundred physicians, practitioners, and patients who bring a quality of intention that has radiated over time to affect 'the consciousness of all the decision makers in the system.'

"Of course, at the time of our initial weekend meeting, none of this could have been foreseen—but you could feel the larger intention that was present," added Otto. "The day after the doctor-patient forum, Ursula and I and the core group of doctors met to clean up the schoolroom we'd been using. We were joined by some patients who'd shown up, unasked, to help. It was like the morning after a big, wild party, when you're hanging out, tired but elated, and ready for whatever happens next.

"With all the help, we finished the cleanup a little ahead of time. Someone saw a chair in a nice sunny spot next to some trees at the entrance area of the school and sat down with a cup of coffee. Another person pulled up a chair and joined in. Soon we were all sitting in a loosely structured circle. Someone volunteered to get the leftovers from the kitchen. When they returned, the grill was already lit, and we joined together to share an impromptu meal.

"I asked the woman next to me what she thought of the forum the day before. She told me she had been very touched by it.

"'Touched by what?' I asked.

"'Well, in a way, I experienced the day like a wedding,' she said.

"A wedding! I couldn't believe it. She had found the perfect words to describe a subtle level of experience that I'd been unable to express. The day had truly been about joining two separate elements of a larger field—the doctors and the patients together in a health care system—in a way that strengthened both and opened possibilities for each. I turned to look at our little wedding party and for a moment felt everything slowing; it was as if a thick, warm light was pouring down upon and around us, linking us in an invisible bond, head to head and heart to heart. The presence of this slowing and quieting light was more real than words can say."

We were quiet for a moment. Then Joseph remarked, "It amazes me how many of the people we've interviewed have described similar experiences. It may just be that part of the process of moving through the bottom of the U is becoming aware of the incredible beauty of life itself, of becoming reenchanted with the world.

"While you were talking, I was thinking that the difference between moving down the U and presencing is that when you are moving down the U, seeing and suspending, your awareness is limited to the current field. Presencing opens and connects you with a larger, underlying field that goes beyond what exists now and opens up this great power and beauty."

"But paradoxically, this requires looking inside, and sometimes groups aren't ready to do that," said Otto. "Moving down the U does not guarantee that you will move up. Some groups hit a real wall and aren't able to quit looking outside themselves, at their 'external' world. They must begin to see, as Joseph says, from the point of view of the higher self and a larger intention, which is always conscious of who you are, and what your work is."

"And when you do that, when you discover what you're here for, the forces of nature also operate in your service," said Joseph. "Then, as you move back up the U, all sorts of things start to happen that aid in the realization of your aims, things you had no right to expect. Somehow, when you're acting from this place, you're not alone—and I think this is just as true for a collective as for an individual."

"Here's where all the weird stuff starts happening," said Betty Sue with a laugh. "When you see what you're here for, the world begins to mirror your purpose in a magical way. It's almost as if you suddenly find yourself on a stage in a play that was written expressly for you."

Part 3

Becoming
a Force of Nature

9.

In the Corridor of Dreams

September 2001

It was early September before we met again on Maple Avenue, but the hiatus didn't seem to matter. As we reflected on the events of the summer, we began to see that what we'd been talking about—sensing, presencing, and realizing a "future that depended upon us"—was now happening in our own lives. Our journey "up the U" was starting to draw us to powerful places and unexpected partners, and the seeds of new initiatives were beginning to make themselves evident. We also discovered that realizing requires continual sensing and presencing: the core capabilities for moving down the U become even more important as new partners join in, and the world and our awareness evolve.

Our conversation eventually turned to three separate meetings held in late June, mid-August, and late August. Though planned separately, they became elements of a single development. In June, Peter and Joseph had met with a group of senior executives from the SoL network for a long weekend of reflection and conversation in the colonial whaling village of Marblehead, Massachusetts. Six weeks later they were together again at the annual SoL Executive Champions' Workshop (ECW) in Stowe, Vermont. And at the close of the summer, Otto and Joseph joined Adam Kahane, Brian Arthur, and several others at John Milton's Sacred Land Trust in south central Colorado, a meeting that sharpened the vision that had crystallized over the summer.

"We had convened in Marblehead to assess SoL's development as a global network," Peter told Otto and Betty Sue. "Many of the founding members were there, including Joseph and me, along with newer members from countries developing learning communities. Only about half the group knew one other in advance, but their shared experience building learning-oriented organizational cultures established a strong connection—so strong that people quickly fell into an open dialogue about what they sensed was happening, not just in the SoL network but in the world."

"The opening conversation was extremely powerful," Joseph agreed. "Every person spoke straight from the heart about the deep fear they were experiencing. They said things like 'We're living in unprecedented times' and that for the first time, they were 'afraid' in the face of the hostility to globalization and the 'imperial size of corporations.' One of the first people to speak said, 'We talk about the digital divide that separates those participating in the global economy from those who are excluded. But this is a kind of sanitized way to talk about the real divide—the social divide—which increasingly separates the haves from the have-nots.'

"Another said his senior leadership is deeply concerned, and added, 'We're actually terrified. Much of the world lives in poverty—the world is splitting apart. The growing social divide can make continued global economic development impossible if it's not rectified.'"

"They all seemed to sense a pervasive unsustainability in our present situation," Peter agreed. "I recall one person saying that senior company officers were dismayed at the extraordinarily dangerous position they find themselves in. He said it was like being in the middle of a game of chess where 'every decision is crucial. Things turn on a dime and the clock is ticking. It's an eerie feeling.'

"Another talked about the 'blatantly unsustainable requirements by Wall Street' that all corporations continually grow at the highest rate possible. And someone else said, 'We all know it's unsustainable. What will it take to redefine business growth so it's consistent with nature, and consistent with life?'"

"When it was my turn to check in," said Joseph, "I was surprised to find myself spontaneously restating what had been said in those final hours in Baja about the state of the world. I told the group about the requiem scenario and why it seemed important. 'If we don't start to recognize the seriousness of our predicament,' I said, 'it could become a self-fulfilling prophecy. But if we do, I truly believe that a profound shift of the whole could start within our own generation.'"

"That opening conversation set the tone for the two days," continued Peter. "Several people commented that they felt as if they'd been called to Marblehead to speak openly about what they were seeing in the world. At the end of the meeting, the group decided to create a joint statement of their concerns that they could share within their companies. They wanted people to see what peers in other leading multinational businesses were thinking and feeling about the state of the world."

"I read that letter on the SoL web site," said Betty Sue. "I was surprised that they would address topics like these so candidly. I worry that as fear and distrust grow, the possibilities for positive collaborative inquiry also diminish. But I was heartened by the fact that people from at least some major corporations can talk openly about such complex problems."

Peter nodded. "I was stunned by how clearly they articulated problems and how intensely this group felt about the urgency of the situation. Something new is happening when senior corporate executives—and these were very pragmatic and well informed people—have issues like these at the front of their minds.

"Since the meeting, I've shared the Marblehead letter[1] with many groups. Almost everyone can identify with what is expressed there. These are not the sorts of words that come out of corporate PR departments or show up in official business roundtable meetings. They are words that come from honest people who trust one another, giving voice to their deepest concerns. Indeed, simply enabling leaders of all sorts to talk honestly with one another may be the most urgent need.

"The letter they eventually wrote concluded by stating: 'Complex, interdependent issues such as these are increasingly shaping the context for strategy. Yet the pressures created by these very issues tend to keep leaders in a continual "doing" mode, with little or no time for reflection and real thinking. We believe that there is a greater need than ever for leaders to meet and genuinely "think together"—the real meaning of dialogue. Only through creating such opportunities can there be any hope of building the shared understanding and coordinated innovative action that the world desperately needs.'"

"I think a growing number of people believe there are profound flaws in the current process of globalization," added Otto. "But those who are in the middle of the largest global institutions and who see these flaws are still a small minority, and the environment of trust needed to think together about these problems is fragile."

"Yes, you can see a sort of split opening within the corporate

The Marblehead Letter

A natural agenda of issues is shaping the future, especially for corporations with global scope.

- **The social divide:** the ever-widening gap between those participating in the increasingly interdependent global economy and those not.
  How long can 15% of the people get 85% of the benefits of globalization?

- **Redefining growth:** economic growth based on ever increasing material use and discard is inconsistent with a finite world.
  How long can we keep piling up more junk in the same box?

- **Variety and inclusiveness:** developing inclusion as a core competence in increasingly multi-cultural organizations.
  Who is the "we"?

- **Attracting talented people and realizing their potential:** developing commitment in a world of "free agents" and "volunteer" talent.
  What are we committed to, really?

- **The role of the corporation:** extending the traditional role of the corporation, especially the global corporation, to be more commensurate with its impact.
  Just how accountable will society expect us to be?

- **The system seeing itself:** the challenges of coordination and coherence in social systems.
  How can we stop going faster while our ability to see further ahead is decreasing?

June 2001

world, both in how we are with one another and in how we think about the whole global capitalist system," Betty Sue said thoughtfully. "I experienced this quite strongly in a meeting that I facilitated with Adam in late July.

"It was a more heterogeneous executive group than you had in

Marblehead; only some of them had extensive experience with organizational learning and deep change processes. In that sense, they were more representative of the corporate mainstream. The topic of the meeting was sustainable development, and everyone was genuinely interested in being there and working together. But they also struggled with 'sensing together' and being able to speak openly about core issues.

"For example, a chairman of a major multinational spoke after dinner one evening about his corporation's commitment to sustainable development. Afterwards a few of us sitting at one of the tables listened to a very successful African entrepreneur say that he didn't accept what the chairman had said at all, because it completely contradicted his experience of how that company operated in his home country. When we suggested that he raise his concern in the group, he said that he couldn't because it would be 'dangerous.'

"But I think the most telling moment of the meeting for me came when a director of one of the largest firms in the world spontaneously stated that he doubted that the present framework of global capitalism could adapt to the new reality. 'I believe deeper changes will be needed,' he added. When he said that, you could almost feel the room freeze. I don't think people knew how to respond to his comment, especially those who really don't want to consider any alternative to the present system. So no one said anything, and the topic didn't come up again."

"There's no question that one of the greatest needs is how to make it safe enough for people in positions of authority to move down the U," said Otto. "It's no wonder that without achieving real depth in sensing, the opening to our higher Self and the movement into truly innovative action simply doesn't occur. Everyone stays trapped in their mental models and acts—or really reacts—to circumstances based on their programming."

"Seeing with the heart requires opening the heart," said Joseph. "That happened in Marblehead, but it doesn't happen often enough when the stakes are high."

"It's really all about how a real sense of connectedness arises, with one another and with the world," Peter affirmed. "Without that experience of connectedness, real sensing and presencing simply won't occur.

"I also don't think we can underestimate the importance of place in all this. There was something powerful about simply being in a place like Marblehead. We need to rediscover the importance of sacred space, those places that are rich in life energy and potential for connection. And that is exactly why we hold the Executive Champions' Workshop in a special place in northern Vermont.

"The meeting itself is actually held in a large tent in the middle of a beautiful field, with nothing but mountains and trees in all directions. At the end of one of these gatherings, I was sitting with Mieko Nishimizu, the Vice President of the World Bank for South Asia. She was talking about all the meetings she has helped organize for heads of state, finance ministers, and the like. She said, 'People often criticize the lack of imaginative, bold initiatives that arise from such meetings, but if they only saw the process that lies behind the meetings, they would understand.' Then, talking about a particular meeting she remembered, she looked around and said wistfully, 'If only we had been able to meet in a place like this.'"

"Which is exactly what we did a few weeks ago, when we were up there," Joseph jumped in eagerly. "I've been part of the ECW for many years, and it's always been very powerful, but this time there was definitely something unusual in the air."

"What's so magical about this field of yours in Vermont?" asked Betty Sue.

"Well, to understand it you need to know a bit of history, but I think the history is relevant for understanding how sacred spaces develop," Peter replied.

"The tent sits on land owned by the von Trapp family, surrounded by the Green Mountains. There's a special sense of peacefulness about the place. That's the first thing that everyone notices. The story of how the von Trapps escaped from Austria is well-known from the Broadway musical and the movie *The Sound of Music*. What is less well-known is the story of their life in the U.S.

"When the family arrived here in 1938, they had no possessions and no money. They made singing tours that took them back and forth across the U.S. for several years and gradually saved enough to settle down. Of all the places they visited, they liked northern Vermont the most because it reminded them of the land around their native Salzburg. In the summer of 1943, they were looking for a place to buy around Stowe but couldn't find anything they could afford. Their train was scheduled to leave in a day. The children were determined not to leave without finding a home.

"'We set up a small chapel in the broom closet of the inn where we were staying. We prayed around the clock for three days,' Maria, now in her late eighties, recalled with a laugh.[2] 'Each of us—there were eight children, from ages three to twenty-five—prayed for one hour, in rotation. Can you believe it?

"'When the morning to leave came, our father had gone to get ready for our departure. When he returned, he told us that a local farmer had decided to sell his land and that we were going right up there to look at it. When we got out of the car, we all knew that this was our future home. We bought the property that day.'

"Maria is an extraordinary woman, with sparkling eyes and long hair braided in the fashion still common in the Austrian countryside. She eventually became a missionary and spent over thirty years in Papua New Guinea. When I commented to her that the beauty and tranquillity of this land moved people deeply, she didn't seem surprised but simply said, 'When we bought this land, we blessed it. We dedicated it to serve God. People feel that.'

"Her story reminded me how we humans contribute to what nature gives us in creating sacred spaces as dramatic as Stonehenge and the cathedral at Chartres, or as simple as a country field."

"For me, the session in Vermont was special because we really tapped into the power a sacred place makes possible," Joseph said. "I left the Marblehead meeting knowing that something was starting to form. The sense of urgency that I'd felt in Baja was also reinforced. I wasn't sure how that might translate into action, but I felt strongly that something would develop soon.

"Peter started by reading some of the quotes from the Marblehead meeting that we just told you. The conversation quickly flowed into an exploration of what would have to happen in order to address such issues on a large scale and then stayed at that level the entire three days. Then, on the last afternoon, we broke into small groups to talk about our next steps.

"I grabbed five other people—the director of a major private foundation, the president of an international NGO, two senior officers of a large U.S. government agency, and the CEO of a Fortune 50 company—and asked them to join me. After I told them about my experiences with Brian Arthur and John Milton and the kinds of synchronicities and support I'd experienced since Baja, they shared remarkably similar experiences. The CEO, who'd always been highly successful at delivering the bottom line, had discovered that what really mattered to him above all else was exactly what John had talked about in Baja—the need for a fundamental shift in our relationships, not just with each other but with all of nature.

"The two government executives talked about a gathering of the top two thousand leaders of their organization, an event that led to their participation in the ECW. Nothing like this gathering had ever happened in their agency or, as far as they knew, in any other large government agency. They'd heard about the state of the planet's living systems from E. O. Wilson and Peter Raven, world-class experts on biodiversity. That had brought them face-to-face with the consequences of a governing assumption behind modern society: that the lives of other species don't matter compared to human desires and needs.

"Later the poet Maya Angelou had shared her journey of self-discovery and healing after being raped as a teenager, a stunning example of 'seeing from the whole' and the power of forgiveness. 'Eventually I had to realize that I was my rapist, that the anger that was in him is in me as well,' she told the group. She ended by quoting an African of two thousand years ago, 'I am a human being; nothing that is human is foreign to me.' After Peter closed the meeting, speaking about what it would mean to tap people's deepest commitments, the executives said it had been like a 'gigantic opening of the heart.'

"When I asked how they'd moved from this opening to seeing their part in creating a different future, they said that many local initiatives had begun in their organization, but there were also strong forces to maintain the status quo. They were at this meeting in Vermont to see if working with other organizations might lead to more sustainable changes.

"Somehow we all found ourselves acknowledging the sense of urgency we felt. We weren't sure of the specifics, but one idea crystallized: we were convinced that we needed to find a way to develop leaders from business, government, and nongovernmental organizations who could work together. None of these sectors alone can address the major issues we're confronting, yet they have little capacity to work together creatively. Confrontations between even the most well-intentioned leaders usually just reinforce polarization. We felt we needed to do something, and agreed to meet in New York on October 11 to start developing a plan."

Joseph paused, then continued. "I flew almost directly from the meeting in Vermont to Colorado. Brian, John, and I had not been together since Baja, and I was particularly pleased that Adam and Otto were going to be with us."

"Once again in a special place," Betty Sue smiled. "I was sorry I couldn't join you, but I remember my first visit there vividly. John's done wonderful work setting up the land trust to protect sites that native people have held sacred."[3]

"He said this site is one of the largest he's found," added Otto. "Mayan shamans told him their ancestors journeyed there from throughout Central and Northern America."

"The first evening we had an early dinner and used the time for everyone to get acquainted," continued Joseph. "I talked about the intention for this meeting, which had formed at the end of our Baja experience, and then related the events that had occurred since then. I concluded with the powerful conversation and commitment we felt in Stowe to work on leadership with people from different sectors. But the most memorable part of the evening came when Otto told a story about a dream he'd had the night before."

"It seemed important to share that dream," Otto said. "I rarely have dreams that I remember, and this one was very intense. When I woke up, I knew I'd been handed a significant message. I just had to figure out what that message was.

"In the dream, I was walking with a group of people, some of whom I seemed to know. We were walking in a crowd of thousands of people, as you would if you were going to a major sporting event. The air was full of anticipation; there was a feeling that something extraordinary was to come. We were walking up the stairs. I had no idea where we were heading, but we were all on our way to a particular destination. As we were about to arrive, the guy next to me said in passing, 'Oh, by the way, you know you're going to give the speech now.'

"'What are you talking about?' I asked the guy. 'What kind of speech and to whom?'

"As we walked the final feet up the stairs, he explained to me that this gathering was a global meeting of the Catholic Church. The pope had just passed away, and some younger leaders of the Church had asked me to give a speech about how to fundamentally reinvent and transform their institution for the years to come. It was, they told me, a unique opening.

"In that moment we'd reached a platform at the end of the stairs, and I found myself standing on the speaker's stage in a massive stadium with about eighty thousand people. The funny thing was that from that particular spot, it felt as if you could connect to each one of them in the most personal way. I felt at one with every single person. I knew them. And they knew me.

"Suddenly, just as at the beginning of a classical music concert, all the thousands of voices started lowering at the same time, without any central guidance. People seemed to be moving into a deep anticipative collective silence. I knew that this was the moment when I was meant to step forward. But I didn't. Something was holding me back. I wasn't really prepared. I was still waiting for an intuition to show up about what to say. And I was also waiting for somebody to officially invite me to step forward. After all, just one person, whom I didn't even know, had told me that I was supposed to give this speech.

"As I stood there hesitating, I was shocked to hear the voices starting to get loud again, as if people had realized, 'Well, maybe nothing's going to happen tonight after all.' With horror, I realized that the chance to step into my real purpose was passing by. In that moment, I saw that the door to the destination of my journey, towards which I'd been traveling all my life, was closing."

"Otto, that's a very powerful dream," said Betty Sue. "As I was listening, I couldn't help but think it could apply to the four of us, or even to our larger collective situation."

"Everyone at Crestone thought that as well," said Joseph. "There was a profound moment of full silence when Otto finished. I think everyone felt the power of that dream.

"Then late in the afternoon of the second day we were sitting in a circle outside when the sky suddenly got very dark. Otto was talking about our understanding of the U process and how it could be the basis for transforming how leaders work together. It started to rain, at first lightly and then more heavily, and we heard rolling thunder approaching.

"Everyone moved into the small open-air cook hut next to where we'd been sitting and huddled together. As Otto spoke about suspending and learning to see, the thunder got louder and louder, and when he reached the idea of presencing, the essence of the U, lightning began striking all around us. The lightning was so intense and the thunder so loud that Otto finally quit trying to talk and said, 'Well, at the bottom of the U, it's all about silence.'

"We all sat without uttering a word as the lightning struck all around us. It was as if nature had taken over and finished Otto's sentence for him."

"It was very intense," said Otto, "but strangely enough, it wasn't frightening, even though the lightning strikes were so close that I could see the flash and hear the thunderclap at precisely the same instant."

"In the midst of the strikes I noticed John smiling serenely," continued Joseph. "When it was over, we continued to sit shoulder to shoulder, knowing we'd been in the presence of something sacred and powerful. Finally, John spoke softly and said that this was 'a punctuation, a real blessing.' We learned later that he'd been struck by lightning when he was much younger and that it had been a critical event in his spiritual awakening.

"That evening John's friend Sara, who'd watched the whole scene from a nearby cabin, noted that the first strike had occurred directly to the east of the meeting site, just across the stream—and that the strikes had continued in a circle in a clockwise direction—eleven in all. Referring to the practice John had first taught us in Baja, she said that Mother Earth had given us our own 'eleven directions ceremony.'

"On the last day, the group took a long hike up into the mountains. As we looked out over the hundred-mile view across the Rio Grande valley we understood immediately what John meant when he said the native peoples called the valley 'the corridor of dreams.' We had come to the right place to crystallize our dreams and prepare for taking the next steps toward their realization."

10.

The Grand Will

Not all visions are equal. Some never get beyond the "motherhood and apple pie" stage—good ideas that unleash no energy for change. Others transform the world. "There is nothing more powerful than an idea whose time has come," said Victor Hugo one hundred and fifty years ago. Yet, the power Hugo refers to remains elusive, carefully guarded by a paradox: there's nothing more personal than vision, yet the visions that ultimately prove transformative have nothing to do with us as individuals.

The resolution of this paradox comes from the transformation of will that starts as we move through the bottom of the U. The seeds for this transformation lie in seeing our reality more clearly, without preconceptions and judgments. When we learn to see our part in creating things that we don't like but that are likely to continue, we can begin to develop a different relationship with our "problems." We're no longer victims. When we move further, from sensing to presencing, we become open to what might be possible, and we're inevitably led to the question "So what do we want to create?" But the "we" in this statement is a larger "we." The visions that arise out of genuine presencing come from "the field knowing itself," a spontaneous expression of discovering the power to shape our reality and our responsibility to an emerging future. As we begin to move up from the bottom of the U, this larger intention becomes accessible to us.

By contrast, many visions are doomed from the outset because those who articulate them, whether consciously or not, are coming from a place of powerlessness. If we believe that someone else has created our present reality, what is the basis for believing that we can create a different reality in the future? In terms of the theory of the U, the problem with most attempts to formulate visions is that they occur "too far up the left side of the U." When this happens, people formulate visions that are disconnected from a shared understanding of present reality and a sense of shared responsibilityfor that reality. If people are still externalizing their problems, they create, in a sense, "externalized visions," which amount to a kind of change strategy for fixing problems which they have not yet seen their part in creating. Only when people begin to see from within the forces that shape their reality and to see their part in how those forces might evolve does vision becomes powerful. Everything else is just a vague hope.

This is why most visions that management teams come up with are superficial. Even if they embody a lot of good thinking, they're still a product of a fragmented awareness, and usually of one or two people's ideas imposed upon the group. As Joseph says, "When people are really connecting to one another and to their larger reality, there's a different feeling in the room. I've learned to trust the visions that arise in this space. It's not that you see it all completely clearly. But you feel the presence of this larger intention, and you just need to work with it. In a sense, real visions are uncovered, not manufactured."

The transformation of will that arises from presencing was beautifully articulated by George Bernard Shaw: "This is the true joy in life, the being used for a purpose you consider a mighty one, the being a force of nature, rather than a feverish, selfish clod of ailments and grievances complaining that the world will not devote itself to making you happy."[1]

Crystallizing Intent

Genuine visions arise from crystallizing a larger intent, focusing the energy and sense of purposefulness that come from presencing. We use the term "crystallizing intent" because of the way a crystal can concentrate or focus light. Crystallizing intent requires being open to the larger intention and imaginatively translating the intuitions that arise into concrete images and visions that guide action. As we explored this capacity in our interviews, we found that the experiences of innovative managers and entrepreneurs were particularly illuminating. While many of them had an intuitive appreciation of moving down the U, their attention was much more focused on the movement upward, of bringing the new into reality.

Nick Hanauer has founded half a dozen highly successful companies and was a board member of Amazon.com for many years. When Joseph and Otto interviewed him, he was working with a small group of people to "reinvent" the educational system of the state of Washington.

When asked about the role of intention in his entrepreneurial experience, Hanauer said, "There's no doubt about the value of being irretrievably committed to something. One of my favorite sayings, attributed to Margaret Mead, has always been 'Never doubt that a small group of committed citizens can change the world. Indeed, it's the only thing that ever has.' I totally believe it. You could do almost anything with just five people. With only one person, it's hard—but when you put that one person with four or five more, you have a force to contend with. All of a sudden, you have enough momentum to make almost anything that's immanent, or within reach, actually real. I think that's what entrepreneurship is all about—creating that compelling vision and force."

Srikumar Rao has had extensive experience both as a manager and as a consultant with a variety of successful companies. At the time of his interview he was chairman of the department of marketing at Long Island University, adjunct professor of marketing at Columbia Business School, and a contributing editor for *Forbes*. Srikumar said that his favorite course was "Creativity and Personal Mastery," in which he taught students to develop, hold, and broadcast their genuine intention. "If you form and hold your intent strongly enough," says Srikumar, "it becomes true."

But how do you develop your intent?

"You become extremely clear about what it is you want to do. Why is it you want to do what you do? How is it a reflection of your values? How does it relate to your unique purpose in life? What is it that you want to accomplish in society? Think about all of the inherent contradictions that are there, and then, if possible, reconcile them. This could take anywhere from a week to decades. This process of refinement—thinking about your intention many, many times—is, in a sense, a broadcast of intention. When you broadcast such an intention, there's very little else you have to do. The broadcast of intention goes out and makes it happen. Your role is to remain keenly aware, patiently expectant, and open to all possibilities."

Speaking about this, John White, one of the original founding partners of the Institute of HeartMath, said, "Often people need greater clarity before they can act decisively and with full commitment. Once they see clearly their heart's intent, their focus becomes like a laser— a powerful, coherent beam, as opposed to an incandescent, incoherent light. An earnest commitment from the heart emerges, vision becomes clearer, broader, and more inclusive of others. Strength of will is replaced by energetic integrity and a knowingness of 'what else is there' or 'I can't afford to not do this.'"

At first, when Hanauer, Rao, and White talked about "being irretrievably committed," "broadcasting your intention," and "laser intent," it seemed to contradict what Eleanor Rosch had described to us as "tuning into" the larger field that has "an intention to be itself." How do you reconcile "broadcasting intent" with "tuning in"? One seems to suggest an ego-centered process, while the other is clearly about transcending our normal, localized sense of self.

As we pondered these interviews, we wondered whether they described entirely different approaches to intention or simply different articulations of the same basic process. But then we began to notice that what many of our interviewees had in common was a particular quality of intention—as if it came from a different source.

Alan Webber, cofounder of *Fast Company*, said that it can be difficult to explain this source of intention to most people. Initially, when people asked him, "Why are you doing *Fast Company*?" his answer was very rational: "'Well, you know, it's a magazine about this and that, and the world doesn't have one.' But I soon realized that those reasons weren't the real reasons. The reason you do something is because you can't not do it. It's hard to explain that to people without sounding like a lunatic."

Darcy Winslow, now the head of women's footwear at Nike, provided another account of the role of sensing and presencing in tapping deep intentions. She was one of a handful of people who began agitating for creating more environmentally sound products and processes at Nike some six years ago. She and her colleagues formed what became the "sustainable business strategies" group, a sort of skunk works to get advanced innovation departments, designers, product managers, engineers, and manufacturing partners thinking differently. Before long, they found that they were "tapping deep passions among people."

"It was never hard to get people to talk about this," said Winslow, "because innovation is really what Nike is all about, and sustainability is totally dependent on innovation." When people started to focus their energies on what that would mean for Nike's products, "the ideas and energy that started to emerge were amazing." Today, Nike has succeeded in establishing standards that are among the highest in its industry for waste reduction and community responsibility in manufacturing. It also has a line of organically grown cotton apparel, has reengineered rubber compounds to eliminate chemical toxins, established solvent-free manufacturing processes, and is systematically trying to move toward a wide range of environmentally preferred materials, such as PVC replacements, in all its products. "We're working to integrate design principles that will require a new business approach, such as designing products that can be one hundred percent disassembled at the end of their useful life, with the various components returning to their original state, for reuse or recycling."

When Peter asked Winslow how she had gotten the idea of Nike being a leader in sustainable products and processes, she said, "It was obvious. You just have to open up to the state of the world and who you really are. Industries face immense challenges to become environmentally sound and ultimately restorative. When we really looked, we saw that Nike is all about life, about fitness and health in the broadest sense. We then began translating this basic intent and who we were—a highly innovative and competitive culture—into how we run the business in all areas. Once we tapped into this as something we really wanted to do rather than something we 'ought to' do, everything that makes Nike great came to the fore. We have a long way to go, and ultimately there will have to be changes in industrywide infrastructures, one of the biggest challenges. But I believe there is a 'tipping point' in consumer interest coming, and we can be part of bringing that about."

Hanauer, Webber, and Winslow's comments suggest that perhaps the least noticed and most important capacity that sets apart some of the most successful leaders concerns their capacity to tap into and focus a larger intention. Although people are sometimes reluctant to talk about this or simply don't know how to do so, when they reflect on their own actions, a different source of action becomes evident. This source lies beyond their preconceived plans or narrow self-interest, and often even beyond their past experiences.

Brian Arthur emphasized again and again the power of crystallizing intention, once you arrive at a place of genuine "knowing." "Intention is not a powerful force, it's the only force," said Arthur.

When operating from this larger intention, the standard model of rational decisionmaking gives way to a different process—simply doing what obviously needs to be done. As Eleanor Rosch says, action arises "as a spontaneous product of the whole."

Stanford's Michael Ray illustrates this point with a story about Will Ackerman, founder and CEO of Windham Hill Music Company.

As a student with one more class to take, Ackerman went to his professor, who also happened to be his father, and said, "I can't take this anymore. I'm dropping out."

"Sounds like a good idea," said his father. "I think I will, too."

Ackerman's father did indeed quit his job after his son quit school. Ackerman then borrowed $5 each from twenty of his friends and started his business. After Windham Hill was an established success and Ackerman had started other businesses, he built a little place for his father in New Hampshire. As Ray tells the story, one night father and son were sitting out on the porch in their rocking chairs, talking about Will's different business ventures, and Will said, "I don't know, Dad. I've got this construction business; I've got this music thing. What should I do?"

His father responded, "You know, I've never made a decision in my life."

At first Ackerman thought, "Oh boy, what a letdown." But then he realized that if you know what's right, you don't have to make decisions. When you know what's right, it's just there for you, and you do it.

Seeds Are Small

Becoming a force of nature doesn't mean that all of our aspirations must be "grand." First steps are often small, and initial visions that focus energy effectively often address immediate problems. What matters is engagement in the service of a larger purpose rather than lofty aspirations that paralyze action. Indeed, it's a dangerous trap to believe that we can pursue only "great visions."

For example, the first initiatives arising out of the health care project in Germany described earlier were started by small clusters of participants who were inspired to take the energy they felt and translate it into meaningful action. None of these local experiments, by themselves, was sufficient to move the whole health care system "to levels three and four," their larger intention. But each served to focus that intention and generate momentum and ultimately confidence in initiating further actions. This simple point clarifies the nature of genuine vision: it is not the grandeur of the vision that matters but what it accomplishes. "It's not what the vision is but what the vision does," says Robert Fritz, an accomplished composer and writer on the creative process.[2] In other words, the only meaningful criteria for judging vision are the actions and changes that ensue.

The nature of genuine vision is beautifully expressed in a story told by Debashish Chatterjee, a respected writer on leadership with the Indian Institute of Management and the J. F. Kennedy School of Government at Harvard University. Chatterjee once asked Mother Teresa what had enabled her to do such great things in her life. "First she looked at me quizzically, as if she was trying to figure out what I could possibly mean. Then she responded by saying simply, 'You cannot do great things. You can only do small things with great love.'"

Fritz says that building the capacity to crystallize a larger intent requires daily practice, working with what he calls "structural tension."[3] Unlike most "visioning exercises," working with structural tension involves crystallizing vision and recognizing present reality and is especially useful in times of stress or daily crises. Paradoxically, Fritz believes that moments of stress or real difficulty are "points of power" in developing vision and integrating it into our lives—if we develop the discipline to first notice how we're truly feeling and be honest in acknowledging "what is," objectively, emotionally, and physically. Becoming more able to simply discern physical and emotional reactions is a powerful practice in suspending and becoming less attached to the stories we tell ourselves about what is going on. Second, we must ask, "What do I (or we) really want?" This sounds simple, but it takes substantial discipline to stop your emotions and anxiety long enough to simply refocus on what matters to you. And finally, we must be able to choose what we want and move on. Even though nothing may change immediately, as you "reenter" a situation, you will notice changes.

The term "crystallizing vision" does not mean making a vision fixed or rigid. On the contrary, visions are alive only in the moment we see and choose them. They have their genuine meaning grounded in the particulars of where we are right now. In this sense, crystallizing is ongoing—continually re-creating the vision freshly in the here and now.

As the idea of vision has become popularized in recent years, its essential meaning has often been lost. Visions are not lofty sentiments or inspiring phrases; they're practical tools. In the simplest sense, a vision is simply an image of what we're seeking to create. The power of some visions over others comes from their source, not their sentiment—and from our ability to continually reconnect with that source. Visions that have power are expressions of deep purposefulness, acted upon in the present moment. Just as the nozzle of a hose intensifies the force of a current of water, so too does a clear vision channel and focus the purposefulness and energy that arise from presencing.

Intentional Work

When our work is informed by a larger intention, it's infused with who we are and our purpose in being alive. Reflecting on *Fast*

Company, Alan Webber said, "The work of doing the magazine is not about getting interviews, and it's not about getting awards. It's about meeting remarkable people who are doing amazing work and getting them to tell their stories in the pages of our magazine so that other people can share that.

"When I find myself worrying about little stuff or whether I'm a hero or a failure, I know I'm listening to the wrong voices. The real voices are all about this conversation that started many years ago about what really matters. What really matters is the capital 'W' Work, and the Work comes out of this magic concoction of the reasons we started down this road in the first place."

When people in leadership positions begin to serve a vision infused with a larger purpose, their work shifts naturally from producing results to encouraging the growth of people who produce results. David Marsing, a senior officer at Intel, once suffered a near-fatal heart attack. He traces the origin of his capacity to lead to the clarity and sense of purpose that arose from the heart attack:

"I died, clinically, in that emergency room. Fortunately, they brought me back. As I lay on the gurney in the emergency room, I knew exactly why I was there: I'd had the heart attack because of the way I was living. I always knew that Intel was a high-stress environment, but I'd thought of myself as somehow above it. I'd been an athlete. I'd worked there for many years. I was tough. But I was also blind. I was blind to what the environment I'd helped to create did to people, including me. As I lay there, I saw all of this very clearly. I also knew that climbing the ladder at Intel was really not very important to me.

"In the hospital and during the months afterward, I discovered that my true purpose was to help people realize that they have more potential than they ever imagined they had. I made a conscious choice to go back into that stressful environment, but to do it with a very different perspective and with much more concentration on my meditative and spiritual processes. I wanted to create environments for people that would help them see their true full potential. I also wanted to protect people from the typical responses that large organizations generate when they're under stress. These responses can be very unhealthy, as I'd discovered firsthand."

Marsing did many things differently when he returned to work. One was to introduce reflective or contemplative practices at alternating weekly staff meetings. He said, "At first people weren't sure if I was serious. Many doubted that it would last. But over time they found these very helpful in slowing down, being much more aware of their environment, and opening up."

Eventually, these new practices and Marsing's new outlook led to one of Intel's biggest successes. Marsing was general manager during the construction and "ramp-up" of Fab 11, Intel's biggest semiconductor fabrication facility and at the time the largest "fab" of its kind in the world. Fab 11 went from start-up to full-volume production in record time, allowing Intel to recoup its $2.5 billion investment not in several years, as expected, but in just five short months.

Awakening

How to find our way to becoming a servant of the whole, where action arises, as Rosch says, "as a spontaneous product of the whole" is an old puzzle. Twenty-five hundred years ago, Lao Tzu wrote:

Do you think you can take over the
    universe and improve upon it?
The universe is sacred.
You cannot improve it.

In the pursuit of learning, every day something is acquired.

In the pursuit of Tao, every day something is dropped.

Less and less is done

Until non-action is achieved.

Tao abides in non-action,

Yet nothing is left undone.[4]

How do we find this space of "non-action, [where] nothing is left undone"?

For some, it takes a trauma or tragedy—like David Marsing's near-fatal heart attack, Otto's experience with the fire, or the diagnosis Fred, the World Bank executive in Jamaica, received—in order to "wake up" and discover what actually matters to us and to find the courage to pursue it. But the awakening is not in the event itself; it is in ourselves. Being a servant of the larger whole ultimately involves a shift in will, accessible to all who come to understand and choose it.

More than twenty years ago, Peter gave a passage from Martin Buber's *I and Thou* to Joseph. Both kept it near at hand, touched by its message of the transformation of will and true freedom.

The free man is he who wills without arbitrary self-will.
. . . He believes in destiny, and believes that it stands in need of him . . . yet does not know where it's to be found. But he knows that he must go out with his whole being. The matter will not turn out according to his decision; but what is to come will come only when he decides on what he is able to will. He must sacrifice his puny, unfree will, which is controlled by things and instincts, to his grand will, which quits defined for destined being.

For Buber the capacity for true freedom arises when we "sacrifice" our "unfree will" to our "grand will." Eventually, we realized that this capacity was exactly what Shaw had referred to as "being a force of nature" and that, in the phrases that followed, Buber beautifully evoked the entirety of the U movement:

> Then he intervenes no more, but at the same time, he does not let things merely happen. He listens to what is emerging from himself, to the course of being in the world; not in order to be supported by it, but in order to bring it to reality as it desires.[5]

11.

In Dialogue with the Universe

inston Churchill once defined leadership as "going from failure to failure without losing enthusiasm." Nothing undermines the creative process more than the naïve belief that once the vision is clear, it's just a matter of "implementation." In fact, moving from concept to manifestation is the heart of creating—which literally means "bringing into existence." And like a river's path from its source to the sea, it is anything but a straight line. Instead, creating is a sort of dance between inspiration and experimentation, as illustrated beautifully by transpersonal psychologist Christopher Bache's reflections on what can happen between teacher and students if the teacher can truly let go and follow the course of what is emerging.

"In lecturing there is a moment that comes when a student has asked a question or when you're searching for just the right example to communicate a difficult concept . . . [when] there is a pause in the flow of your mind, a break in the continuity of your thinking. These moments are choice points, opportunities for intuition to transform an otherwise predictable lecture into a lively improvisational exercise." In those moments, "I discovered a small door in the back of my mind. This door would sometimes open and through it slips of paper would be passed to me with suggestions written on them—an idea, an image. I found that, if I took the risk and used this gift, something magical would happen. . . .

"When the magic happened, the walls of our separateness came down temporarily . . . [and] my students and I tapped into levels of creativity beyond our separate capacities. On a good day, the room was so filled with new ideas that after class I too sometimes copied down the blackboard, having caught glimpses of a deeper territory of new concepts unfolding in our dialogue. . . . Truth spoken directly from the heart and skillfully illumined by the mind has a power that cannot be eliminated even in academic settings."[1]

As Bache's comments suggest, often we learn what is emerging only as we move into action. The key is to act and remain open—so that the "small door" does not slam shut in our haste and because of our focus on the task at hand.

Prototyping

A recurring theme in our interviews with entrepreneurs and innovators was the importance of fast-cycle experiments or rapid prototyping as a way of avoiding getting stuck in plans or trying to completely figure out "the true nature of the emerging whole." Indeed, the true nature of an emerging whole can't be accessed fully without engaging in concrete experiments, improvisation, and prototyping. What we begin to intuit starts to become clear and real for us in a totally new way once we consciously endeavor to make it manifest and stay open to the feedback that effort elicits. All the business and social activists that we talked to embodied this principle.

John Kao, a highly successful businessman, musician, and entrepreneur, founded the Idea Factory in San Francisco to help large companies achieve breakthrough innovations. For Kao, prototyping is at the heart of every creative design process. "Prototyping is modeling or simulating your best current understandings precisely so you can have a shared set of understandings that enable communication, especially among people with very different discipline bases. That allows you to break that prototype and iterate cycle until you get to some desired outcome, which you could not have predicted in the beginning."[2]

For engineers, prototyping is a way of testing new design ideas embodied in physical (or computer-based) models. Prototyping in living social systems preserves the engineer's commitment to testing, with two important differences. First, it is more open-ended and exploratory. As Kao says, in engineering "you start with a specification and then, if you do all the things that specification says, you get to the end point—usually by excluding all the other branches of the tree. But design enables you to travel down any branch that's relevant to get to that end point." Second, in living systems we ourselves are "the prototypes"! As Gandhi said, "We must be the change we seek to create."

When shifting from visioning and crystallizing to prototyping, we reenter the sphere governed by the primacy of the concrete particulars. Prototyping is not about abstract ideas or plans but about entering a flow of improvisation and dialogue in which the particulars inspire the evolution of the whole and vice versa.

In its essence, prototyping accesses and aligns the wisdom of our head, heart, and hands by forcing us to act before we've figured everything out and created a plan. A tenet of prototyping is acting on a concept before that concept is complete or perfect. People concerned about success often want to slow down and plan or take more time to become comfortable with a course of action—but that may be exactly when you need to act. In Robert Redford's movie *Bagger Vance*, Bagger tells his pupil, a gifted but unsure golfer, "Don't think about it, feel it. The wisdom in your hands is greater than the wisdom of your head will ever be."

Effective prototyping requires the capacity to stay connected and grounded in your deepest source of inspiration and larger will while simultaneously learning to listen to all of the feedback your actions elicit. If you're open, the larger environment will continually tell you what you need to learn. The feedback you get from experiments will give helpful clues about how to shape, mold, and concretize what is beginning to form—but only if you learn to listen and set aside your negative reactions to "not getting it right" from the outset. This is a secret that highly creative people know tacitly. The entrepreneur, inventor, and founder of Polaroid, Edwin Land, had a small plaque on the wall of his office that read, "A mistake is an event the full benefit of which you have not yet turned to your advantage."

For a group that has moved through the bottom of the U, prototyping means becoming a vehicle in which a larger field to manifest itself. This is the principle of creating living microcosms of an emerging whole, of "being the change you wish to create," the key strategy in "moving up the U." Bache adds that when we stay connected to this larger field, what he calls "Sacred Mind," our actions become part of a larger pattern of synchronous developments that could have never been planned and are even difficult to explain after the fact.

Staying connected to the larger will while in action builds on the capacities for sensing, presencing, and crystallizing intent: the capacity for prototyping isn't actually separate from these but includes and grows from them. The result is action shaped by the field of the future rather than by the patterns of the past.

Creating and Adjusting

People often believe that you need to know how to do something before you can do it. If this were literally true, there would be little genuine innovation. An alternative view is that the creative process is actually a learning process, and the best we can possibly have at the outset is a hypothesis or tentative idea about what will be required to succeed. Robert Fritz characterizes the essence of the creative process as "create and adjust."[3] We learn how to do something truly new only through doing it, then adjusting.

Throughout this prototyping process, we may go through many small "U's," sensing and acting, which then produce more awareness and modified actions and even visions. This is what Kao refers to as "prototype and iterate," and what Brian Arthur describes as "act swiftly and with a natural flow." This create-and-adjust process may take hours, days, or years.

For example, starting in the mid-1990s, a small group of SoL members sought to organize a collaborative learning community focused on sustainability. While other corporate sustainability groups already existed, none was based on organizational learning principles and tools.[4] This group believed that the cultural and business changes required to transform traditional business models to incorporate social and environmental well-being were immense and that significant progress would be impossible without companies working together to build new learning capabilities. Eventually, this effort became the SoL Sustainability Consortium—but only after many false starts over more than three years. Along the way, many meetings and workshops were organized, but none generated a shared commitment to work together in an ongoing way.

"Many companies participated in these meetings with enthusiasm," said organizer Sara Schley, "but we just never quite reached 'takeoff.'"

"It was clear that people cared about sustainability issues personally," her co-organizer and husband, Joe Laur added, "but they struggled with how to make them salient in their organizations."

Harley-Davidson's Tim Savino, another of the organizers, put it more bluntly: "I knew this was really important, but I think for many at Harley at that time, accepting the notion of 'sustainable business practices' was roughly equivalent to embracing communism." Still Schley and Laur persisted, forgoing other work and dedicating their energy to creating the consortium.

Groping for how to get more traction within the businesses, the group decided that what was needed was a CEO meeting. If they could get enough top people into one room and get them to acknowledge the importance of these issues, then surely that would engender the commitment of the organizations. This turned out to be the most discouraging meeting of all and led to some important lessons on collective prototyping.

In early 1998, about a dozen CEOs and executive VPs met in Boston, along with the heads of several major environmental organizations. Each was enthusiastic about the strategic significance of environmental issues. They all came from organizations that seemed to support change. Everyone said the right thing. People gave presentations on environmental deterioration and on the necessity of redesigning processes to reduce waste and energy consumption, and several offered impressive case studies of their own organizations' environmental accomplishments.

But when the formal presentations were over and people began to talk informally about why they had not accomplished more, the major reasons offered were adverse government regulations, indifferent investors, and other external limits. Not surprisingly, when the conversation turned to what the group might do together, most of the emphasis focused on pressuring the U.S. federal government to be more pro-environment and convincing investment analysts that environmental improvements were worth spending money on. The energy in the room at the end of the meeting was at rock bottom. "It was a real eye-opener just how powerless the 'powerful' felt when it came to achieving real changes," commented Laur afterward.

The next day, Peter called Ray Anderson, the CEO of Interface, a U.S. floor covering manufacturer, who had helped to organize the meeting, and was then the co-chair of President Bill Clinton's President's Council on Sustainable Development.

"We both just admitted that the meeting had been a failure," says Peter. "We were very disappointed that there was so little real energy in this group and so much hand-wringing over external forces that were keeping people from doing what they knew was important. At the end of the conversation we both agreed that we didn't know what was needed, but 'whatever it is, it's not what we're doing so far.'

"That conversation with Ray turned out to be pivotal for me. On the one hand, we came up with no new ideas at all. But somehow, just being completely honest with one another about what had happened and about how we felt was important. That letting go left us open and, within a month a very different strategy emerged."

Instead of inviting CEOs, the organizers would invite a group of managers who were experienced with organizational learning. This group might include executives, but it would also include local line managers, internal consultants, and staff. The key was to invite people with real experience in successfully achieving significant change who also cared personally about social and environmental issues. "We decided to go with passion and commitment rather than the org chart," said Laur later. "Without even fully recognizing it, we naturally gravitated toward a group with an ability to 'be the change' they were seeking to create," said Peter. "As it turned out, this group, which met in Cambridge in January 1999, became a microcosm of the larger collaborative we were trying to create."

In the ensuing years, the number of corporations and governmental and nongovernmental organizations involved has grown, and the consortium itself has generated many diverse initiatives that are starting to play out on a larger scale.

A highlight of that January meeting in Cambridge was John Elter's story of a group he led when he was at Xerox that created Xerox's first fully digital generation of copiers. Attendees were inspired by the technical accomplishments of the team and particularly their "zero-to-landfill" vision, which had arisen among groups of engineers returning from wilderness solos.[5] "Why," they asked, "if nature creates no waste, shouldn't we do the same?" Elter's team, later nominated for the U.S. National Medal of Technology, pioneered design innovations that resulted in a product with only about two hundred parts (versus two thousand for its predecessors), all of which went together with clips and screws for disassembly, ninety-two percent of which could be remanufactured and ninety-six percent recycled.

Although the product met or exceeded all of Xerox's sales targets, the company was having financial difficulties, and Elter was about to retire, potentially taking with him an extraordinary knowledge base in design for remanufacture. Today, along with some of his brightest protégés, he has joined Plug Power, a start-up fuel cell manufacturer and another member of the consortium—following CEO Roger Saillant, who left Ford as one of its most accomplished executives to head up Plug Power. Together they are bringing world-class technical and managerial expertise into a struggling industry that could be vital to the transition toward renewable energy sources. And as Elter says, "We aim to make zero to landfill the norm of the fuel cell industry."

Listening to Feedback

Prototyping effectively requires cultivating a capacity to listen to the feedback that an initial effort elicits from the environment. But as the consortium story shows, this isn't always easy. Something that in retrospect was clearly preliminary and poorly conceived, at the time often seems like "the right idea." It's easy to become attached to something that takes a lot of effort to create. Plus, being open to listen to what the environment is saying isn't the same as reacting to every criticism as a failure to be corrected. Successful prototyping requires something in between the extremes of either ignoring feedback or overreacting to every disconfirming signal.

Speaking of his experience with *Fast Company*, cofounder Alan Webber said, "A visual representation of my experience would look like a semipermeable membrane that keeps accepting signals. Stuff comes through and stuff goes back out, and there's a constant dialogue with your environment over whether the idea is pregnant or not, whether the environment is supportive or hostile, and whether the idea is perfect the way you've conceived it or needs to be further evolved.

"If you're open in relation to your idea, the universe will help you. The universe, as it turns out, is a very welcoming place. So if you're open, it wants to suggest ways for you to improve your idea.

"Now, that said, the universe sometimes offers suggestions that suck. Part of the adventure is listening to those ideas and suggestions and trying to make your own calculations about which ones are helpful and which ones are harmful. You don't want to be closed and say, 'No, this idea came from my mind fully hatched, and if we can't do it the way we've conceived it, I'm not going to do it at all.' On the other hand, if you listen to everybody else's suggestions, you go mad. You have to be taking in energy and ideas and tweaks and listening to what the world is trying to tell you with an honest ear. At the same time, you have to keep the integrity of what you're doing and maintain that sense of personal conviction that the initial conception was an honest and good one."

Tara Poseley, a thirty-five-year-old senior officer at the Gap, echoed Webber's experience. In the last few years, Posely, in her own words "a serial innovator," has pioneered three new business units, each of which is among the most profitable and fastest growing in the company. After Joseph and Otto explained the model of the U to her, she described her way of operating as "going through the U every day."

When she founded Gap Body, Poseley began by immersing herself in marketing information about the identity of the dominant players in the business and how they operated. Then, believing that there was a great opportunity for a new approach, she developed a business plan, which she presented to the senior management committee of the company. It was the first formal presentation she had ever made to senior management, and she came with a huge set of slides. After the first few slides, she looked around the room and realized that she was losing her audience. In that moment she decided to shift her entire approach and, turning to a rack of prototype garments behind her, began handing them out as she spoke directly to the CEO and other senior officers. At the end of the meeting, the CEO gave her the green light to move ahead.

Poseley told us that this was a moment of significant learning for her. "Yes, you have to have the vision," she said. "And you have to have the deep intention that goes with it. But you also have to have an incredible capacity for self-observation and course correction in real time. The universe wants to help. But you must be able to observe and listen."

Rediscovering Purpose

When you move from crystallizing intent to prototyping, you move from the domain of ideas to the domain of action. Not only does this make what is emerging more tangible, it eventually leads to a new level of clarity about the underlying purpose animating the entire undertaking.

After the initial patient-physician dialogue forum in Germany, a number of prototyping initiatives started. Many of the participants, such as Dr. Gert Schmidt and his colleagues, left the forum with the intention "to move our system from levels one and two to levels three and four. To do this, we needed new types of processes and tools that would allow us to make the whole visible to the players in our system in the most concrete and practical ways. We decided to start by prototyping some conversational platforms that would convene people from different institutions around practical issues and topics.

"At first we brought together representatives from all the main organizations of a particular health region. We had two or three nice meetings—but nothing really substantial emerged. We then realized that we'd been limited in our thinking to an overly institutional approach.

"Now we take a different approach. We start by defining 'the practitioners'—the people who really face the everyday problems and can make or influence decisions in their own institutional subsystem—in short, people who need one another in order to take effective action. At the meetings, we talk about all the issues in a very open manner, focusing on creating short-term solutions and implementing them.

"These groups form around specific issues and problems, sometimes on very short notice. When the issue is dealt with, the group dissolves. Currently, we have ten of these groups operating. And they all work much more effectively than our earlier groups did."

One of these ad hoc action groups focused on the results of a diabetes study. The team was selected based not on formal representation of institutions or expert knowledge, but on their status as key practitioners in the system—physician's assistants, for example, and diabetes patients. One of the strategies that emerged from their work was to engage women who lived in the countryside as activists for developing and promoting new habits of living and eating. "This very decentralized approach addresses the real issues of chronic diabetes patients," said Schmidt, "which have nothing to do with needing more or better drugs and everything to do with locally embedded infra-structures for becoming aware and living differently."

Another innovation was a regional emergency service that brought rural physicians inside and outside the hospital into a single, fully inte-grated, and self-directed system. This system has a single phone num-ber that everyone in the region can call at any time, around the clock. Patients have immediate access to a physician who can offer instant advice, direct the question to the nearest physician on call, or send out the emergency van with a doctor.

As a result, patients in emergency situations feel more secure because they have immediate access to competent physicians. When less qualified professionals responded to emergency calls, not only did patients feel they were not getting quality attention, but vans were often sent out unnecessarily. Using the heavily powered, expensive emergency vans more wisely has lowered costs. In addition, physicians have benefited in unexpected ways. Sitting at the "pulse of the region" in the new emergency service headquarters, "you begin to get a sense of the region as a whole," one physician said, which feeds back natu-rally into recognizing what's needed, which "has facilitated important learning processes for physicians, emergency care staff, firefighters, and others who worked more in isolation from one another in the past."

Continual prototyping has also built a sense of momentum and self-determination. "We experience the difference when we visit our col-leagues in other regions," said Schmidt. "In these meetings, the style of conversation is still the way it used to be in our meetings. They talk about the 'others'; for example, they may say, 'But the insurers will think this and do that.' We no longer pose these questions. We either go straight to these people and ask them directly, 'What are you thinking? What are you doing? What are you up to?' or we simply don't bother about them at all. We don't worry about what others may or may not think. We focus our time on where we can best make a difference."

"Shifting the system to levels three and four" has come to mean helping people live in healthier ways, fostering professionals' awareness of the system as a whole, and building a greater sense of self-determination. It has also become manifest in both quantitative— such as zero patient complaints—and highly personal outcomes. Characterizing his work experience, one physician commented, "When I drive through our region at night, in the woods by myself at 3 AM, I no longer have the feeling I'm alone." Another said, "My relationship to patients has become more like a partnership, a thinking together. I'm more able to elicit and reformulate the thinking of the patients and to help them become aware of what they really want." Said another simply, "I've rediscovered the joy of work."

When Otto asked Dr. Schmidt how he would account for all these changes, he responded that the "experience of shaping something is a source of power. When you have better knowledge about how the system and whole region work, and you get to know a lot of people, you end up having a different access to making things work. Before all this, for instance, I used to postpone awkward conversations forever. Now I simply do it. We're in a different situation today because we're seeing the whole more clearly, and the whole net of personal communications and relationships is more in flow."

As a field of prototyping activity in a large system evolves, the deeper purpose becomes embedded in so many ways that it ultimately becomes transparent. "When you consider that this started as a purely physician-driven initiative, it would have been impossible to predict the depth or breadth of the changes that have taken place," says Otto's colleague Ursula Versteegen. "It's evolved into dozens of projects involving hundreds of different institutions and individuals throughout the entire region. What started as prototyping became an organic metamorphosis, the emergence of a landscape of continual innovation that now we all take for granted."

Staying Connected

As occurred in the German health care work, the movement from presencing and crystallizing into prototyping can lead to many parallel prototyping efforts. While the proliferation of prototyping experiments is often essential, it can also lead to fragmentation and even unnecessary competition. One key to avoiding this is to keep the prototyping efforts connected to one another. If this can be done, multiple prototyping efforts can, over time, build larger social networks and a critical mass for change.

There is no single "right" way of maintaining these connections. For example, larger groups can be organized into "rapid prototyping teams," and then the teams can coach one another. As collections of prototyping efforts evolve, it can be useful to set up a distinct team whose job is to coordinate across all the teams. Bringing a number of prototyping groups together regularly, face-to-face, to share what they are accomplishing—and especially what challenges they are confronting—can lead to further connections and ways to help one another.

What matters is that staying connected becomes a strategic priority. The energy of prototyping will draw many new, action-oriented players into an initiative. Most will come with little appreciation for the history of learning and relationship building that has been responsible for success in the past and will lack awareness of the larger community that has developed. The centripetal forces of fragmentation can be overwhelming if there is not a clear vision of the larger community of prototyping activities as the real microcosm of large-scale change.

Synchronicity: The Field Knowing Itself

Perhaps the most important aspect of crystallizing intent and prototyping is one that people rarely talk about. When people connect with their deeper source of intention, they often find themselves experiencing amazingly synchronistic events. In his classic *Synchronicity: An Acausal Connecting Principle*, Carl Jung defined synchronicity as "a meaningful coincidence of two or more events, where something other than the probability of chance is involved." Jung's definition artfully juxtaposes two seemingly contradictory notions: "coincidence" and "something other than . . . chance."[6] Synchronicity seems to bind together just such opposites: intentionality and fortuity, action and luck, causality and "acausality."

Intel's David Marsing told Joseph that "Synchronicity is about being open to what wants to happen." For him, what Rao called "the broadcasting of intention" is evident by the way "many people sense and are drawn together around a new possibility that's unfolding." And, he added, "It's usually more than one person who senses it and who wants to help. I rarely find myself in this sort of place alone. You don't even have to advertise—there's something about the situation that resonates with people who have a similar intent and a similar set of principles and values. They're drawn to it, and then magic begins to unfold."

While synchronicity can't be controlled, it also isn't random—indeed, one of the primary consequences of the entire U movement is that the power of synchronicity is brought more reliably into play. This starts with the opening that occurs in suspending and continues with the "surrender into commitment" that arises in presencing. As W. H. Murray of the Scottish Himalayan Expedition said, "The moment one definitely commits oneself, then providence moves too."[7] It would be wrong to say that highly successful innovators expect magic to occur, but they somehow accept it quietly, as an almost inevitable part of the process. You can hear this in Alan Webber's comment that "The universe, as it turns out, is a very welcoming place." Or, as Tara Posely put it, "The universe wants to help."

Perhaps what we call magic or synchronicity is simply what it feels like, from our personal vantage point, to be part of a field knowing itself and to be taking action informed by the whole. When forced to understand the increasingly frequent magic in his classroom, Christopher Bache—like Eleanor Rosch, Rupert Sheldrake, and others with whom we spoke—came eventually to think of a larger field. "When these synchronistic resonances first began manifesting in my classes, I thought of them as paranormal exchanges taking place between separate minds. . . . Eventually it simply became more elegant to conceptualize these phenomena as symptoms of a unified learning field that underlay and integrated the class as a whole.

"The most important observation that pushed me toward the . . . field view of these events . . . was the sheer magnitude and intensity of the forces that were involved. Too many people's lives were being too deeply touched for me to conceptualize what was happening in terms of resonances with my individual energy.

". . . about fifteen years ago, students started coming up to me after class . . . [saying things like] 'You know, it's strange you used the example you did in class today, because that's exactly what happened to me this week.' . . . My students were finding intimate pieces of their lives showing up in my lectures. . . . Students also began to tell me that it was uncanny how often my lectures answered as if on cue questions they were feeling but were not asking." He eventually discovered that students were also reporting similar coincidences with one another. As one student said, "'Each quarter seemed to bring new and unexpected changes and synchronicities. I entered into a web of relationships and meetings with people that profoundly influenced my life.'"[8]

When he discovered Sheldrake's writings, Bache gradually came to see his own experiences not as something extraordinary or paranormal but as a natural feature of a living system. In a sense, he and his students were starting to pay attention to something subtle among them and were learning how to cultivate it further, what Bache calls "Sacred Mind," "the unbounded awareness within which all individual experience occurs, the living matrix where minds meet and engage."[9]

Sadly, Bache writes, "our culture has not taught us to recognize the presence of this broader mental field, let alone how it functions." For example, "atomistic models of mind do educators a great disservice because they desensitize us to the subtler textures of the teaching experience . . . . Even the exceptional exchange—when the teacher 'awakens the student's hunger for learning'—is still seen as an interaction between ontologically separate minds."[10]

After many years of exploring and thinking about Sacred Mind, Bache has concluded that it is too limiting to think of such fields as just a product of "non-ordinary states of consciousness." Rather, he has come to see them as "the inner lining of everyday life." Spiritual disciplines that "awaken the individual to the transcendental depths of experience" offer one pathway to experiencing this larger mental field. But there's a second path. Through genuine engagement within teams or groups, as in Bache's classroom, we discover Sacred Mind "'hidden' in plain sight . . . alive within our everyday collective experience."[11]

And when we do, we discover, as Rosch said, that "action becomes action that supports the whole, that includes everything and does everything that's needed." But of course, the action is not just "our action." It is the by-product of participating more consciously in dialogue with an unfolding universe.

Realizing and the Craft of Institution Building

November 2001

When the four of us met again in the fall, it was the first time we had been together since the events in New York on September 11, 2001. We all felt that 9/11 was a painful reflection of the forces behind the "requiem scenario" and a confirmation of the importance of the deep learning process we were trying to understand. Joseph started by updating us on the October 11 meeting held to carry forward the work begun in Vermont.

⁓

"When our group from Stowe met in New York, we were just a few blocks from what is now called 'Ground Zero.' It was profoundly moving to be there, and we couldn't help but reflect on what the event might mean in light of our vision for transforming leadership. We talked about how much it should be attributed to the 'insanity' of religious fanaticism, and how much to other causes."

"As one person put it," Otto added. "One person's 'religious fanatic' is another's 'heroic martyr.' Although September 11 can be seen in many lights, we all agreed that the impetus that had brought our group together—the need to bring diverse leaders from business, government, and civil society together to work toward more sustainable patterns of globalization—was more urgent than ever. We spent a lot of time in conversation about the forms the initiative could take, but in the end what mattered most to all of us was getting started right away."

"We agreed that the initial prototyping process should start with a new round of sensing interviews," continued Joseph. "If nothing else, September 11 told us that we simply have to understand the state of the world as experienced by diverse world citizens—to learn how to 'sense' globally, rather than to impose one group's solution onto others. Within a few weeks a network of people had started to conduct another thirty interviews in seven different regions around the world. Two overarching themes arose from the interviews: the current global crises and an emerging new global consciousness.

"Wendy Luhabe, an influential entrepreneur and mentor to women and young entrepreneurs in South Africa, summed up many others' comments saying, 'There's a leadership crisis in the world. If you look at what's going on in the Middle East, or in Zimbabwe, or in the Enron corporation, or in the American elections, or in the position the Bush administration is taking to alienate the U.S. from the rest of the world, you'll see that all these things have a similar pattern of the old dominant forces struggling with the emerging new force of people who are saying, "We're no longer prepared to just sit back and watch the world go to ruin." The old power forces are resisting the new. And the new is showing up in young people, and in women. Unless we can create space for people to participate in managing the world and in creating a different future, we're not going to arrest what appears to be the inevitable.'

"Father Xabier Gorostiaga of Nicaragua, former president of the University of Central America, said we're not merely experiencing a security crisis after September 11, but 'a profound crisis of civilization,' of what our sense of life is: 'The world does not know where it is going.' He said that the 'Washington consensus' model of democracy has widened the gulf between what he called 'two citizenships.' Today there is a 'citizenship of the globalizers and the globalized; a citizenship with the capacity of playing in the market and a citizenship with no capacity; a citizenship that possesses, knows, and has power, and another citizenship that does not possess, does not know and has no power.'"

Otto took up the thread: "I thought Alok Singh, a young member of the global youth network Pioneers of Change, put it succinctly. 'Our systems are failing, and their failures are coming to the surface: they do not serve people. The current crisis will not go away because we're just operating on the symptoms.'

"I found the same sense of breakdown when I did follow-up interviews with people from the German health care project. While many were encouraged by experiments like the new emergency care network, they also felt they were trying to 'fix a dying system.' One said, 'Maybe what's needed right now is to stop trying to keep the system alive artificially and perform a controlled emergency shutdown.'

"This experience of the entire system as 'dying' applies not only to health care but also to education, agriculture, and government. People said that there are simply no high-leverage strategies that will make any difference as long as we continue to avoid integrative approaches that involve all these areas. When I said I expected our current system to hit the wall sometime within the next decade, almost no one agreed with me. Many said the system would crash much earlier, and some said that it wasn't going to happen in the future because it was already happening now."

"Those in the middle of the breakdowns also spoke most powerfully about the second theme—that integrative solutions are inseparable from a new personal awareness," Joseph added. "One of the people Otto interviewed was Nicanor Perlas, a leader in a nationwide civil society movement for sustainable development in the Philippines and recipient of the Right Livelihood Award, also known as the Alternative Nobel Prize. He said that globalization means we have to become 'more aware of how deeply we're interconnected as human beings across all of society. It also means that each of us is confronted with the fundamental choice of participating in patterns of development and interaction that are either life-destroying or life-enhancing.'"

"When we asked people where they see this new awareness and spirituality in action," continued Otto, "many said that unless we looked at the level of local community development, we were missing the point. Several of the young leaders we interviewed were involved in community projects in the developing world. As one young woman from Finland put it, there isn't a world solution on a grand scale. Common solutions that could work for everybody are impossible to find; they are 'against nature.'

"A wonderful example of an alternative to the 'Washington consensus' model of global economic development is the national dairy farmer's cooperative in Gujarat, India. It has made India the largest producer of milk in the world and given millions of dairy farmers across the country livelihood and self-reliance. To date, one hundred thousand village cooperative societies have been established, governed by elected boards comprised mostly of villagers. 'We're not in the dairy business,' Amul's managing director, Mr. B. M. Vyas, says. 'We are in the society-building business. Business is not the goal. Business is a means to build a society that is just and fair and that empowers the poor. Democracy is not sitting in the Parliament in Delhi—it is starting at the grassroots level and giving the ordinary man a chance. That value addition is a thousand times more than producing the Intel chip.'

"This new round of sensing interviews is already causing some subtle changes in how we're thinking about our goals. Over and above cross-sector projects on systemic change, we should be fostering a global community of local leaders. Interviews are also confirming something Adam said in the New York meeting: that women and young leaders must have a critical role moving forward. This had been a powerful conclusion from the civic scenario work he'd done, and is something that corporate leaders often overlook."

"I think the interviews are also clarifying our first major step in making this initiative real," said Joseph. "We need to bring together a meaningful cross-section of the types of people we've been interviewing, a kind of strategic microcosm of the types of leaders who need to be working together to create the first set of projects, perhaps at the next ECW. We could include community and youth leaders along with executives from business and government."

"This seems like a good example of exactly what we've been talking about," said Betty Sue. "Your new round of interviews became an important prototyping exercise, and the learning from them is evolving your understanding and vision. As I was listening, it seemed to me that the capacities that we've been identifying and using over the past year are now being embodied in this new initiative you're working on."

"I think so, but this is still in its very early stages," Joseph replied. "I imagine we'll go through several more iterations before we know the form it will finally take."

"But as a particular type of learning process, I think we *can* say a bit about what happens when groups complete the whole movement of the U," said Peter. "Like any learning process, completion means realizing—bringing into reality enduring changes that are both external and internal. The external changes include obvious consequences or achievements. For an organization that also includes new organizational practices, or ways of doing things and working together. Clearly, for example, this leadership initiative is about developing networks of leaders from business, government, and non-governmental organizations who can work together.

"The internal changes show up on two levels. First we come to embody a new capacity for action. What once required conscious effort happens effortlessly, almost automatically. We know we've learned to walk or ride a bicycle, or write a sonnet when we can produce these outcomes reliably. Just so, organizations can embody new capacities by developing new domains of competence embedded in assumptions and institutional norms. But learning also creates new domains of meaning. It shifts our awareness and understanding. We see the world in new ways. What was invisible to us becomes visible, like when you learn a language while living in a different culture and gradually come to 'see' that culture in a new way."

"The real difference is that more superficial learning and change processes are abbreviated or distorted versions of the U movement," Otto affirmed. "The learners don't access capacities for suspending habitual ways of seeing, and they fail to connect with the deeper source of action that arises from becoming 'present' to future possibilities. That's why the embodiment and understanding that arise in completing the U movement also differ from what occurs in more typical learning processes—collectively moving through the U can lead to creating entirely new institutions or truly transforming existing ones."

"One way shifts in organizational meaning and understanding show up is through governing ideas," said Peter. "Bill O'Brien, the former CEO of Hanover Insurance, used to say that the fundamental problem with most businesses is that they're governed by mediocre ideas. Maximizing the return on invested capital is an example of a mediocre idea. Mediocre ideas don't uplift people. They don't give them something they can tell their children about. They don't create much meaning."

"I think talking about lofty guiding ideas leaves many people cold today," Betty Sue said. "What business doesn't have a mission or value statement? Enron had a corporate value statement, as did WorldCom, Tyco, and countless other firms that have ultimately been devastated by violations of their own codes of conduct. None of these value statements functioned as an adequate check to executive abuse of power."

"That's the difference between good ideas and governing ideas," replied Peter. "Ideas move from good ideas to governing ideas when they become the foundation of an organization's system of governance—that is, when they become a source of decision-making power. Having lofty value statements obviously doesn't necessarily empower people to speak up against practices that violate those values. Real governing ideas must be married to processes and norms that enable people to live the organization's values and purpose. That might mean, for instance, established ways that people can challenge executive actions effectively, embedded in a culture that both respects and continually challenges authority. Otherwise, people can only do so by putting themselves at personal risk, which means that corrections inevitably occur too late. Most value and mission statements combined with traditional authoritarian governance structures are worse than useless—they breed cynicism and become a smoke screen for business as usual. Discovering governing ideas that generate real meaning and building the commitment to translate them into how we live and work together is hard work—the work of moving down the U not once, but repeatedly."

"And to do that requires infrastructures for sensing, presencing, and realizing," added Otto. "There are few examples at this point, but I think Shell's scenario process, when it truly engages people in discovering their assumptions about the world, is probably a good instance of a sensing infrastructure in the business world. From what I've heard, Unilever's 'learning journeys'—taking managers out of their familiar environments and into places they would never otherwise go—help people connect with one another and open sources of inner knowing that enable both sensing and presencing.[1] Infrastructures for realizing would probably need to support rapid prototyping of the sort tht John Kao talks about. They key is to have infrastructures in all three areas, and I think that is very rare."

"Yes, but this doesn't mean that sensing, presencing, and realizing don't occur in real organizations, even if the capabilities aren't embedded in well-established routines and behaviors," added Joseph. "We've all seen groups move through the bottom of the U and make profound changes in how they operate, many of which endure for years."

"Like Visa," said Peter. "Joseph and I worked closely with Dee Hock, Visa's first CEO, during the founding of SoL. Not many people realize it, but Visa International is arguably the largest business in the world, with over $3 trillion in transactions and a market value approaching a trillion. Yet to many it doesn't even look like a business. It's organized as a self-governing network of more than twenty thousand member institutions that are also its owners. It's governed by a constitution that stipulates how governing boards are elected, the rights and obligations of members, how new members are admitted, and how members can be disqualified. In short, one of the world's largest corporations operates as a self-governing democracy.

"What really strikes me in light of what we're talking about is that

Visa emerged from a profound collective journey through the U. It started with the chaos of the early days of the credit card industry in the late 1960s, in the midst of a massive financial collapse brought about by overexpansion. Amidst a spreading perception that the whole industry was doomed, Dee headed a small group of executives who had been convened by Bank of America in order to immerse themselves in the reality of the situation. The deeper they dug, the worse it looked. The system they'd all created could never solve the problems to which it had given rise. This realization forced them, in Dee's words, to abandon their 'old perspective and mechanistic model of reality' and to cease thinking of 'the jargon of banking and payment systems.' Gradually a 'change in consciousness occurred. . . . We were not in the credit card business. . . . We were really in the business of the exchange of monetary value.'[2]

"Lying awake one night during the middle of an intense week-long meeting, he suddenly realized that 'no bank could create the world's premier system for the exchange of value. No hierarchical stock corporation could do it. No nation-state could do it. . . . It was beyond the power of reason to design such an organization. . . yet, lying there, [I was reminded] how evolution routinely, effortlessly tossed off countless varieties of much more complex organisms and organizations—rain forests, marine systems, weather systems, cheetahs, whales, body, brain, immune system—with seeming ease.'[3]

"When he awoke the next morning, he found himself asking if an organization could be patterned on biological concepts and methods so that it could evolve to continually organize and invent itself. 'What if we quit arguing about the structure of a new institution and tried to think of it as having some sort of genetic code?'[4]

"The genetic code became Visa's purpose and principles, its governing ideas, and the core governance processes spelled out in its constitution.[5] The subsequent work of prototyping and institutionalizing took over four years, but in the end Visa International was formed, more or less in its current form."

"That's a great example of the U movement in action," said Otto. "I think Dee's term for organizations like Visa—*chaordic*, how order emerges from chaos—is a powerful metaphor for the entire U process."

"Yes, it is," said Betty Sue. "When I read his book, you also get the feeling of Dee as a real 'force of nature' throughout the process—that creating Visa was truly his calling. But his story also makes me wonder if we'll discover that our journey together is really about coming to understand democracy itself. We live in societies that espouse democratic ideals and have certain mechanisms of democracy, like voting, but by and large our institutions function very autocratically—often literally like small dictatorships. I've been thinking about this more and more lately. Maybe we're just at the beginning of the age of democracy and self-governance. What if the past two hundred years have been a sort of preparation and initial prototying period? What if democracy itself is really in its early stages of development?"

"I had a premonition of that when I watched the fall of the Berlin Wall," Otto said. "It felt as if we were entering a transitional period. Act One was the collapse of the Soviet Union and the communist block. Act Two is what we are witnessing now: the limits of the U.S. brand of capitalism and democracy are becoming painfully obvious. Maybe Act Three concerns the emergence of a new constellation of global forces.

"What would happen if rather than thinking of democracy as something we inherit, like a suit of clothes passed on from our grandparents, we thought of it as a learning process—one where we've only taken the smallest baby steps so far, and new prototypes will come."

"There's a real question, however, as to whether the present prototype can tolerate new prototypes, or whether it contains its own form of totalitarianism," added Peter. "Remember, Betty Sue, when that one brave person in your July meeting asked if 'the present framework of global capitalism can adapt to the new reality?' No one responded."

"That's certainly a big question for many of the world's emerging countries," said Betty Sue. "They often feel that there really is no alternative to the Washington consensus.

"Perhaps our openness going forward will depend on one other message in Dee's story, that is, our connection to nature—learning to live by natural principles and giving up our attempts to control. It's interesting that, in his real moment of crisis, Dee awoke to what he knew about living systems and evolution."

"One thing I really appreciated about Dee was that he was brutally realistic about how much the 'Newtonian mind' has been conditioned to believe that someone must be in control," said Joseph. "That's why we're continually trying to gain control and to avoid being controlled. When one person tries to control another, it invariably backfires. Why do we think someone must control larger systems like schools or corporations? Dee says it's because we see that system as more like a machine than a living being. I think he's right. It's not surprising that machine thinking has produced institutions that make it virtually impossible for us to live in harmony with nature, and with one another."

"So what we're saying is quite simple," said Peter. "Our capacity for democracy grows from our connection with nature. As we lose that connection, isolation, fear, and the need to control grow—and democracy inevitably deteriorates. It's easy to forget that a deep connection with nature provides the inspiration for genuine democratic thinking. Perhaps this is what Walt Whitman was trying to warn us about over a hundred years ago. There's a passage of his I've never forgotten, and now I think I know why.

> We have frequently printed the word Democracy. Yet I cannot too often repeat, that it is a word the real gist of which still sleeps, quite unawakened . . .

It is a great word, whose history, I suppose remains unwritten, because that history has yet to be enacted.

It is, in some sort, younger brother of another great and often used word, Nature, whose history also waits unwritten. [6]

Part 4

Meeting Our Future

13.

Leadership: Becoming a Human Being

December 2001

We met a few weeks later on a snowy day in December. We had all been thinking about the things people said in the second round of 'sensing' interviews.

"The idea that we're experiencing a crisis in leadership probably isn't new, but I heard it in a new way," said Betty Sue. "If we're at the end of an era, I think it's clear that a new kind of leadership is called for."

"New realities have certainly demanded new thinking about leadership before," said Peter. "One of the oldest ideas about leadership is that 'with power must come wisdom'—an idea that seems to date from the period when larger city states were forming in China and

Greece about twenty-five hundred years ago. As larger organizations with greater institutional power were coming on the scene, people recognized they needed to deal with the dangers such organizational power could bring. I don't think it was a coincidence that Plato's dialogue with Glaucon about the philosopher king in the *Republic* was written within a hundred years of the time when Guan Zhong and later Confucius laid the foundations of Chinese thinking about leadership. In many ways, the two sets of ideas are remarkably similar, each articulating a philosophy of moral development so that this new organizational power wouldn't be abused.

"I can't help but think that we're in a very similar period today. Globalization is reshaping societies and cultures on a scale that has never happened before. Yet the old idea that those in positions to influence such organizations' power must be committed to cultivation or moral development has all but completely disappeared. I doubt that few have even thought what such cultivation means—what it takes to develop a capacity for delayed gratification, for seeing longer-term effects of actions, for achieving quietness of mind. The ancient Greeks and Chinese believed such cultivation required a lifetime of dedicated personal work, guided by masters."

"But many people seem to feel these old ideas don't speak to the realities of today's technology-driven world," said Betty Sue. "Our leaders are more likely to be technologists than philosophers, focused on gaining and using power, driving change, influencing people, and maintaining an appearance of control."

"Yes, old ideas are not very popular," agreed Peter. "Somewhere in the last generation or two, the very word 'old' became a pejorative term. Now it's synonymous with worn-out and obsolete, and 'new' automatically means improved and superior. This might be perfectly fine in talking about machines, but it's tragic for living systems.

"Several years ago, Debashish Chatterjee, a good friend and well-known author on leadership[1] opened a seminar on leadership at MIT by saying, 'I've been guided in my work by the notion that older is often better. If an idea has been around for a few thousand years, it's been submitted to many tests—which is a good indicator that it might have some real merit. We're fixated on newness, which often misleads us into elevating novelty over substance.'"

"And with the loss of valuing the 'old,' elders passed from our midst," said Joseph, "wisdom was replaced by technical expertise, and aging came to be seen as a long descent from youth and vigor to old age and infirmity." He frowned. "I think the costs of these shifts for human happiness and social stability have been incalculable."

"The connection to the ancient Greeks and Chinese really strikes me," said Otto. "Of all the interviews I've done, none was more interesting than the one with Master Nan Huai Chin in Hong Kong. Even though Peter helped make the introduction, we've never talked about my visit. I think that much of what we're coming to understand about the U movement was laid out long ago in Chinese culture, although its meaning is all but lost today. Nan is regarded by many in China as the most important living *chan* (Zen) Buddhist master, although he is little known outside of China. He's also a Taoist master and a—some would say 'the'—eminent Confucian scholar. He's written over forty books, which have sold tens of millions of copies in China, mostly on the black market until recently. He is also reputed to be the greatest living expert on Chinese medicine, ancient poetry, and feng shui, the art of physical design—as well as being a leading military strategy and the former kung fu champion of China."

Peter smiled as Otto caught his breath. "Master Nan's accomplishments seem almost impossible to comprehend in one person. One of the senior U.S. State Department officials in China, who told me that traditionally, advisers to the emperors were expected to be masters and integrators of all the Chinese traditions, said, 'He may be the last in this tradition.'"

"I'm not surprised," Betty Sue laughed. "Our modern cultures don't encourage following that kind of path. But Otto, are you saying that Master Nan recognized the U theory?"

"Actually, it was more than that. We started off by talking about his most recent book at that time, a new interpretation of one of the Confucian classics, *The Great Learning*.[2] It's an essay that was originally recorded twenty-four hundred years ago and has been a mainstay of Chinese culture ever since. As one of my interpreters, Dr. Zhao, put it, 'Every emperor respected it, because it talks about how to become a leader.' Still, despite superficial familiarity, its deeper meaning has been lost. The other interpreter, Ken Pang, said that since the Ch'ing Dynasty—the last line of Chinese emperors, which started in 1644— there has been a 'dogmatic interpretation' of the work, which eventually 'contributed to the downfall of that dynasty.' Master Nan then added that the core of the Confucian theory of leadership formation rests on the idea that 'if you want to be a leader, you have to be a real human being. You must recognize the true meaning of life before you can become a great leader. You must understand yourself first.'"

Joseph nodded. "Bill O'Brien used to say, 'The success of an intervention depends on the inner condition of the intervener.' That's far more important than techniques or strategies for change."

"Right," Otto agreed. "In this sense, the cultivated self is a leader's greatest tool. This idea is a cornerstone of traditional thinking about leadership in indigenous cultures, as it was in ancient China and India.

"But one reason this traditional view has been largely discarded is that it's difficult. It's the journey of a lifetime. And much of the practical know-how that might have once guided individuals on this journey has passed out of the mainstream of contemporary society, even in those societies like China that still preserve elements of their ancient teachings. The distinctiveness of Master Nan's new interpretation is to show that *The Great Learning* actually presents a detailed theory of leadership cultivation.

"'If you want to be a great leader,' he said, 'you need to enter seven meditative spaces. These seven spaces—awareness, stopping, calmness, stillness, peace, true thinking, and attainment—can look like one step, but actually, it's a long, long, long process.'

"Pang explained that the established interpretation of the first two steps, awareness and stopping, had become that each person needed to be aware of their position in society and not overstep it. 'The emperors would say that you have to know where to stop, you have to listen to everything I say, you have to be subservient.' Master Nan's interpretation of 'stopping' in *The Great Learning* is very different. He says that the original meaning was 'stopping the flow of thought.'

"Professor Zhao said it's important for leaders because people who haven't achieved this state will be obstructed by all kinds of different emotions—greed, fear, anger, anxiety—that will prevent them from making 'right judgments.'

"Master Nan told a story about a famous Chinese prime minister when China was still divided into many small states. The man's son was arrested and about to be executed in a neighboring state. The man wanted to send his youngest son to rescue him, but his oldest son objected. 'Sending your youngest son means you don't think I'm capable,' said the oldest son. 'Send me.'

"The man relented and sent his oldest son to rescue the son in prison. The oldest son found a minister who was very close to the emperor and pleaded with him, offering him money for the release of the brother. The minister said he would help. Soon it was announced that the emperor would release all prisoners. Hearing this, the oldest son thought, 'Terrific. I don't need to give the money I had promised to this guy, since all prisoners will be released.' But the minister had convinced the emperor to release all prisoners as an act of magnanimity, to enhance the emperor's reputation and benefit the entire country. When the minister learned that the eldest brother was now withholding the money, he went back to the emperor and persuaded him to release all the prisoners except the son, who was executed.

"When the eldest son returned to his family, carrying the body of his brother, the father's apprehensions about sending the eldest were confirmed. Why? Because the father knew that the eldest son worked very hard for his money and wouldn't want to give it away, while the youngest son didn't have the same attachment to money.

"'Attachment affects our ability to judge, and our knowing,' Zhao told me. 'That's what it means when you don't know how to stop.'

"'In Buddhism,' Pang said, 'thinking is like a waterfall. You look at a waterfall, and you just see water coming down. It's like a curtain of water. But everyone knows that the waterfall is really composed of water drops. Thinking is the same. Our mind runs so rapidly that we perceive our thinking as if it's a waterfall. But if you're aware, if you're able to stop, you know that thinking is just tiny drops.'

"'Thoughts,' Nan said, 'pass one, one, one, like that. Most people can't see the gaps between the thoughts. Advanced cultivators learn to see that 'thoughts change every moment, every second. We're always being cheated by our thoughts,' taking them as reality.

"Stopping begins to occur spontaneously as soon as we're able to see our thoughts. 'As soon as you're aware, you're already stopping,' Pang told me. 'Not until we stop can the essential question appear. Before "stopping," our goals and aims are more likely to be a reflection of our past than what's really needed now.'"

Joseph leaned forward with excitement. "The parallels of the Confucian theory to the movement down the U sound pretty remarkable. Becoming aware of yourself and the world by stopping the flow of thought sounds exactly like Francisco Varela's comments on suspension and removing ourselves from the habitual stream of thought."

"They are," replied Otto. "And as Master Nan explained the remaining five stages, the parallels continued. He did a quick summary, saying, 'Once you actually stop, you move to the third stage: *samadhi*, or calmness. When you reach true calmness of mind, then you'll be able to reach true quietness or stillness. You'll be in a state of peacefulness in which you can truly think. When you can truly think, then you can attain the goals that you're supposed to achieve.'

"The seven meditative spaces of leadership basically consist of two movements. The first movement could be called the 'way in,' which is to move from normal awareness to a place of true stillness, what we've called the bottom of the U. The second movement could be called 'the return,' which is about returning to more normal levels of activity with new awareness, without losing the presence of the deepest point. This is the whole movement we've been working to understand, albeit in a different language. And the parallels at specific spaces are striking. For example, Nan said that when the mind becomes truly calm and you enter the first stages of *samadhi*, you begin to see 'the life process at work.' That sounds very much like what we've been calling redirecting, or re-orienting our attention to the living process behind whatever is immediately visible."

"So, taken together, the first three spaces—awareness, stopping, and calmness—are all about connecting deeply to present reality, the essence of sensing, and moving down the U," Joseph said.

"Right," said Otto. "And when I asked if it was valid to consider these three spaces as seeing reality more deeply, Pang responded, 'This is the only way to see present reality.'

"Nan also commented on a shift in our awareness of the self, which we now know is part of what happens at the bottom of the U. Embedded in this steady stream of thoughts are habitual thinking patterns that shape our most basic experiences and beliefs, including our standard notion of self. We take our concept of our self as reality. But Nan said, 'Thoughts are not a person. Thoughts change all the time.' According to *The Great Learning*, stillness and peace arise when we penetrate through everyday thoughts to our deeper experience. When this happens, Nan says, 'you get rid of the habitual view of the self.'"

"What Varela described as discovering the 'virtuality of the self' and Ohashi as the 'alien self,'" Joseph affirmed.

"Yes. Later Nan said, 'We say "we," the human. Actually, this is just a symbol representing something. Ultimately speaking, there is no such thing as a person. It doesn't really exist.' "[3]

"This is exactly what Ohashi was talking about when he spoke of the 'nothingness' that 'enables my existence,'" said Peter. "This illusory aspect of our everyday awareness of self is very hard for Westerners to grasp but foundational to traditional Eastern thought. There is a wonderful poem attributed to a Chinese sage, Wu Wei Wu:

> "Why are you so unhappy?
> Because ninety-nine percent of what you think,
> And everything you do,
> Is for your self,
> And there isn't one. [4]

"I think that one of the fundamental ideas of Buddhism is that the reality of the phenomenal world is emptiness. This connects directly to the physical science understanding that all manifest phenomena are in flux, including our bodies and physical selves. We reify these through our thought, which creates the appearance in our awareness of substance, but this appearance is illusory. The really key notion of Eastern philosophy in general is that another dimension of reality exists that is not phenomenal, that is actually substantial and enduring, and that this reality is accessed as we're able to control our thought. This is why the physicist David Bohm spent ten years in conversations with the Indian philosopher Khrishnamurti, exploring parallels to his theory of the implicate order, the generative field underlying manifest reality. I think it also explains why many scientists we've interviewed are serious practitioners of Eastern disciplines today."

"Practice and cultivation are critical," said Otto. "The Confucian theory concerns long-term individual 'cultivation' or development. Although he says no fixed amount of time is required, Nan talks about 'entering these spaces' as a 'long, long process' of leadership cultivation—in Eastern terms, possibly the journey of many lifetimes. In this sense, the Confucian theory complements the theory of the U. While we've been trying to understand the underlying capacities this movement requires, traditions like Buddhism, Taoism, and many others offer rich tools and methods to develop these capacities. But, none of this matters if we're not personally committed to our own cultivation.

"Although I didn't see the full connection to the U process at the time, I said to Master Nan, 'First you slow down and look deeply into yourself and the world until you start to be present to what's trying to emerge. Then you move back into the world with a unique capacity to act and create. This seems to be very much what *The Great Learning* teaches about leadership cultivation. Does this make sense to you?'

"He affirmed that this was a correct interpretation of his thinking, but not the only one. He said, 'Maybe, later in your life, you will also arrive at other interpretations.'"

"You know, it's amazing how we can pursue a question and eventually come to a place that wise people have reached before and 'know it for the first time,'" Betty Sue said. "But I think it's also important to point out that while leadership cultivation has been the main part of wisdom traditions of the past, it will be different in the future. The leadership of the future will not be provided simply by individuals but by groups, institutions, communities, and networks.

"One of the roadblocks for groups moving forward now is thinking that they have to wait for a leader to emerge—someone who embodies the future path. But I think what we've been learning with the U process is that the future can emerge within the group itself, not embodied in a 'hero' or traditional 'leader.' I think this is the key going forward—that we have to nurture a new form of leadership that doesn't depend on extraordinary individuals."

"I totally agree. But what does that imply in terms of personal cultivation?" asked Otto.

"I think it's more important than ever," replied Betty Sue, "but for more people. Plus, the cultivation will occur within and among larger collectives of people. We need to learn the disciplines that will help cultivate the wisdom of the group and larger social systems."

"This is the defining feature of our era regarding leadership," Peter stated. "In a world of global institutional networks, we face issues for which hierarchical leadership is inherently inadequate. This is the big difference between our world and the context that led to the leadership ideas of Confucius and Plato twenty-five hundred years ago.

"We see this all the time as we work with CEOs of even global corporations. It's easy for people on the outside to greatly overestimate their power. I remember one man saying half jokingly that he always imagined that when he finally made it to the top of the company, he would look under his desk and he'd see these levers he could pull to make things happen. He said it was a sobering experience to finally get there and look under the desk and discover there were none. I think this is no different for heads of state. What distinctive power does exist at the top of hierarchies is usually skewed toward power to destroy rather than the power to build. In a few weeks, a CEO can destroy trust and distributed knowledge that took years to build. The power to wage war is far greater than the power to wage peace."

"As models of leadership shift from organizational hierarchies with leaders at the top to more distributed, shared networks, a lot changes," said Betty Sue. "For those networks to work with real awareness, many people will need to be deeply committed to cultivating their capacity to serve what's seeking to emerge.

"That's why I think that cultivation, 'becoming a real human being,' really is the primary leadership issue of our time, but on a scale never required before. It's a very old idea that may actually hold the key to a new age of 'global democracy.'"

14.

Science Performed with the Mind of Wisdom

At the International Institute for Applied Systems Analysis outside Vienna, Austria, many years ago, a senior officer from the United Nations closed his presentation by saying, "I've dealt with many different problems around the world, and I've concluded that there's only one real problem: over the past hundred years, the power that technology has given us has grown beyond anyone's wildest imagination, but our wisdom has not. If the gap between our power and our wisdom is not redressed soon, I don't have much hope for our prospects."[1]

What if science, like democracy, is an unfinished project? What if the mainstream view of science and the technology it engenders—which increasingly shapes modern society—is but one early prototype, a prototype with great power but also significant limitations?

And what if a new science is emerging, one that might, by its nature, better integrate knowledge and wisdom?

Our interviews with leading scientists from diverse fields, combined with our own experiences, have led us to conclude that the movement through the U is inseparable from an unfolding revolution in the modern scientific worldview; indeed, the theory of the U is but one expression of this movement. Both the theory of the U and this revolution are based on an understanding of reality that differs fundamentally from the world of Newtonian billiard balls, where change arises from one object colliding with another, and the greater the force the greater the change. Just as the theory of electromagnetic fields, and, later, of quantum fields transformed the Newtonian worldview of isolated particles, this emerging science potentially transforms the particle nature of the isolated self.

Connectedness is the defining feature of the new worldview—connectedness as an organizing principle of the universe, connectedness between the "outer world" of manifest phenomena and the "inner world" of lived experience, and, ultimately, connectedness among people and between humans and the larger world. While philosophers and spiritual teachers have long spoken about connectedness, a scientific worldview of connectedness could have sweeping influence in "shifting the whole," given the role of science and technology in the modern world.

The new integrative science has roots in the relativity and quantum theory revolutions in physics of the early twentieth century, but it also draws on much more recent developments in physics, biology, cognitive psychology, and medicine, to name a few. And while many innovators within established Western scientific fields are contributing to its development, there is also an increasing influence from outside Western science—for example, non-Western medicine and the scientific traditions of indigenous peoples. In fact, at this stage, there is still little consensus on even the major dimensions of a more integrative scientific worldview—its ontology (basic assumptions about reality), epistemology (basic assumptions about knowing), or methodology.

The lack of consensus is inevitable: it took more than two centuries for the scientific paradigm pioneered by Galileo, Newton, Kepler, and Descartes to coalesce as the core of Western science. Another century or more passed before the basic paradigm infiltrated mainstream society through applied technologies, public education, and the spread of Western scientific thinking into leadership and management.

Undoubtedly, what emerges from this newest revolution will be a synthesis of the old and the new. Just as the Newtonian paradigm did not disappear from twentieth-century physics, many tried and tested aspects of established scientific understanding and method will be integral to any future worldview. So too will be the human and social dimensions of change, because the emerging scientific worldview is as much about us as it is about "science."

Twenty years ago, Joseph met with the eminent quantum theorist David Bohm in London. Bohm, a former colleague of Albert Einstein at Princeton, whom Einstein regarded as an intellectual successor,[2] told Joseph, "The most important thing going forward is to break the boundaries between people so we can operate as a single intelligence. Bell's theorem implies that this is the natural state of the human world, separation without separateness. The task is to find ways to break these boundaries, so we can be in our natural state."[3]

Unlike the Newtonian paradigm, theories such as the U that connect human development, awareness, and institutional change may be crucial to the new scientific worldview—and to the speed with which it influences society. We may not have the luxury of waiting two to three centuries for a science of connectedness to create a wiser society.

Fragmentation

Science and art—two of the oldest activities in human culture—are both dedicated to investigating reality. Art, wholly dependent on the direct experience of the artist, deepens our understanding by asking, as the painter Gauguin put it, "Where do we come from? What are we? Where are we going?" Native science, the traditional science of indigenous peoples around the world, similarly seeks to foster an understanding of the universe in ways that nurture our connection and relationship to the earth and the whole of the natural world.[4] How, then, has modern science developed in such different ways?

The basic problem is "fragmentation," said Bohm, a way of thinking that "consists of false division, making a division where there is tight connection" and of seeing separateness where there is wholeness.[5] Bohm called fragmentation—in our view of the universe and of ourselves as separate from one another and nature—"the hidden source of the social, political, and environmental crises facing the world."[6]

This fragmentation is reflected in the rigid academic divisions among scientific subjects—chemistry, physics, biology, psychology, astronomy, geology, zoology, physiology, economics, sociology, and so on—that thwart systemic understanding across boundaries. In fact, the further one advances in any scientific discipline, the more narrow it tends to become. This carries over into all fields in modern society, to the extent that what it means to be "an expert" today is knowing a lot about a little.

More subtly, our fragmented mind-set is evident in the traditional scientific focus on studying isolated things. For hundreds of years, the prototypical "thing" was the atom, long thought in the West to be the most basic building block in nature. By the middle of the nineteenth century, physicists had started to see that the atom itself could be further fragmented, leading initially to seeing it, too, as made up of still smaller things: neutrons, protons, and electrons. But this whole infinite reduction to smaller and smaller things eventually broke down in the twentieth century, leading physicists into an entirely new domain of quantum energy fields, "electron clouds," and probabilities rather than definitive statements about the subatomic world.

The belief that understanding lay in studying isolated things has largely persisted in the social sciences and still dominates everyday affairs. It led economists to focus on isolated "rational actors" in explaining how markets worked. It led Freud to explain human behavior in terms of its "atomic constituents"—the ego, superego, and id — and biased the whole field of psychology to focus on the individual apart from family, work, and larger networks of relationships.[7] Even collective phenomena in the social sciences are often studied as if they were isolated things. Studies of effective teams in work settings, for example, typically focus on roles, tasks, and interpersonal dynamics, ignoring the fact that a team's effectiveness often depends on how it interacts with the larger organizational context.[8] Similar dynamics play out in public affairs. Political conflicts are driven by people defining threats in the form of external "enemies," all the while failing to see the network of dysfunctional relationships that bind our enemies and ourselves together.

Atomistic thinking shapes almost all management actions. Organizational performance is measured by adding up the performance of isolated "business units." When there are difficulties, individuals are fired or individual business units sold off, with no account taken of larger systems that may have caused the problems—or the consequences for know-how embedded in the social networks severed by the changes. A veteran senior engineering manager of a former Fortune 100 company that had all but collapsed had a simple explanation for its unexpected demise: "One reorganization too many. After the last 'reorg,' the social networks collapsed. People simply did not know who knew what or how to get the help that they needed."

Measurement

Ironically, a primary agent driving the ascent of fragmentation in science and society is one of science's greatest tools: measurement. Not only is quantitative measurement an invaluable tool of the scientific method, it's an indispensable aid to management discipline. But it can easily become elevated to a sweeping generalization about reality. When this happens, people start to believe that something is "real" only to the extent that it's measurable. Managers know this assumption as the familiar dictum "You can't manage what you can't measure," or "People pay attention only to what gets measured."

Not only does overreliance on measurement doom modern society to continuing to see a world of things rather than relationships, it also gives rise to the familiar dichotomy of the "hard stuff" (what can be measured) versus the "soft stuff" (what can't be measured). If what's measurable is "more real," it's easy to relegate the soft stuff, such as the quality of interpersonal relationships and people's sense of purpose in their work, to a secondary status. This is ironic because the soft stuff is often the hardest to do well and the primary determinant of success or failure. For example, engineers know that the best technical solutions often fail to be implemented, or are not successful when they are, because of low trust and failed communication.

The problem is not measurement per se. The problem is the loss of balance between valuing what can be measured and what cannot, and becoming so dependent on quantitative measures that they displace judgment and learning. When this happens, you see managers "driving" organizations to meet quantitative goals set at the top, with little serious effort to build new capacities required to achieve sustainable levels of improved performance. The resulting "management by fear," in the words of the famous quality management pioneer W. Edwards Deming, pervades modern institutions, from businesses driven to meet Wall Street expectations to schools driven to improve scores on standardized tests.

As the physicist Fritjof Capra points out, it's not possible to measure a relationship. A few leading management thinkers and organizations seem to have come to a similar understanding. The accounting theorist and coinventor of activity-based costing (ABC), H. Thomas Johnson, says, "Quantitative thinking originated when Galileo proposed the idea of studying motion as a concept separate from the object moving."[9]

Quantifying aspects of a system separate from the system as a whole became a cornerstone of Western science and eventually Western management, where managers think nothing of setting arbitrary cost or production targets to drive change. Yet you cannot measure velocity or profits without fragmenting these measures from a larger whole, something a handful of companies have come to understand. For example, Toyota's market capitalization exceeds the sum of Ford's, General Motors', and DaimlerChrysler's (and has for most of the past two decades). Johnson shows that Toyota has no centralized cost-accounting system that enables top managers to drive "disembodied (cost) targets." Instead, its superior cost and financial performance stems from "sophisticated measurement practices implemented locally where they can enable human judgment and learning about the whole, rather than displace them."[10]

Unbroken Wholeness

In short, the fundamental insight of twentieth-century physics has yet to penetrate the social world: *relationships are more fundamental than things*. "At all levels of life," writes Capra, "from the metabolic networks inside cells to the food webs of ecosystems and the networks of communications in human societies, the components of living systems are inter-linked in network fashion."[11] While the slow acceptance of this idea reflects the inevitable delays in an alternative worldview's gaining credibility, the evidence is mounting. Moreover, the extent of the interrelatedness of nature may be far greater than almost anyone might have imagined.

In a lecture at University College in London in the mid-1950s, Bohm described an implication of the quantum theory and the idea for an experiment that captivated a young physicist in the audience, J. S. Bell. Bell worked out the theory more fully, as well as the means to test it experimentally.[12] The results of the experiment and its many successors, demonstrating what's now known in physics as "nonlocality," have been called "one of the most shocking events in twentieth-century science."[13]

Bohm had predicted that when an atomic particle is split in two and the spin of one portion of the split particle is altered, the spin of the other portion would also change—instantaneously, regardless of the distance that separated them! Years later Bohm wrote, "It is an inference from the quantum theory that events that are separated in space and that are without possibility of connection through interaction are correlated, in a way that it can be shown is incapable of a detailed causal explanation."[14]

Bell's theorem and nonlocality reveal a level of interrelatedness that defies common notions of cause and effect, the cornerstone of the Newtonian world. Today, scientists are engaged in many experiments to explore the extent to which such interdependence exists at more "macroscopic" levels beyond atomic particles.

For example, a recent study has shown that random number generators (RNGs) around the world behaved in highly nonrandom ways on September 11, 2001. RNGs are computer programs that generate numbers that meet statistical conditions for randomness, as required for various research applications. They are shielded from electromagnetics, telecommunications, and all other known forces that could cause systematic biases. In other words, these are computer programs that are supposed to be insulated from all external influences and are tested regularly to assure that this is so. An ongoing monitoring study of thirty-seven RNGs around the world showed the extent of the anomalous behavior on September 11. A recent report in the *Foundations of Physics Letters* documents an abnormally high average variance, autocorrelation (correlation among successive numbers generated by each program), and "internode" correlation (correlation among the different programs) across this global network—on average, the probability of what was observed was less than one in a thousand. Moreover, the minute-by-minute behavior of these statistics across the global network matches the chronology of the terrorist attacks, with the non-random behavior starting around 5:00 A.M. and peaking around 11:00 A.M., Eastern (U.S.) daylight time, staying extremely deviant into the evening. In the words of the authors, the "substantial deviations from chance expectation" on September 11 have potentially "profound theoretical and practical implications." They conclude that "it is unlikely that [known] environmental factors could cause the correlations we observe" and that, barring demonstration to the contrary, "we are obliged to confront the possibility that the measured correlations may be directly associated with some (as yet poorly understood) aspect of consciousness attendant to global events."[15]

Bell's theorem and current research such as the RNG studies suggest an interdependence that extends beyond the "external" world, linking thought, emotion, and measurable phenomena, potentially on even a global scale.[16] This "unbroken wholeness," as Bohm referred to it, challenges a cornerstone doctrine of Western science, first articulated by René Descartes more than three centuries ago. Concerned that science had to escape the oversight of the Church, which had imprisoned pioneers such as Galileo, Descartes said that science should concentrate itself totally on manifest or "extended" phenomenon, *res extensa*, and leave aside any speculation or investigation into inner or "mental phenomena," *res cogens*. While scientists eventually achieved a rapprochement with the Church, the Cartesian split between the inner and outer has shaped science ever since.

The Blind Spot

Victor Weisskopf, a member of the famed Manhattan Project and the head of the MIT Physics Department for many years, once spoke about how he had become a scientist. "When I was a little child I would sit under the piano as my grandmother played Beethoven. Though it was very long ago, I can still remember how I felt as the music washed over me. That is when I became a physicist." Similar feelings of joy and connection and the curiosity they excite have led many other people to become scientists, too. Unfortunately, the cultivation of ever-richer experiences of connection is limited by the Cartesian disregard for the inner state of the scientist.

"The blind spot of contemporary science," says cognitive scientist Francisco Varela, "is experience."[17] In our everyday lives, this means living as "naïve realists," taking our experience for granted, as if our physical senses operate like a sort of camera recording separate external objects. According to Varela and Humberto Maturana, an experimental biologist and architect (along with Varela) of the Santiago Theory of Cognition, a pioneering theory of the biological foundations of perception, naïve realists operate as if "what we see *is*."[18] This would appear to be less true for scientists, who do not rely on sensory data so much as sophisticated instruments to see beyond the senses. But great scientists are distinguished not by their instruments but by their refined capacity to imaginatively examine the awareness their instruments enable. This was the heart of Goethe's method for a more holistic science—cultivation of the capacity to see the living phenomena that become manifest in concrete forms. Einstein is said to have claimed that "intuition was more important than IQ" and that he "never discovered anything with my rational mind." He was famous for his "*gedanken* (thought) experiments," experiments based on his remarkable imaginative capabilities. His basic insights leading to relativity theory, he said, had been discovered imagining himself "traveling on a light beam." Maturana says that "love, allowing the other to be a legitimate other, is the only emotion that expands intelligence."

When people encounter stories such as Weisskopf's experience with music, or hear physicists such as Bohm talk of "separation without separateness" or Einstein talk of intuition, or a biologist such as Maturana speak of love, they may easily dismiss what they hear as "philosophizing." But to do so misses an essential point: these views of the world and of life directly reflect their understanding as scientists. For Weisskopf, real understanding was as much in the body and emotions as in the head, and the strange world of quarks, mesons, and Z-bosons of modern physics had to be "felt" as much as "thought." Bohm's fundamental theoretical contribution concerned "the wholeness of nature" and the continual interplay of the "explicate (or manifest) order" with a subtler "implicate order," where awareness, space, and time are all interdependent. For Einstein, the universe seemed to be telling us one overarching truth, the truth of infinite interdependence. Maturana's understanding of perception centers on the fact that we're not passive observers of an external world; rather, we know our world through interacting with it, and our emotions can limit or enrich that interaction. In short, these statements reflect scientists crossing the epistemological divide between subject and object to address the "blind spot" of which Varela speaks.

A Reflexive Science of Living Systems

Another sign of an emerging integrative worldview in science are the new conceptual frameworks that integrate fragmented academic fields. "Complexity theory is really a movement of the sciences," says the economist Brian Arthur. "The movement that started complexity asks, How do things assemble themselves? Complexity looks at interacting elements and asks how they form patterns and how the patterns unfold, patterns [that] may never be finished [because] they're open-ended. This caused some negative reactions: traditional science doesn't like perpetual novelty. Newtonian laws are supposed to be unchanging. But anything complicated and interactive seems to unfold and develop new structures."

The aim for a more integrative science may be to understand living systems. Capra proposes a synthesis of diverse developments in physics, chemistry, and biology that identifies three basic characteristics of living systems: they create themselves ("autopoeisis"); they generate new patterns of organizing, or "self-organize," in ways that could not be predicted from their past ("emergence"); and they're aware, in the sense of interacting effectively with their environment ("cognition").[19] In developing this synthesis, Capra draws on the work of many leading scientists, including Maturana and Varela, for an understanding of self-creating and awareness, and on the Nobel Laureate chemist Ilya Prigogine's theory of emergent patterns of organization in chemical reactions.

Biologist Rupert Sheldrake's theory of "morphic fields" focuses specifically on the innate potential of living systems to evolve. When Otto interviewed him in 1999, Sheldrake said, "My interest in these ideas first developed while I was doing research on the development of plants at Cambridge University, asking questions about what biologists call morphogenesis, the coming into being of form." Sheldrake was especially interested in the variety of forms that arise from simple origins: "How do plants grow from simple embryos into the characteristic form of their species? How do their flowers develop in such different ways?" The reductionist approach to the problem is to say that all morphogenesis is genetically programmed. Yet, Sheldrake wondered, if all the cells have the same genetic programming, how do they develop so differently? This question eventually drove him to imagine a radical alternative: that invisible blueprints he called "morphic fields" underlie the form of growing organisms. For "self-organizing systems at all levels of complexity, there is a wholeness that depends on a characteristic organizing field of that system. Each self-organizing system is a whole made up of parts, which are themselves whole at a lower level. At each level, the morphic field gives each whole its characteristic properties and makes it more than the sum of its parts."

Sheldrake believes that the morphic fields of living systems themselves evolve, a process he calls "morphic resonance," whereby every embodiment of a living system simultaneously contributes to a larger morphic field and to its evolution. "Any given morphic system, say a giraffe embryo, 'tunes in' to previous similar systems, in this case previous developing giraffes. Through this process, each individual giraffe draws upon, and in turn contributes to, a collective pool of memory of its species." He draws a parallel to the psychologist C. G. Jung's "collective unconscious": for humans, "morphic fields extend beyond the brain into the environment, linking us to the objects of our perception," making us, individually and collectively, "capable of affecting" our larger world "through our intention and attention."

The logical extension of such views is to think of the entire universe as a living, emergent system, transcending the traditional scientific split between the "physical" and "life" sciences. One of the most comprehensive attempts at an integrative theory of an emergent universe was Bohm's "implicate order." In their meeting in London in 1980, Bohm told Joseph that the implicate order is a language rather than "a description of reality." Moreover, it's a language where "you can't associate each word with a thing." Such association, he explained, is how fragmentation arises, such as when we attach a noun label to an aspect of our awareness and it immediately becomes separate and fixed in our minds. In the language of the implicate order, meaning comes from "the whole . . . like in music [where] you can't say one note means anything . . . [or] an impressionist painting [where] when you step back, you see a picture, but there is no correspondence between the spots of paint and what you see in the picture."[20] The explicate order—in Bohm's analogy, the individual notes or dots of color—is manifested in physical reality, but inextricably connected to the implicate order, the underlying whole—the concerto or painting—out of which they arise. Henri Bortoft, the physicist who helped us understand Goethe's science, was a former student and colleague of David Bohm, and the subtle observational capacities he explained as being necessary to appreciate living systems—what he called "exact sensorial imagination"—seem vital to appreciating Bohm's implicate order as well. The basic challenge of understanding Bohm's theory is that it is not about an external reality called "the implicate order" so much as it is about a way that we can be in the world that reveals a deeper level of interdependence. This is why, beyond its mathematics, the theory defies didactic description in a noun-verb language such as English. The theory of the implicate order is by its nature reflexive: beyond a certain point, the only way to evoke a sense of the theory is through personal experiences, especially those experiences when the mind becomes still.

Many years ago, Peter had an experience in midwinter in northern Maine that left a lasting impression about the implicate order. One morning he skied about a mile out onto a frozen lake. It was a calm, beautiful morning, and the sun was just rising. He sat on a rock along the shore of a small island looking across the windblown snow on the lake toward the mountains in the distance.

"It was very quiet, and my mind was so still that I found, after a while, that I had to actually make an effort to form a thought. After a while I gave up and just sat there. Suddenly, I saw that the shape the wind had made in the snow was identical to the shape it had made on those mountains. I did not *think* this thought—I *saw* this directly. The two were the same. In that instant, my sense of time changed completely. One pattern had been formed in two or three days, and one in two or three hundred million years. Yet they were exactly the same, both arising out of the same implicate or generative order. In that moment, my normal experience of space and time vanished, and with it my normal experience of being outside nature."

Undoubtedly, many "radical" integral theories such as the implicate order and morphic fields will be found to be incomplete and perhaps even significantly flawed. But they do illustrate how scientists from diverse fields are thinking seriously today in ways that promise to revolutionize how we understand a systemic, living world. Perhaps more important, these understandings cannot be put into the old box of abstract statements about an "objective" universe. Appreciating the universe as an emergent living phenomenon can be done only "from the inside," through cultivating the capacity to understand the living world *and* ourselves as an interconnected whole. This starts the journey toward a science, as Eleanor Rosch put it, "performed with the mind of wisdom."

Science Performed with the Mind of Wisdom

Perhaps the defining feature of such a science will be that it enhances life. "I chose biology because I loved animals," Sheldrake told Otto. "But I soon realized that the kind of biology I learned involved killing everything and cutting it up. Ever since, I've been driven by the question, What would it take to develop a science that enhances life?"

Such a science will, by its nature, be developmental. The physicist

Arthur Zajonc is a leading scholar of how scientific understanding evolves with different levels of awareness.[21] For Zajonc, in a more integral science, "the theme of human development is an essential feature of . . . scientific investigation."[22] Zajonc means human development in a broad sense, not just the intellectual development characteristic of current scientific training. For example, the capacity to observe starts with learning how to "remain with the phenomenon as the primary source of cognition," which in turn requires "development of the mind-body system in ways that Western education has largely neglected." Zajonc's studies of light led him to discover Goethe's theories of color and view of developmental science—expressed beautifully in Goethe's simple statement "Every object well contemplated opens up a new organ within us."[23] In other words, in order to develop a science that enhances life, we must become more alive.

But as Zajonc, Rosch, and many others have told us, this is not a matter just of method but of intent. Rose von Thater-Braan, one of the organizers of an integrative learning center for the study of indigenous knowledge and native science[24] says, "The many differences between native science and Western science start with intent. The common purpose that drives modern Western science is to understand nature in order to better control—some would say commodify—nature." By contrast, in native science, "The fundamental intent is to become more human and to learn how to live in harmony with nature and with one another. Native scientists may invent technologies to make their life easier, but these are always secondary to human development."[25]

Many of the scientists cited above have spoken powerfully regarding the type of intent needed to give rise to a more integral science. For Bohm, the imperative is to evolve our awareness, so that it might naturally become more whole, more in line with our connectedness to the world. Without such awareness we're blind to the impact of our current ways of thinking. "Thought," as Bohm often said, "creates the world and then says, 'I didn't do it.'" Einstein spoke of the "optical delusion of our consciousness," whereby we experience ourselves "as something separate from the rest." "Our task," he said, "must be to widen our circle of compassion to embrace all living creatures and the whole of nature in its beauty."[26] Maturana's work embodies his commitment to "a manner of co-existence in which love, mutual respect, honesty, and social responsibility arise spontaneously from living instant after instant."[27] He says that we become more human through realizing "that we do not see the world as it is but as we are" and reminds us that "no human being has a privileged view of reality." When we forget our contingent view of reality, we lose our capacity to live together; as Maturana says, when one person or group asserts that only they see "what is really going on," they are actually making a "demand for obedience."

Our Faustian Bargain: Shifting the Burden to Modern Science and Technology

The intention driving mainstream science cannot be addressed separately from the imperative to apply scientific know-how to create new technology. Science and technology together create the reinforcing engine that drives the modern world.

As we all know, our society relies on the power that comes from technology. It is this power that has reshaped the world and continues to do so. It is this power that holds the promise for great benefit—and unprecedented destruction. It is this power that drives wealth creation and the economic incentives for research and development. And it is this power that preserves a status quo that undermines human development in ways that few of us see.

No matter how exciting a more integral science might be, little is likely to change until we understand the forces that have led to our dependence on modern technology and the part we all play in maintaining those forces. It is not just the desire for power that drives modern technology. It is the fear that we cannot live without it.

In the fall of 2001, just after September 11, Peter gave a presentation at the annual Systems Thinking in Action conference, where "a picture that had been kicking around in the back of my head for years suddenly became clear. The extraordinary events and the group of people who had managed to travel from around the world to convene catalyzed one of those 'blinding flashes of the obvious.' I realized that our growing reliance on modern science and technology and our growing sense of disconnection and powerlessness both arose from the same underlying 'shifting-the-burden' dynamic."

"Shifting the burden" is an archetypal systemic structure that arises when people act to ameliorate the symptoms of a problem and end up becoming more and more dependent on these "symptomatic solutions." For example, taking two aspirin to relieve a headache seems innocent enough and indeed may be perfectly appropriate. But what if the source of the headaches is stress from work and family commitments that simply exceed your capacity? In that case, the "successful" medical intervention may actually mask a deeper problem. Not facing the real problem may cause it to get worse: continuing to take on more work will increase the stress and eventually make ever more powerful drugs necessary. After a while, you can't imagine coping with your intense lifestyle without regular medication; you have "shifted the burden" to what was initially seen as a onetime fix, headache relief. If this pattern is not corrected, eventually you do not have just an overwork problem, you have a drug addiction problem. Indeed, the overwork problem may be forgotten as the difficulties of coping with your addiction intensify.

Shifting-the-burden dynamics can arise whenever people face difficult problems and there's a difference between "symptomatic" and "fundamental" solutions.[28] Symptomatic solutions are "quick fixes"—

like taking an aspirin—that address the symptoms of a problem without dealing with deeper causes and more fundamental solutions—like reducing overcommitment. Shifting-the-burden dynamics recur in diverse situations, but they always follow the same systemic pattern. The symptoms of the problem can be addressed either through a symptomatic solution or a fundamental solution. Only the latter will relieve the symptom by addressing its underlying causes. This simple systemic structure gives rise to shifting-the-burden behavior over time when we opt for the symptomatic solution and stop there. The symptomatic solution, two aspirin, relieves the problem symptom, the headache. But this short-term improvement reduces the perceived need for a more fundamental solution—reducing overcommitment. As the fundamental sources of the problem are ignored, symptoms (the headaches) get worse, the symptomatic solutions get more intense (we use increasingly powerful drugs) and the ability to address fundamental causes of the problem atrophies. Finally, increasing reliance on symptomatic solutions usually brings unintended side effects, like health problems which demand more attention.

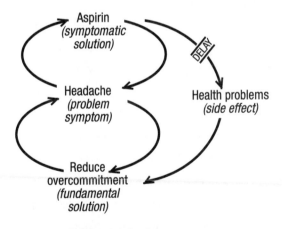

Shifting the Burden

Shifting the burden to aspirin to relieve a headache, rather than addressing the fundamental problem, overcommitment.

We tend to think of addiction as a personal problem. But the shifting-the-burden dynamic shows that it's actually a systemic phenomenon that recurs at many levels. Just as people can become addicted to prescription drugs, alcohol, or cigarettes, companies become addicted to cost cutting to improve profits, governments become addicted to lotteries to raise revenues, and the agriculture industry becomes addicted to pesticides and chemical fertilizers to improve crop yields. Shifting the burden is one of the most common and insidious patterns in a modern society that demands quick solutions to difficult problems. Because it's so common, the shifting-the-burden dynamic typically goes unnoticed. Individuals and institutions fail to see how their capacities for fundamental solutions are eroding until the dependency and side effects build to overwhelming proportions, eventually leading to unavoidable breakdowns.

Western culture's growing reliance on reductionistic science and technology over the past two hundred years fits the shifting-the-burden dynamic remarkably well, revealing a play of forces that create growing technological power and diminishing human development and wisdom. The picture that Peter drew for the conference attendees that morning started with the innate human drive to influence our lives, to make things "better" or in some way more in line with what we care about. This "desire for efficacy" might be the desire to help a sick child, to solve a pressing problem, or to feel secure. One basic way to expand our efficacy is through modern science and technology. But another is through integrated (emotional, mental, physical, and spiritual) growth and enhanced wisdom. This means growing in our sense of connection with nature and with one another and learning to live in ways that naturally cultivate our capacity to be human.

The two approaches are not mutually exclusive, but it's easy to shift the burden to technological solutions and thereby lose sight of developing our own capacities. So we use hand calculators and forget arithmetic. We rely on our cars to take us everywhere and lose the joy of

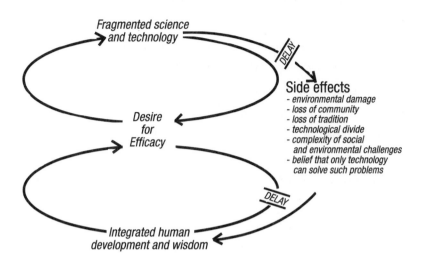

Fragmented science
and technology

DELAY

Side effects
- environmental damage
- loss of community
- loss of tradition
- technological divide
- complexity of social
  and environmental challenges
- belief that only technology
  can solve such problems

Desire
for
Efficacy

DELAY

Integrated human
development and wisdom

Shifting the Burden to Science and Technology

This diagram shows a generic systemic pattern—shifting the burden—
that has influenced Western society for several hundred years by fostering
an increasing reliance on science and technology at the expense of human
development. In shifting-the-burden dynamics, the more often symptomatic solutions such as advances in fragmented science and technology
are used, the more the capacity for fundamental solutions atrophies, leading to an even greater need for symptomatic solutions. Many of today's most
pressing problems, like environmental damage and the technological divide,
arise as longer-term side effects of the shifting-the-burden process, creating still more problem symptoms requiring more technological responses.

walking. We relieve the symptoms of an illness through modern medicine without learning how to heal ourselves. We buy a larger car in
order to feel more secure instead of learning how to understand one
another and create personal security for one another. Most of us have
little idea of our capacity to create the qualities we truly value in living, because our culture has encouraged shifting the burden away from
this sort of knowledge for a very long time. By giving us perceived
power, modern technology reduces the felt need to cultivate our own

sources of power. After a while, power through our technology is all that we know.

There is nothing inherently wrong with technology: advances in technology can further our understanding of the nature of the universe as well as enrich our lives. But like many shifting-the-burden situations, the dangerous aspect of our growing reliance on modern technology is the way it distracts attention from more fundamental sources of progress. The growing gap between technological power and wisdom arises not from technological progress alone but from the way it interacts with more integrative human development. After a while, the very need for such development is all but forgotten. Today, we basically define progress by new developments in technology rather than by any broader notion of advance in well-being. Thus, the ever-widening gap between our wisdom and our power is not accidental or due to bad luck. It arises from a basic structure we enact in modern society. It will continue to get worse until we see this structure.

Seeing is getting harder because one of the most insidious side effects of our reliance on a fragmented science and technology is the increasing complexity of our social and environmental challenges. Historically, human beings faced a very different world of social and environmental issues. If we polluted the local river, the results were right there for all to see. Either we cleaned it up, or we all suffered the consequences. If we were unable to get along with our neighbors, the conflict was between us. Our problems, however severe, were relatively local, close in time and space to where we lived.

But today, many of the negative social and environmental side effects of actions manifest on the other side of the world. A corporate decision made on one side of the world can literally change lives on the other side. This is true for countries as well. The way we live in the U.S., for example, affects people around the world. We have great difficulty seeing these effects. Then when people in other countries oppose or challenge us, we have great difficulty understanding their actions. This is the technical definition of complexity in systems thinking, when cause and effect are no longer close in time and space. As complexity increases, the need for wisdom grows, even as our wisdom atrophies.

We have two basic options if we truly want to reverse the growing gap between our power and our wisdom. One is to somehow stop or limit the expansion of technology. Such a strategy has been advocated by many who stand up to fight technological progress and its application through global economic growth. The other is to strengthen our fundamental response—to find ways that lead to increasing reliance on enhancing human development and wisdom. The highest leverage will come from strategies that inherently do both. The emerging integral science has this potential: to expand practical know-how and human development as two aspects of the same process. While it would be naïve to assume that such a science will simply displace the present fragmented science, it's safe to say that without such a development, the likelihood of reversing the shifting-the-burden dynamic is low.

Perhaps most important, this scientific revolution is not just about the "scientists" but about all of us.

A New Path

"Mind and world are not separate," said Rosch. "Mind and world are aspects of the same underlying field. . . . Since the subjective and objective aspects of experience arise together as different poles of the same act of cognition, they're already joined at their inception. . . . If the senses don't actually perceive the world, if they are instead participating parts of the mind-world whole, a radical reunderstanding of perception is necessary."

Bringing this new understanding of perception into day-to-day work led Greg Merten, general manager of Hewlett-Packard's Ink Jet Supplies Operations, to host a series of several-day seminars with Humberto Maturana. The rationale for confronting practical engineers and managers with seemingly esoteric subjects such as the "biology of cognition" and the "biology of love" was obvious to Merten. "HP prospered historically because it had a set of guiding values that expressed a way of being in the world that our founders, Dave Packard and Bill Hewlett, simply lived. As the company grew, we lost sight of how to conserve those values at the top. Training for executives focused on learning about the business rather than learning about one's effectiveness in relationship with others on behalf of the business. We became more of a 'business' rather than a human community. Why should it be surprising that being a human community hinges on understanding humanness?

"When I say, 'We see the world not as it is but as we are,' I'm offering it as a timeless leadership lesson consistent with Humberto's groundbreaking work in the biology of cognition. We all tend to think of ourselves as objective observers, but none of us are. If I want to see things change 'out there,' first I need to see change 'in here.'

"At the heart of the challenge facing HP—and lots of other businesses—is the way information moves around the world. In order to grow in line with our business, new ways of experiencing information will be needed. When Humberto says that 'love is the only emotion that expands intelligence,' it reminds us that legitimacy and trust are crucial for the free flow of information and for how information gets transformed into value. We will need to use the heart more, which means the quality of our being and relationships with one another become more and more central in allowing an organization to flourish."

Seeing the emerging whole can start from many places: from the outlines of a new, more integral science, the imperative to work together differently, or the evolution of spirituality. In Hong Kong,

Master Nan said, "What has been lacking in the twentieth century is a central cultural thought that would unify all these things: economy, technology, ecology, society, matter, mind, and spirituality. There are no great philosophers or great thinkers who've been able to develop the thinking that unifies all these questions." The decline in integrative awareness and thinking has been replaced by a focus on business and making money as a default common aim. When Otto told Master Nan he thought human culture was on the verge of a new spiritual awareness, Nan agreed but said that it might not develop as most expect. It "will be a different spiritual route from that of the past, either in the East or West. It will be a new spiritual path.

"As early as the forties, many Westerners began seeking spiritual liberation through Hinayana Buddhism, Mahayana Buddhism, Tantric Buddhism, and meditation. But they haven't gotten into the center: What is human nature? Where does life come from? What is life for?

"What was important for the ancient leaders of China—to develop a culture that respected these questions—is important again today. But the future will also be different because of the progress of the past several hundred years. It's timely that the old theories be reexamined and combined with science. They should not be believed in rigidly."

The tendency of our interviewees to focus primarily on either moving down or up the U bears out this absence of an integrating thought. Scientists—such as Varela, Rosch, and Bortoft—probe the deeper processes of observation. "People of action"—such as Hanauer, Webber, Posely, and Kao—offer compelling accounts of the deeper dimensions of creating. But the key lies in transforming both our capacity to see and our capacity to create. In effect, the U theory suggests that the central integrating thought of which Nan speaks will emerge from building three integrated capacities: a new capacity for observing that no longer fragments the observer from what's observed; a new capacity for stillness that no longer fragments who we really are from what's emerging; and a new capacity for creating alternative realities that no longer fragments the wisdom of the head, heart, and hand. Or, as Otto puts it, "What's emerging is a new synthesis of science, spirituality, and leadership as different facets of a single way of being."

The inventor Buckminster Fuller used to say that all of us are scientists; in other words, we all have the capacity for primary knowing, for seeing the generative processes of life. Today we've put science on a pedestal, where it occupies a position similar to that of religious institutions in the past. Scientists have become people who tell us how things "really" are, and most of us have become passive recipients of their knowledge.

Fuller had a very different view. For him, science was "putting the data of your experience in order." He believed that the future lay in cultivating the scientist in all of us. If science is an unfinished project, the next stage will be about reconnecting and integrating the rigor of scientific method with the richness of direct experience to produce a science that will serve to connect us to one another, ourselves, and the world.

15.

Presence

January 2002

It was midwinter before the four of us were all together again, sitting in a circle in Otto's study on Maple Avenue. Just over a year had passed since our first meeting, but in many ways it felt like a lifetime.

~

"So much has happened over the last year that when I look back to our first meeting, it seems as if we're living in a different world today," said Betty Sue. "People are more aware of the dangers we face and perhaps more receptive to the issues underlying the requiem scenario. But ever since Joseph asked, 'What will it take to shift the whole?,' I've been wondering: if shifting the whole requires deep change on a scale that most of us have never experienced, are we ready for this kind of change?"

"Jiro Nonaka, who coauthored *The Knowledge-Creating Company*, calls this 'a time of clashing forces,'[1] and I'd have to agree," said Peter. "It's a time of extraordinary crosscurrents. Things are getting better, and things are getting worse. On the one hand, people seem much more open to talking about large-scale issues that have no simple solutions, like those the Marblehead group identified, and more large organizations are working seriously to address them. But most of the problems eliciting these responses are getting worse, and there seems to be more and more of a backlash to maintain the status quo. Traditional mind-sets and institutional priorities are under great threat, and they're fighting to preserve themselves—which, if you think about it, is exactly what you would expect in times of epochal change."

"I always worry about the temptation to seek a simple story in fearful times like these," said Betty Sue. "Simple stories of good guys and bad guys may ease our anxiety in the short term, but oversimplifying is exactly what we don't need right now."

Peter nodded. "The rise of fundamentalism around the world is part of the backlash to preserve the status quo. Someone in a recent SoL program said, 'I worry much more today about unquestioned answers than about unanswered questions.' Whether religious or political, fundamentalism allows us to avoid deeper issues and the real need to listen to one another."

"The irony is that thanks to our global media we all witness dramatic events virtually simultaneously," said Betty Sue. "But even though we receive the same images, we don't experience the same thing. What many Americans see in events like September 11, or in the conflicts in the Middle East or Africa, is very different from what many Europeans or Arabs or Asians see. If anything, these common images highlight the deeper differences in our worldviews. I think people are increasingly aware of these differences, and that awareness raises our anxiety level even further."

"It's almost as if we're living in a split world," said Otto. "Plus, the clashing forces Nonaka talks about show up personally, as well as publicly. On the one hand, many people are experiencing a profound opening. But we're also experiencing a buildup of pressure, tension, and anxiety. Time is speeding up. The people and organizations we work with are just like me, struggling to simultaneously speed up and slow down. As the need for reflection and deeper learning grows, the pressures against that need being fulfilled grow too."

"But the opening is occurring, and if anything, our most recent sensing interviews and projects in places like Guatemala and South Africa show that those people on the periphery of the first-world mainstream society are most open," said Joseph.

"Something seems to be shifting," said Betty Sue. "But the changes are subtle and probably fragile."

"Very fragile," Joseph concurred. "Many of our interviewees over the past five years talked about profound personal experiences that altered their worldview and then said that they'd never told anyone else what they told us. The opening that is occurring is disorienting, and people can easily feel alone."

"Do you remember the movie *The Shawshank Redemption?*" asked Peter. "There was a very poignant part of the story where a man who had been in prison for most of his life finally gets released at the age of seventy or so. But he has no way to live in the world outside of prison, and he ends up committing suicide. I believe that little story is a lesson for all of us. It reminds us of the difficulties of adjusting to a reality that differs from the world that's familiar and comfortable, even if that reality is one where we're 'free' and aligns much more with what we truly value.

"I think our culture's dominant story is a kind of prison. It's a story of separation—from one another, from nature, and ultimately even from ourselves. In extraordinary moments—like Otto's fire story or Joseph's experience in Baja—we break out of the story. We encounter a world of being one with ourselves, others, nature, and life in a very direct way. It's beautiful and awe-inspiring. It shifts our awareness of our world and ourselves in radical ways. It brings a great sense of hope and possibility but also great uncertainty. It can also be hard suddenly finding ourselves outside the story that has organized our life up to that point. It's wonderful to be free, but also terrifying.

"I think our interviews show that more and more people are getting out of 'prison' today, and many, like young people and those outside the Western mainstream, were never fully in the prison in the first place."

"The whole situation is exactly what Plato described in the allegory of the cave," said Otto. "If you have been living all your life in a cave, looking at shadows moving across the wall, suddenly finding yourself outside can be blinding."

"Speaking from firsthand experience, that allegory is more than just an interesting story," said Peter. "Our culture's dominant story is not something external, it's part of us, and it's certainly part of me. The pressures to pull myself back into the cave or prison, to go back to my habitual ways of living, can be overwhelming sometimes.

"There's an old saying in Buddhism, 'There's nothing more difficult than changing yourself.' It's one thing to have momentary transcendent experiences, to be outside the prison or cave, but it's another to stabilize the awareness they bring. But going back into the cave can also be painful, because you no longer quite fit there. You're now aware of real limitations in your traditional way of living. So you can feel caught between two worlds. Part of you wants to flee the sunlight and return to the cave, but you are also more and more out of sync with life in the cave."

"It makes me wonder whether the most important part of the

interviews is simply helping people see that they're not alone," said Betty Sue.

"People really want to tell their story," Otto agreed. "But they often fear being seen as part of some weird minority. They may not know that many people are having experiences much deeper than the mainstream worldview can account for."

"The cultural historian Thomas Berry says that the primary problem of the present era is that we're 'in between stories'," said Peter. "Berry says the old story that bound Western culture, the story of reductionistic science and redemptive religion, is breaking down. It simply no longer explains the world we are experiencing or the changes that confront us."[2]

"Maybe more people are wandering outside the cave than we realize, or at least getting close to its edge," said Betty Sue. "At the heart of a culture's dominant story sit core myths, and these myths shape how we make sense of the world. In addition to reductionistic science and redemptive religion, other core myths are breaking down—like the story of the 'hero.' We can no longer simply wait around for a great leader to come along and save us. While many people might still be hoping for this, I think fewer and fewer believe it will happen. And the economic myth we've been in for most of the past century isn't serving us well either. I think people are waking up to the inadequacies of the economic myth—they're questioning whether short-term self-interest will solve our problems."

"These are the stories that defined life in the cave," said Peter, "different threads of the story of separation. But outside the cave we don't yet have a new story that's clear enough, simple enough, and widely understood enough to serve a new community of thought. I think we are trapped between stories."

"David Bohm said that his theory of the implicate order was first and foremost a language, a new way of thinking and talking together," noted Joseph. "Maybe the first need is not for a new story. It takes a long time to develop a new dominant story in a culture. Perhaps what we need now is a new language with which we can start to think and talk coherently about these things."

"Maybe that's what we're doing with this theory of the U," said Betty Sue. "We're trying to develop a language that can help people think and talk together about how the whole can shift. We know so much about the problems of the world today that it's easy to fall into fear and denial. What we need is a language of hope and possibility that's grounded in ideas and experiences emerging from innovators in science, business, and communities.

"So if people need a language with which to think and talk about a different way of being in the world, and if we think the U theory might provide such a language, where are we now?"

"The basic ideas have become much clearer to me over the past year," said Peter. "The movement down the U, transforming our habitual ways of seeing, describes a clear progression that I think people can understand. Likewise, moving up the U, transforming the source of our awareness, is certainly familiar to entrepreneurs in all domains."

"And the insights of people like Rosch, Webber, Ray, Bortoft, Rao, Hock and Varela have given us a much more precise way to describe the capacities and subtle distinctions involved in both movements," said Otto.

"I've found that real understanding comes for many people we work with if they can remember a time when they've truly surrendered to their commitment," said Joseph. "Once they've experienced the periods of synchronicity that follow, they're left with a burning question as to how to bring this about again more reliably.

"Clearly, people relate to the U theory in different ways. Some appreciate the distinct capacities in moving down and then up the U. Others just seem to grasp the whole of it and aren't really interested in the different capacities and aspects. Others respond to the idea of

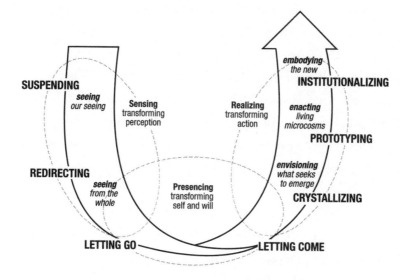

Seven Capacities of the U Movement

The entire U movement arises from seven core capacities and the activities they enable. Each capacity is a gateway to the next activity—the capacity for suspending enables seeing our seeing, and the capacity for prototyping enables enacting living microcosms—but only as all seven capacities are developed is the movement through the entire process possible.

seeing with the heart and opening up to something beyond yourself, and to spontaneous action in support of the whole."

"In my experience, the part that people struggle most to understand," said Betty Sue, "is the bottom of the U—*presencing*."

"Yes, that is really is the 'heart of the heart,' as Eleanor Rosch puts it," said Peter. "It's the essence of the whole theory, and perhaps what we really may be discovering about shifting the whole."

"The mystery at the bottom of the U . . . ," said Betty Sue slowly. "In the end, it may be impossible to give a very complete explanation of it. Some things are beyond human comprehension, and it's actually unwise—some would say irreverent—to try to analyze them too far."

"Why irreverent?" asked Joseph.

"In the sense that to be reverent is to be humble in the face of 'the gods'—something larger than your mind can encompass."

"Maybe this is as it should be," said Peter. "I agree that it would be unwise to boil it down into an 'official account.' But I think that our experiences and ways of thinking about presencing are different in subtle ways, and it would be useful to tease out these differences.

"What do we mean by 'presencing' and the capacity to have a different relationship to the future? In particular, Joseph and Otto, you often talk about becoming aware of 'a future seeking to emerge.' This seems to imply that the future has intentionality, which is not something that most people would readily connect with. Is this consistent with your experience?"

"Yes, I think so," said Joseph.

"My view may be a little different," said Otto. "To me, presencing is about 'pre-sensing' and bringing into presence—and into the present—your highest future potential. It's not just 'the future' in some abstract sense but my own highest future possibility as a human being."

"What about the implied intentionality in the phrase 'seeking to emerge'?" asked Peter. "How do you see that? Do you mean there's something out there called a 'future potential' that *wants* to become present?"

"Yes," said Otto, "but it's a level of reality that's not exterior to or separate from our highest self—what Michael Ray called 'your Self,' with a capital *S*. I'm not thinking about a separate future, something 'out there' that calls to me. That would be just like seeing my current reality 'out there'—another dualistic 'subject-object' perception. At the bottom of the U, this sort of dualism no longer exists.

"The key is that your highest future possibility is related to your own highest purpose or intention. It's more an intention you build for yourself, for your life, perhaps even before you are born."

"Do you mean this intention develops prior to this lifetime, over several reincarnations or embodiments?" asked Peter.

"Well, to me, it's a legitimate question," said Otto. "It goes beyond my conscious experience, but I think it's a perfectly legitimate hypothetical lens to use for looking at things. We must remember that probably half the people in the world do believe in reincarnation. It's just not a notion that's part of our Western, materialistic culture."

"In other words, we shouldn't reject it automatically," said Peter.

"Right," said Otto. "The important point is that in exploring this future potential, you aren't exploring a future someone else has written for you. It's more intimately connected with your evolving, authentic Self—who you really are. It's much more fluid, more open, more in dialogue with you. And yet, at its core, it's connected to the alien part within ourselves that Ohashi was talking about. This is why Martin Buber said that 'it stands in need of you in order to be born.' I've experienced this element—the evolving future field—as a being that is actually *looking at me*. In the moment you feel that gaze, you feel the world stopping. After that you're no longer the same."

"Yes, but there's an 'it' there," said Joseph. "This is where my experience is a little bit different, Otto. When Buber says 'bring it to reality as it desires,' that suggests that there aren't one or two or an infinite number of possibilities waiting to be brought to fruition. For me, it's being an instrument of life itself, to accomplish, in a sense, what life or God, or however you want to put it, wishes for me to accomplish."

"So, Joseph, coming back to this issue of intentionality, it sounds to me as if you're very comfortable with the idea that life has an intention," said Peter. "For you, Buber's term 'as it desires' feels right."

"It does. The more I've worked with that quote over the years, the more I've felt that it describes explicitly what I experience. For me, 'Bring it to reality as it desires' means using ourselves as an instrument for something better to emerge, being open to our larger purpose.

"I believe that everyone is born with a destiny or a purpose, and the journey is to find it. That's the way I read Robert Greenleaf's work on servant leadership: the ultimate aim of the servant leader, the quest, is to find the resources of character to meet your destiny, and to find the wisdom and power to serve life that way.[3]

"Each time the idea of what we're now calling the Global Leadership Initiative has surfaced in the past year—first as a seed of possibility in the conversation in Baja, then again in Marblehead, until it finally became clear in Stowe—I had a very distinct and centered feeling that this is exactly what I was meant to do. I know that the experience may be different for other people, but for me this is the track laid out for me, this is the future waiting for me. I think when you click into your destiny there's a feeling of being solid and grounded. Your anxiety falls, your concern is lowered. Even if it's highly ambiguous, which it invariably is, you just have this feeling that 'I'm going to take the next step and it's going to work out,' and it does."

"The felt sense you talk about definitely resonates with me," said Otto. "And yet, I wouldn't necessarily assume that path was laid out by—call it God or something else. Maybe we as human beings participate in the process of laying down that path to a much higher degree than we understand."

"I also recognize what Joseph is talking about," said Betty Sue, "and I would add that what troubles some people about the phrase 'instrument for something better to emerge' is that it sounds as if you're an unthinking tool or slave. I think there's an act of commitment that must occur first which actually creates the capacity to be an 'instrument'—or, as I like to imagine it, a dancer with life. It changes your life entirely when you make that commitment.

"In the Bible, the prophet Isaiah says, 'Here am I, O Lord, use me.' But without free choice or free will, that dance with destiny may not begin."

"I understand the fear of losing autonomy, but that is exactly the opposite of how I experience it," said Joseph. "Buber said it beautifully: 'Freedom and destiny are solemnly promised to one another and linked together in meaning.'[4] When the sort of commitment you're talking about happens, you feel as if you're fulfilling your destiny, but you also feel as if you're freer than you've ever been in your life. It's a huge paradox."

"I think that's because there are two types of freedom: outer freedom and inner freedom," said Peter. "Outer freedom is what we usually mean when we talk of freedom: whether or not forces outside me are limiting my actions. Inner freedom is more subtle. It concerns the extent to which our actions are governed by our habits. We can appear free in the sense of no one is controlling us, yet our actions are completely predetermined by our habitual ways of thinking and acting in reaction to our circumstances.

"I believe the freedom Buber is talking about is the latter, the awakened awareness that I am now more free to do whatever is required to contribute toward my destiny, less constrained by my past habits."

Betty Sue nodded. "To me, that movement and intention, that willingness to surrender, actually creates the field in which presencing occurs. But that moment of presence is profoundly paradoxical. *Here* is the mystery—an opening up to some depth or dimension that's beyond description. This is not just another space or capacity, this is something distinct."

"This is the call to service that most of us deny throughout our whole life," said Joseph, "this call to give ourselves to something larger than ourselves, and to become what we were meant to become."

"That reminds me of something Master Nan said," Peter added. "Remember what he said about the last of the seven spaces of the Confucian theory: 'Then you can attain the goals that you're supposed to achieve.'

"Still, I have one qualm, and it's not with the ideas we're describing but with the language we're using. We're talking about an experience that's very real to each of us, and it's natural to talk in ways that are consistent with our own culture and heritage. But 'responding to one's calling' or 'God's will' might not communicate across different cultures and might even suggest that what we're talking about is only a Western notion. That, for me, would be a great loss. You know, you rarely, for example, encounter the word 'God' in Buddhism."

"What word would Buddhists use?" asked Joseph. "Call to *life*, perhaps?"

"It would require more than just a change in the word," said Peter. "Actually, I think the whole way we approach this is, in some ways, more Buddhist than Western.

"My understanding of Buddhist theory is limited, but I think it starts with a process orientation—in other words, an approach that emphasizes a process of cultivation. The potential problem in talking about a 'call to God's service' is that it still could be quite conceptual—my *interpretation* of what God wants me to do. The real distinction is *concept* versus *experience*: the experience of being uplifted into God's service, or life's service, or service of the universe, or whatever terms we use versus a belief in such service.

"Now, this is a very slippery distinction, so the Buddhist approach rests on rigorous disciplines of cultivation that start with paying attention to our present way of living and the role of thought in the prison we've created for ourselves. As we said before, until we can start to master our own thought, to 'pacify the mind,' we won't be able to escape this prison of our own thinking. Only then can we be open to what's emerging.

"The core of the Buddhist theory here is that the human exists in two interdependent orders.[5] One is the manifest domain, the domain of manifest phenomena, both tangible and intangible. The other is the infinite, the absolute, the transcendent, the universal beyond form, beyond thought, beyond any 'thing'—typically referred to as 'Suchness.' And the human exists, literally, where these two orders intersect, what's called the '*Tathagata-garbha*' in the oldest texts. The Sanskrit term, *Tathagata*, which was originally one of the terms for the historical Buddha, Siddhartha Gautama of Sakyamuni, over time became synonymous with Suchness or the absolute. The Sanskrit *Garbha* means "matrix" or "womb." So the human is said to exist, by our basic nature, in the matrix of interaction between the absolute and the manifest. We don't exist in one or the other but in both, because—and this is a key to the Buddhists' nondualistic worldview— the manifest does not exist without the absolute, nor the absolute without the manifest. They're inseparable, interpenetrating. According to Buddhist theory, enlightenment is possible because we exist in the absolute as well as the phenomenal.

"From this point of view, what we're calling 'presencing' is possible because of this womb, where the absolute and the manifest interact. I think a Buddhist would say that presencing can arise to the extent that we develop the capacity, individually and collectively, to extend our conscious awareness in both domains. Normally, we're habituated to the phenomenal or manifest domain, paying attention only to what's tangible, even to the point of seeing ourselves as a material thing, our body. But we inherently have this much greater capacity, which can be cultivated."

"And this movement in the U's deep learning cycle offers a language for describing this process of cultivation," said Betty Sue.

"Yes, especially when we think of the U over an extended period of time. That's why it corresponded to a high degree with the Confucian theory of leadership development as Master Nan explained it," Peter said.

"So what the major Western religions conceive of as a transcendent, exterior God, the Eastern religions conceive of as immanent," said Otto.

"Right."

"Isn't the key point really that study, meditation, and other forms of individual cultivation over an extended period of time are essential to build the capacity to be an 'instrument' of service?" asked Betty Sue.

"Yes, exactly," said Peter. "It's not just a matter of belief or wanting to be an instrument. You must develop the capacity. That's why I was saying the Buddhist notion is about the process of cultivation. There are three basic areas in which you must work. First, you must meditate or 'practice'—you must have a discipline of quieting the mind. Second, you must study—the sutras, the Koran, the Torah, the Bible—whatever helps to develop a theoretical understanding. And you must be committed to service, what the Buddhists would call 'vows.' Your cultivation grows out of all three.

"This emphasis in Buddhism on cultivation has been lost to mainstream Christianity, but it's present in Christian mysticism and in the more esoteric schools of other Western religions, like the Sufis in Islam.

"One other key point is the Buddhist notion of when and how theory matters. A Buddhist would say, 'First you must emphasize practice and service.' Until your mind truly starts to quiet, all this talk about ideas and theory is just intellectualizing, and can actually get in the way of your cultivation.

"But there comes a time when you need theoretical understanding. When your practice has led you to experiences that you can't understand, you need a better theory. Otherwise, if you try to understand these transcendent experiences with 'profane,' or, we might say. 'materialistic,' ways of thinking, your cultivation will be set back."

"This is exactly what we've been saying about the ex-prisoners needing a suitable theory and language!" Betty Sue exclaimed. "It's why I've come to see our work together as basically learning how to articulate a theory, a way of making sense and communicating. Obviously, spiritual traditions of all sorts have provided such languages for a long time. But we need languages that fit the present time—that can deal with the collective as well as the individual, and that transcend traditional boundaries of tribe, nation, and culture."

"Right," Peter agreed. "But new theory is useful only to the extent that enough people's experiences have brought them to a point of needing different ways to see things and they can recognize they are not alone in this need. So the interviews and sharing individuals' and groups' experiences of presencing are also important."

"You know, one of the things we've been seeing is that many people are having these types of experiences outside organized religions altogether," Otto commented, "in social or community contexts. In fact, much of the discussion of spirituality that people have now is very personal. Their spiritual encounters are outside of the boundaries of organized religion."

"That's an important point," said Peter. "The flip side is that I find attempts to synthesize across religions to be pretty sterile—for example, value statements. The UN Universal Declaration of Human Rights is a good thing. It was written with sensitivity, trying to be acceptable to different religions. But I think it misses the whole point. I think what we're saying is that the foundation for this transformation has to be experience, not concept, and these experiences of the transcendent must show up 'where we live our everyday lives.'"

"And they are showing up," said Joseph, "just as they have for each of us, in the middle of our societies and communities and organizations, where people are finding extraordinary power when they surrender into their commitment."

"That's consistent with the breakdown of mainstream institutions, and of people's faith in them," said Betty Sue. "Because people no longer trust traditional institutional forms and structures, if any one institution sets itself up as the protector of such experiences, it will backfire. Because the potential for presencing is immanent, it can occur anywhere. No one, or no institution can lay a unique claim to it."

Otto nodded. "As the avant-garde artist Joseph Beuys says, 'Today the mysteries or the magical no longer take place in churches but in the main station,' in the midst of everyday life."

"And because of this we need languages for talking about these experiences and this deep process of change that are not only not religious, but are also not jargon," continued Betty Sue.

"In particular, I still have difficulty with the phrase 'shifting the whole.' I always find myself thinking that it refers to some sort of coordinated action on a global scale. I'm afraid that when people hear it, they may just give up. After all, who acts on a global stage? The CEO of a huge global corporation or the president or prime minister of a country or a high official in the UN do occasionally, but not most of us. Do you see what I'm wrestling with?"

"Yes," said Peter, "I've had the same reaction at times. It's as if we define ourselves out of the picture with language like that."

"But everything we're learning from people like Bohm, Bortoft, Kabat-Zinn, Rosch, and so on, back to Goethe, says that is wrong," said Otto. "The emerging whole manifests locally. It manifests in particular communities, groups, and, ultimately, in us as individuals."

"So," said Betty Sue, "you're saying that while the phrase 'shifting the whole' could sound like an integrated global agenda, it actually means almost the opposite?"

"It all depends on how you use the word 'whole.' What we're talking about is sensing the unfolding whole within each of us, within the present situation, and acting in service of it," said Otto. "The other notion of whole, the 'integrated global agenda' notion of whole, is what leads to the dead end that Bortoft calls 'the counterfeit whole.'"

Joseph smiled. "Another paradox. Serving the emerging whole means paying attention to what's right here within my awareness, what's completely local, and surrendering to what's being asked of me now."

"So we have a new systems axiom," said Peter. " '*What is most systemic is most local.*' The deepest systems we enact are woven into the fabric of everyday life, down to the most minute detail.

"This is so important for us to understand. We, every one of us, may be able to change the world, but only as we experience more and more of the whole in the present. This is the 'evolving consciousness' that Bohm said was necessary to appreciate the implicate order. Now I see that it's also the cultivation of awareness to 'see the absolute in the manifest,' as the Buddhists would say."

"And only as we learn to use ourselves as instruments for something larger than ourselves to emerge, wherever we act," said Otto "as parents or citizens or community organizers or managers in global corporations.

"And that makes me realize we haven't talked enough about the shadow side to all of this."

"When I was in Vienna recently, I watched an interview with the secretary of Adolf Hitler on TV," said Otto. "It was incredible. She described the last weeks in Berlin in 1945 and what it was like as a few people continued following their insane agenda—even as the bombs were crashing down left and right and they were obviously heading to oblivion.

"Throughout the interview she kept saying that she couldn't remember certain aspects of her experience. She couldn't remember her emotions or what she was feeling. As the war drew closer and closer to the end, she was operating almost on 'automatic pilot.' All her emotions, her capacities to sense and to feel, never mind knowing what her deeper purpose or will was—she couldn't remember any of these. They were 'deep-frozen,' so to speak.

"But something happened as she was telling her story. By the end of the conversation, her face was entirely transformed. As she described the final days of total collapse, you could literally see her horror become etched on her face—particularly around her eyes. As she experienced her emotions, as they 'thawed,' she connected emotionally with the events in ways that she could not when they had actually happened.

"Apparently, after the war and for the remainder of her life, she did volunteer work anonymously in low-profile organizations. She died the day after the interview was aired for the first time. A few days before that, the interviewer, a well-known Austrian artist, happened to have a last brief conversation with her. In that conversation, she said to him that, finally, for the first time, she could start to forgive herself.[6]

"If Hitler is an example of evil, this interview gives an interesting way to think about how evil works. It's a freezing of deeper capacities. That's what keeps you going. It took her a half century to make sense of that."

"That's a perfect example of becoming an instrument of a will that's not your own," said Betty Sue. "And that is exactly why people talk about the danger of becoming an instrument. You can become some kind of robot. You're not in the generative matrix. You're dehumanized."

"I think this story is for all of us," said Joseph. "What Otto was just describing was the opposite of what we're talking about, which is serving life. This was serving death."

"I don't think we're describing very unusual things right now," said Peter. "Obviously, this is a stark example, and we're on the 'other side,' talking about 'them,' those other people. But we're describing the life of most of us working in most organizations: when we're used as an instrument to serve something other than life, we lose our feelings and our capacity to sense. We just go through the motions. This happens to people all the time, for example, in corporations whose purpose is to make money for the sake of making money."

"You know, the people in Nazi Germany thought they were serving the future—just a different future," said Betty Sue.

"Exactly," said Peter. "And, just like Hitler's secretary, when we're in this sort of situation, we justify our actions by the need to keep things going, to protect what exists and carry out the tasks at hand. Just like her, we say, 'Well, this is just what has to be done for now. It will be over soon, and then we'll be able to do something different.'"

"Peter, your comment about this characterizing the life of many people in modern organizations really hits me," said Joseph. "I'll never forget one particular interview I had with a senior executive. As our conversation progressed and he opened up more and more, he began to talk about all the compromises he had made in his life in order to 'climb the ladder' in the corporation. He hadn't really thought a lot about it at the time; it seemed that he was just doing what he had to do to be successful. He said exactly the same thing, that he had totally lost his capacity to feel and sense. Eventually he just looked at me and said, 'I don't really like the person I've become.'"

"So the shadow side of being an instrument is losing our sense of autonomy, our will, and the real ability to make choices," said Otto.

"Yes, and our humanity—our capacity to sense and feel," said Betty Sue.

"But if we're really honest, isn't this exactly what's playing out for all of us in the larger world, as we all enact the process we call 'globalization'?" queried Peter. "If you asked any of us, or virtually any citizen of today's global society, if we actually want to destroy species as a result of our purchasing decisions, we would all say, 'No, of course not!' Wouldn't any of us respond exactly the same if you asked us if we wanted to create global warming and melt the polar ice caps, or if we wanted to prevent people in developing countries from gaining access to clean drinking water because it's owned by soft drink producers whose business expands because we buy their products? Yet this is exactly what's happening. Our purchasing decisions are mediated through the network of institutions that span the world to bring us the goods and services we buy. Like your executive, Joseph, we're just doing what we think we need to do to be successful, and I suspect if we could really see the consequences of our actions, we wouldn't like ourselves very much.

"I wonder how different we are from Hitler's secretary, really? We're all in the bowels of this giant machine, the modern global economy, being used as instruments to serve its ends. We create the machine collectively, but we feel trapped individually. We've shifted the burden so much to the machine that we don't see a lot of options, even though they may really be there. We can't go off into the woods and live happily off the land anymore. So we 'deep-freeze' our ability to sense what's actually going on. We deny the larger consequences of our way of living."

"It's the prisoner scenario again, isn't it?" said Betty Sue.

"Yes," said Peter. "We live in the cave and dull our senses accordingly."

"And we've also ruined other people's options to live differently," said Joseph.

Betty Sue nodded as Peter said, "That's why this notion of being an instrument is so tricky. We can get all excited about it, because we know the potential of it, but it also touches deep fears. At some level, we recognize that we're already being used as instruments beyond our choice, at least at some level."

"That is why you need the call to service and the call to cultivation," said Otto.

"That's right," Peter said. "There's no other way out of this. We may not be able to change the larger systems overnight, but we can commit to the continual development of awareness and the capacity to choose. That's why personal cultivation is so important. It keeps you sensitive and 'in the matrix,' so to speak."

"The capacity to choose is key," said Joseph, "and that's always linked to our awareness.

"Not long ago Adam and I met Carlos Barrios, a Mayan priest chosen by his people's elders to learn and spread understanding of the Mayan vision of unity and harmony in the world. It was a remarkable meeting, much like those with Brian Arthur, John Milton, and the others who catapulted us on the journey of discovering the U. The Mayan vision is inseparable from the Mayan calendar, and as Carlos was explaining this to us, I recalled John Milton's comment that the Mayans were really 'the masters of time.' The Mayan calendar, as Carlos explained it, is composed of multiple cycles of varying lengths. Perhaps the most famous of these cycles is the *Bolopumí*, or 'The Long Night.' Five hundred years before Cortes landed in Mexico, beginning the European colonization of native peoples, the Mayans had established the *Bolopumí* as starting in 1518, the year he landed. The calendar said that this cycle would be a period of darkness, when materialism would take root among the peoples of the world and when people's hearts would become cold. The *Bolopumí* lasts nine cycles of fifty-two years each, or 468 years. The calendar then describes several different shorter cycles, marking a period of transition. Carlos said that the last of these transitional cycles signals that 'a new child is born,' a thirteen-year cycle that began on August 17, 2001. A youth becomes an adult in Mayan culture on his thirteenth birthday. Carlos said that this cycle represented 'an opportunity to create a new world,' but 'this child will be born among great chaos and upheaval.'

"When Carlos said this, I took out my calendar and found that August 17 was the day when the six of us sat in that circle in Stowe and committed to creating what I think will be called the Global Leadership Initiative. Carlos said that this was not surprising—that all around the world generative choices were being made on that day.

"The call is clear: for the whole thirteen-year period, we must do all we can to create this balance and connection with one another. 'We're facing these problems,' Carlos said, 'because of our lack of relationship, not just with one another but with all of nature. My purpose is to help the human race understand that it is facing self-destruction unless there is a return to balance and harmony with nature.'

"While he was speaking, John Milton's words in Baja flashed

through my mind: 'The fate of the human species is still very much in our hands—there must be a profound transformation of our spirit and mind and of our relationships to each other and to the earth.' It's as if we must be conscious and aware that every choice we make has the power to affect things one way or another. And those choices are a direct result of how deeply we're sensing and presencing.

"People are justifiably skeptical about prophecies, but I think that, when used wisely, they have the same function as scenarios, like the requiem scenario. We can see them as predictions, but if we do, they lose their power. Their greatest impact is on how we see the present and the choices our new seeing reveals. The forces at play in the world are of our own making. I know in my heart that we do have the power to create different forces if we have the will to learn to see."

The day was drawing to a close as Betty Sue asked, "So if we had to summarize our understanding right now of the core of presence and the U in a sentence, how would we do it?"

"A profound opening of the heart, carried into action," said Joseph. "As Phil Lane, a Native American teacher, says, 'The longest road you will ever walk is the sacred journey from your head to your heart.'

"I sort of snuck in two sentences there," he added.

We laughed, then Otto said, "For me, the core of presencing is waking up together—waking up to who we really are by linking with and acting from our highest future Self—and by using the Self as a vehicle for bringing forth new worlds."

"I'd say it's the point where the fire of creation burns and enters the world through us," Betty Sue continued.

"Someone recently asked me how I would explain all of this to an eight-year-old," said Peter. "Without thinking, I replied, 'we have no idea of our capacity to create the world anew.'"

Epilogue

"With Man Gone, Will There Be Hope For Gorilla?"

April 2002

We met the last time on Maple Avenue on a beautiful spring morning. Trees were just beginning to blossom, and the sound of children playing across the street filled the room. The conversation began slowly.

"You know, one question still lingers for me," said Betty Sue. "Remember when I was pushing you all before about what happens at the 'bottom of the U' and we concluded that something shifts in our sense of purpose? Not purpose in a purely individualistic sense, but as Otto says, the opening to a larger self and to a larger purpose.

"I'm wondering if what we've been exploring is really all about purpose in some sense. If more and more 'ex-prisoners' are being drawn to deeper levels of awareness of a larger purpose, do you think a *collective* sense of purpose might be developing, which could accelerate the whole U process wherever it's occurring?"

"There are many levels of 'collective.' Which do you mean?" asked Peter.

"Well, potentially at all levels—from the purpose of a group working together to the purpose of humans as a whole."

"It's possible. But I think the question of human purpose is almost impossible for us to ponder in our present state.

"Do you remember *Ishmael*—the novel by Daniel Quinn, the conversation between the man and the gorilla?[1] That book had a great impact on me. It showed so clearly how and why we've become more and more separated from nature since the beginnings of the agricultural revolution—what Quinn calls the advent of 'totalitarian agriculture.' But there's a part of the story I never understood that's stuck in the back of my mind for years.

"The book begins with the narrator answering an ad in the paper— something like 'Teacher seeks student. Must be intent on saving the world.' He goes to a nondescript office building, finds the office specified in the ad, and enters a darkened room. As his eyes gradually adjust, he realizes he's sitting next to a large pane of glass. On the opposite side sits Ishmael, the gorilla who placed the ad.

"The conversation that ensues is actually a journey down the U. Ishmael guides the narrator in learning how to 'see' some of our deepest assumptions—assumptions shared by virtually all modern societies that are now so taken for granted that it's almost impossible for any of us to realize their impact."

"When I first read the book, the whole idea of a telepathic conversation between a man and a gorilla seemed completely contrived," said

Otto. "Then I realized that a dialogue with a member of another species is a powerful way to draw out shared assumptions that we can't see on our own."

"Like the *seeing* that arose from Joseph's 'conversation' with the whales and the sea lion," said Betty Sue.

"Right," said Peter. "But there's something very interesting in that first scene. Do you remember what's behind Ishmael?"

"There's a sign behind him, hanging on the wall," said Otto. "But I don't remember what it says."

"It says, 'With man gone, will there be hope for gorilla?'"

"What do you make of that?" asked Betty Sue.

"It clearly confuses the narrator in the story, who seems to regard it as a kind of koan, some sort of verbal puzzle," Peter replied. "He expresses frustration at the sign's ambiguity and then proceeds to ignore it, and it's never referred to again until the end of the book."

"It is a strange question. All the evidence suggests that gorillas would be much better off without humans," said Otto. "Their survival, and many other species,' is threatened by our way of living. But the sign seems to suggest the opposite."

"It does," said Peter. "But as illogical as the sign appears to be, I actually think it poses the question that the narrator's whole journey down the U is about and perhaps ours as well.

"As you say, we humans are the threat to the gorilla's survival, as everyone trying to protect the gorilla from extinction would quickly acknowledge. If man were gone, the gorilla would need no protection from man. So why would Ishmael ask whether there would be 'hope for gorilla' if man were gone? Given our current way of thinking, it makes absolutely no sense. And that, I think, is the whole point.

"Ishmael is asking a truly radical question: Might the gorilla really need man, not just for protection but for something more? This is a question we've stopped asking. It's a question about our purpose as a species, about our purpose within the larger web of life, within the universe. I think we've stopped asking this question because we no longer see ourselves as part of that universe. We see our purpose only in human terms: what we want, how to make things better for us. We don't wonder how we might contribute to life as a whole, and that's why questions of purpose—like Betty Sue's—are basically meaningless to us today."

"Which means we really have no larger purpose at all," said Joseph. "We simply live to meet our needs and to pursue our selfish aims, building a world fashioned in human terms. How can you have a larger purpose if you're separate from the larger world?"

"We consider the living universe around us as nothing more than 'natural resources' that exist solely for us to take and use," said Peter. "We even treat DNA, the very program of life, as something for us to exploit as fits our needs with no thought of how it might affect other specied.

"The environmental movement is mostly focused on how we can be 'less bad,' how we can take or destroy less. But what if humans, as a species, actually have a purpose? What if we have something distinctive to contribute—something to *give* rather than just *take?*"

"In this sense, the requiem scenario is simply saying that we're at the end of the line as 'takers,' as Quinn would put it," said Otto. "It's one thing for a village or even a nation to take more than it leaves. But we humans in toto are now taking at an unprecedented rate globally.

"What you're saying is that no alternative path forward may exist without rediscovering why we're here—because only then can we start to see what we actually have to give."

"Yes, and that will require us to think differently, to think as if we are part of the universe. The ancient Anasazi, like many native peoples, believed that they needed to conduct their dances and ceremonies in order to maintain balance in the universe. If they neglected this duty, not only they but countless other forms of life would suffer. Maybe all of this is about rediscovering what our dance is—today, in the modern world—and who we, the dancers, are."

"So seeing our collective journey down the U as rediscovering our purpose actually reveals this deeper question," said Betty Sue. "Who are we? Are human beings fundamentally separate or inseparable from nature? We need to re-experience our place in the universe before we can see how it needs us as well as how we need it. And this is no mere intellectual discovery. Remember the grief you felt in Baja, Joseph?"

"I'll never be able to forget it. It was like the grief you feel when you lose someone you love. But it wasn't just a single loss. It was more like discovering that I had a family I'd never even known about—and that my family was suffering."

"And out of the grief you found your connection to the purpose that Ishmael's question suggests," continued Betty Sue.

"Yes," Joseph answered. "For me, it has to do with our stewardship responsibility today and in relation to new possibilities for life, even if we have no idea what these new possibilities might be."

"Perhaps they'll come from the collective intelligence emerging in global networks," said Otto, "what Nicanor Perlas calls the 'real message of globalization,' becoming 'more aware of how deeply we're interconnected as human beings across all of society.'"

"I believe that's a real possibility, but only if we can open our hearts to finding our place," Betty Sue said.

"And when we do, we'll discover that the connectedness works in *both directions*," said Peter. "Perhaps the sea lion's suffering that you sensed, Joseph, is her loss of relationship with us, as well as our loss of relationship with her."

"Like a family that's been split apart," said Joseph, nodding.

"I think this larger purpose has been implicit in our conversations all along," said Betty Sue. "The field of the future is what comes into play when we come into the presence of an understanding of why we are here. We must first know this in intimate terms, like Joseph found in Baja. But the expanded self at the bottom of the U naturally encounters a larger purpose."

"At that point we experience ourselves as both 'a part' of the whole and the whole," said Otto. "Isn't this exactly what David Bohm told Joseph in London, about 'the natural state of the human world'— 'separation without separateness'?"

"But the assumption of separateness is so deep that I can't imagine what it will take to dislodge it," said Peter. "I think that many people hoped that September 11 would tell us that all of us can be affected by any of us. But in the aftermath of that 'wake-up call' is showing that such events can also invoke great fear and may even have the opposite effect, leading to more defensiveness and reinforcing separateness."

"Fear can only separate us," said Otto. "Maturana says, 'Love is the one emotion that expands intelligence' because love connects us."

"Maybe we just need to learn to see what research like the random number generator experiments shows—how subtle and extensive the fields in which we participate actually are," said Joseph.

"And to see that maybe evolution doesn't end with us," said Peter.

"Near the latter part of the book, Ishmael tells a very funny story about coming upon a jellyfish at the beach and asking the jellyfish to give its account of how it got to be. The jellyfish traces in detail the evolution of bacteria into multicellular organisms and then more complex aquatic organisms, until, Quinn says, the jellyfish 'turned pink with pride' and said, "but finally *jellyfish appeared!*""[2]

"Well, it's nice to know that maybe we don't have a monopoly on species myopia," said Betty Sue, laughing.

"But as silly as it sounds, we do act as if evolution stopped with us, that 'we're it,' the whole point of nature's four-billion-year project on this planet Earth. It would probably shift things to realize that may not be so. Maybe we're here to enable what comes next, and maybe our state of awareness will influence what comes next."

"It certainly would up the stakes for getting our act together," said Joseph.

"It would," Peter agreed with a smile. "And I think you're right, Joseph—some of the new research might help us recognize and understand that we're part of this living, generative field—and that we influence it just as it influences us. I was reminded of this all over again when Fred Matser visited recently from Holland. Fred set up a family foundation that supports researchers around the world doing work that could contribute to deeper understanding of life.[3] As he was leaving, he gave me a present, a book based on the research of Masaru Emoto of Japan. I thanked him, said good-bye, and set the book aside.

"When I looked at it a couple of days later, I was stunned. The book was composed mostly of pictures—beautiful pictures—of water. Emoto has developed a way to apply magnetic resonance imaging to photograph the crystals formed when water freezes.[4] His results are controversial and clearly exploratory. For many reasons they are also difficult to replicate, so I think it is best to view them as part art, and part science. Still, as best I can tell, some scientists are taking the work seriously.[5]

"Emoto says he has long been fascinated by water because we are mostly water. At the time of a human conception, 'water accounts for about ninety-five percent of the fertilized egg.' As adults, it accounts for about seventy percent of our body weight, roughly the same percentage of the surface of the earth that is covered by water. Although we live on 'the water planet,' 'What we learned from these experiments,' he says, 'is that we do not know anything about water.'"[6]

"What's so mysterious about water?" asked Otto.

"I'll show you," answered Peter.

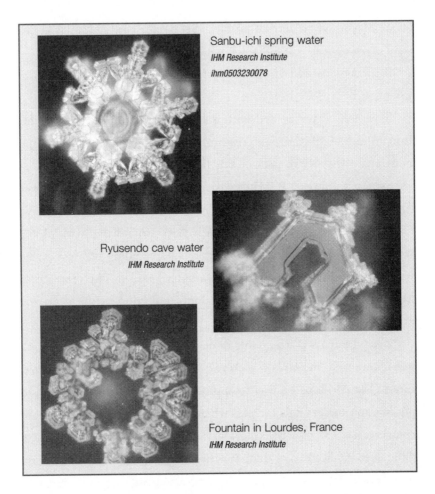

Sanbu-ichi spring water
IHM Research Institute
ihm0503230078

Ryusendo cave water
IHM Research Institute

Fountain in Lourdes, France
IHM Research Institute

"For starters, there is the simple fact of how beautiful water actually is. The first half of the book is made up of photographs of water crystals from different sources around the world. That these crystals—formed from the most common substance on earth—are so beautiful is, for me, a powerful experience of reconnection, like Joseph's experience in Baja. Each photograph is a representative from a sample of one hundred crystals photographed from each source.[7]

"But not all the water is so beautiful. There are also photographs of water from polluted urban sources, which often form only partial structures. Conversely, crystals from places where the people regard the water as especially pure or healthy—remote springs, deep wells,

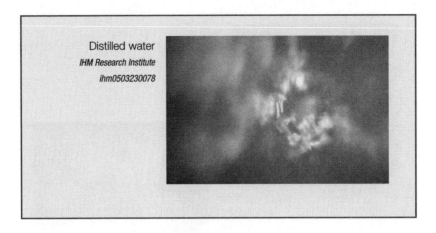

Distilled water
IHM Research Institute
ihm0503230078

and water noted for its healing qualities, as at Lourdes—are stunningly complex and beautiful. In short, healthy water forms beautiful crystal structures, and polluted water does not.

"That's just the beginning. In the second half of the book, Emoto presents photos from different experiments, all using distilled water. Distilled water is almost biologically inert and therefore forms very simple crystals, or crystals that are so underdeveloped that they have almost no distinct structure.

"For example, he shows pictures of distilled water crystals after the water has been exposed to music. The distilled water is put into a vial and placed in front of speakers through which music is played. Then one hundred samples of the water are frozen and the crystals photographed."

"You mean that these beautiful crystals come from the exact same distilled water that forms virtually no crystals on its own?" asked Joseph.

"Yes. The only difference is the music and how it affects the water. What struck me was how the crystals seem to visually reflect the essence of the music—the geometric precision of Bach, the balance of order and flow of Mozart, the beautiful simplicity of folk music. It's as if the water were not only influenced by the music but absorbs and reflects its character.

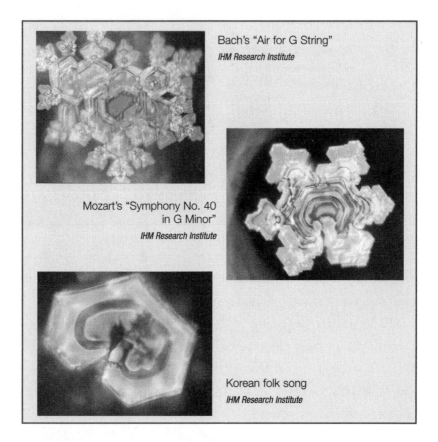

Bach's "Air for G String"
IHM Research Institute

Mozart's "Symphony No. 40
in G Minor"
IHM Research Institute

Korean folk song
IHM Research Institute

"Emoto has conducted many other experiments with water, such as taping printed words or names on the vials of distilled water. For example, the word 'beautiful' in Japanese (or other languages) produces exquisite lacy crystals, while the word 'dirty' produces undeveloped crystals that you could only call ugly."

"This is astonishing," said Joseph. "But at the same time, it doesn't surprise me at all. Water is alive, and the universe is more interdependent than we can imagine. This is consistent with everything we've been saying."

"What these pictures say to me is that thought creates reality," said Otto. "That's why even the smallest acts arising from real clarity at the bottom of the U may have consequences beyond what we can imag-

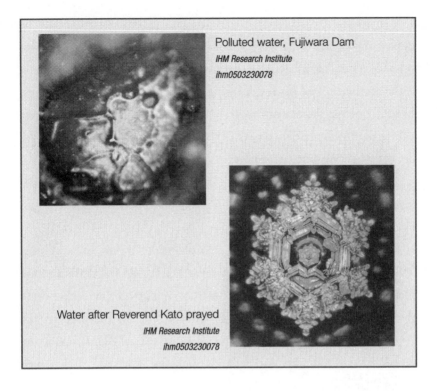

Polluted water, Fujiwara Dam
IHM Research Institute
ihm0503230078

Water after Reverend Kato prayed
IHM Research Institute
ihm0503230078

ine. The interdependency of the universe extends from the micro to the macro, from the visible to the invisible."

"Emoto has begun to experiment with this idea directly," continued Peter. "For example, in one experiment they took water from a highly polluted reservoir and froze it. The samples had virtually no crystal structure. Then an elder priest, Reverend Kato, sat next to the reservoir and prayed for one hour for the well-being of the water. When they then took new samples of the water and froze it, the crystals were stunning.

"Well, as the resident skeptic, I don't know what to think about what causes the patterns in these pictures," said Betty Sue. "I'd like to see more research. But they are wonderfully suggestive as powerful metaphors of the realms of energy we can't see but which we affect, and which have a deep effect on us."

"Obviously, skepticism is necessary, and in time there should be opportunities for others to replicate Emoto's pilot studies," Peter rejoined. "Eventually, flaws in his methods may well be found. But it is the consistency of his results with so many other emerging studies, like the random generator research, that seems important. All suggest a level of interdependence between thought and reality that defies the conventional Western worldview.

"Plus, for me, the sheer beauty of the water crystals is very moving, and that beauty reminds me, in a way that's beyond words, of this interconnectedness."

Looking up from the book, Joseph said, "Bohm used to say, 'Thought creates reality and then says "I didn't do it."' I think these pictures and some of the other research findings simply corroborate the experience of being one body with all life. As the capacity for experiencing this grows, maybe we'll move out of denial about the power of our thoughts and feelings. Imagine if we did, how much might change."

"Perhaps we would begin to develop awareness commensurate with our impact, wisdom in balance with our power," added Otto.

"I don't know, but I do know that this is the work of all of us," said Peter. "All our contemporary cultures have played a part in the journey of separation, and we must all be part of the reversal. As this happens, we may reconnect powerfully with one another also.

"Two weeks ago, I was in Egypt for the first SoL Executive Champion's Workshop held in an Arab country. After September 11, many of us felt this was vital, and with the help of BP in Egypt and a group of Arab companies working on organizational learning capabilities, we were able to organize the program. We met at a resort next to the Red Sea, south of Cairo. On the last evening, we had a dinner on the beach for the participants and their families. After dinner, I asked everyone to come into an adjoining open-air pavilion for 'a surprise.' Showing the water crystal slides that evening, with Egyptian music playing in the background and a full moon rising over the Red Sea, was an experience I'll never forget. It felt like such a privilege to have the opportunity to share with fellow human beings what it means to be human—to see our world in its beauty and share that beauty.

"Afterwards, as we walked back along the beach to our rooms, an executive from Saudi Aramco I had come to know during the program came up to me. He was educated in the West, speaks flawless English as well as several other languages, and, like many of his contemporaries, is stretched between two worlds, the modern world and his traditional Saudi culture. What touched him that evening was not just the beauty of the water crystals, but the memory of his grandfather's teaching.

"'My grandfather taught me that when you are sick, you should take a bowl of water and you should read to it,' he told me. 'If you know the Koran, read the Koran. But it doesn't really matter what you read, so long as it is something that has real meaning to you. Then you take the water and wash yourself with it, and you will get well. Now I understand what my grandfather was trying to teach me.'

"I have only the dimmest appreciation of what all this means. But in that moment, I felt the two of us bound to a common destiny far more powerful than our differing cultures, one in which there was equal room for old wisdom and new science.

"Bill McDonough, the American environmental architect, says his work has led him to a simple question: 'What will it take for us to become indigenous once again?'—not as we were, but as we might be?

"I think if we can find our place, we will find our purpose."

Notes

Introduction

1. According to physicist and philosopher of science Henri Bortoft; see H. Bortoft, *The Wholeness of Nature: Goethe's Way Towards a Science of Conscious Participation in Nature* (Hudson, N.Y.: Lindisfarne Press, 1996).
2. See "Conversation with Rupert Sheldrake: Morphic Fields," interview by C. O. Scharmer, London, September 23, 1999, www.dialogonleadership.org.
3. See "Conversation with Henri Bortoft: Imagination Becomes an Organ of Perception," interview by C. O. Scharmer, London, July 14, 1999, www.dialogonleadership.org.
4. Ibid.
5. A. P. de Geus, *The Living Company* (London: Nicholas Brealey Publishing, 1997).
6. *The New York Times*, June 24, 1993, 1, 9.
7. C. O. Scharmer, "Theory U: Leading From the Emerging Future," Habilitation Thesis (2004), www.ottoscharmer.com; C. O. Scharmer, *Ästhetik als Kategorie strategischer Führung* (Aesthetics as a Category of Strategic Leadership); *Der*

ästhetische Typus von Organisationen (Stuttgart: Urachhausverlag, 1991); C. O. Scharmer, *Reflexive Modernisierung des Kapitalismus als Revolution von innen:Auf der Suche nach Infrastrukturen einer lernenden Gesellschaft* (Reflective Modernization of Capitalism: Toward Infrastructures of a Learning Society) (Stuttgart: Schäffer-Poeschel, 1996).

8. J. Jaworski, *Synchronicity: The Inner Path of Leadership* (San Francisco: Berrett-Koehler, 1996), p. 181.

9. J. Jaworski and C. O. Scharmer, "Leadership in the Digital Economy: Sensing and Actualizing Emerging Futures" (Cambridge, Mass.: Society for Organizational Learning and Beverly, Mass.: Generon Consulting, 2000), www.dialogonleadership.org; C. O. Scharmer, W. B. Arthur, J. Day, J. Jaworski, M. Jung, I. Nonaka, and P. M. Senge, "Illuminating the Blind Spot," 2002, www.dialogonleadership.org. A shortened version of this paper was published in *Leader to Leader* (Spring 2002), pp. 11–14; C. O. Scharmer, "Self-Transcending Knowledge: Sensing and Organizing Around Emerging Opportunities," *Journal of Knowledge Management*, 5, no. 2 (2000); pp. 137–150; C. O. Scharmer, "Presencing: Learning from the Future as It Emerges," paper presented at the Conference on Knowledge and Innovation, Helsinki School of Economics, Helsinki, Finland, May 25–26, 2000, www.ottoscharmer.com; C. O. Scharmer, "Organizing Around Not-Yet-Embodied Knowledge," in G. V. Krogh, I. Nonaka, and T. Nishiguchi, eds., *Knowledge Creation: A New Source of Value* (New York: Macmillan, 1999), pp. 36–60; C. O. Scharmer, "Theory U: Leading From the Emerging Future" (introduction to a forthcoming book with the same title), 2004, www.ottoscharmer.com; P. Senge and C. O. Scharmer, "Community Action Research," in *Handbook of Action Research,* P. Reason and H. Bradbury (Thousand Oaks, Calif.: Sage Publications, 2001), pp. 238–249; K. Käufer, C. O. Scharmer, and U. Versteegen, "Reinventing the Health Care System from Within: The Case of a Regional Physician Network in Germany," MIT Working Paper WPC 0010, 2003, www.dialogonleadership.org; U. Versteegen, K. Käufer, and C. O. Scharmer, "The Pentagon of Praxis" in *Reflections: The SoL Journal*, 2, no. 3 (2001): pp. 36–45; K. Käufer, C. O. Scharmer, and U. Versteegen, "Breathing Life into a Dying System" in *Reflections: The SoL Journal*, 5, no. 3 (2004): pp. 1–12.

10. More information about the interview project, and many of the interviews from which these quotes are drawn are available in their entirety at www.dialogonleadership.org and as a link on the SoL Web site, www.solonline.org.

Chapter 1

1. J. Miles, "Global Requiem: The Apocalyptic Moment in Religion, Science, and Art," keynote address, fiftieth anniversary, Cross Currents Consultation, Association for Religion & Intellectual Life, printed in *Cross Currents*, 50, no. 3 (Fall 2000): pp. 294–309; www.crosscurrents.org/milesrequiem.htm.

Chapter 2

1. This idea and those in the rest of this paragraph owe a special debt to an essay on "Interbeing" by the Vietnamese monk Thich Nhat Hanh, in Hahn, *The Heart of Understanding* (Berkeley, Calif.: Parallax Press, 1988).

2. For examples of the culture changes involved in continuous flow and lean manufacturing, see J. Womack, *The Machine That Changed the World* (New York: Scribner, 1990), and T. Johnson and A. Broms, *Profit Beyond Measure* (London: Nicholas Brealey Publishing, 2000).

3. D. Bohm, *Thought as a System* (London: Routledge, 1994); D. Bohm, *On Dialogue* (London: Routledge, 1996).

4. D. Bohm and M. Edwards, *Changing Consciousness: Exploring the Hidden Source of the Social, Political and Environmental Crisis Facing the World* (San Francisco: Harper, 1991), p. 6.

5. M. Ray and R. Myers, *Creativity in Business* (New York: Doubleday/Currency, 1986).

6. One area where managing "the judge" within us has been explored extensively is in the creative phase of writing. See B. Flowers, "Madman, Architect, Carpenter, Judge: Roles and the Writing Process," *Proceedings of the Conference of College Teachers of English*, (Texas) 44 (Sept. 1979), pp. 7–10.

7. For more on the research from Project Zero and this theory, see H. Gardner, *Frames of Mind: The Theory of Multiple Intelligences* (New York: Basic Books, 1993 [originally published 1983]), and www.pz.harvard.edu.

8. See "Conversation with W. Brian Arthur: Coming from Your Inner Self," interview by J. Jaworski and C. O. Scharmer, Xerox Parc, Palo Alto, Calif., April 16, 1999, www.dialogonleadership.org.

9. W. Isaacs, *Dialogue and the Art of Thinking Together* (New York: Doubleday/Currency, 1999), p. 41.

10. Real conversations are always more complex than simple examples like this,

and building the capacity to suspend assumptions in work settings can benefit from tools such as the "ladder of inference," scenarios, or other methods for exposing assumptions or mental models. See, e.g., P. Senge et al., *The Fifth Discipline Fieldbook* (London: Nicholas Brealey Publishing, 1994), pp. 235–293, or Isaacs, ibid.

11. See "The Cauldron," in Senge, et al., *The Fifth Discipline Fieldbook*), pp. 364–373.

12. Ibid; also W. Isaacs, *Dialogue and the Art of Thinking Together* (New York: Doubleday/Currency, 1999).

13. See P. Senge, et al., *The Dance of Change* (London: Nicholas Brealey Publishing, 1999).

14. See M. Waldrop, *Complexity* (New York: Simon and Schuster, 1992).

Chapter 3

1. M. Buber, *I and Thou*, trans. Ronald Gregor Smith (New York: Scribner Classics, 2000), pp. 23–24.

2. Varela was director of research at the National Institute for Scientific Research.

3. This project is described in detail in a "learning history." See G. Roth and A. Kleiner, *Car Launch* (New York: Oxford University Press, 2000).

4. P. Senge, et al., *The Fifth Discipline Fieldbook* (London: Nicholas Brealey Publishing, 1994), pp. 84–190.

5. H. Bortoft, *The Wholeness of Nature*, p. 264.

6 E. Schein, *Organizational Culture and Leadership,* 2nd ed. (San Francisco: Jossey-Bass, 1992); E. Schein, *The Corporate Culture Survival Guide* (San Francisco: Jossey-Bass, 1999).

7. See, e.g., P. Senge, et al., *The Fifth Discipline Fieldbook*, pp. 245–252.

8. Then professor and director of the Center of Mindfulness in Meditation, Healthcare, and Society at the University of Massachusetts, Kabat-Zinn, whose MIT Ph.D. is in neurobiology, is the author of *Wherever You Go, There You Are* (New York: Hyperion, 1994) and many professional as well as popular writings on mindfulness.

Chapter 4

1. Campbell was quoting the philosopher Schopenhauer.

Chapter 5

1. A. Kahane, *Solving Tough Problems: An Open Way of Talking, Listening, and Creating New Realities* (San Francisco: Berrett Koehler, September 2004).

Chapter 6

1. W. B. Arthur, "Increasing Returns and the New World of Business," *Harvard Business Review* (July–August, 1996), pp. 100–109.

2. J. Schumpeter, *Capitalism, Socialism and Democracy* (New York: Harper, 1975 [orig. published 1946]), pp. 82-85.

3. W. B. Arthur, J. Day, J. Jaworski, M. Jung, I. Nonaka, C. O. Scharmer, and P. Senge, "Illuminating the Blind Spot," *Leader to Leader* (Spring 2002), pp. 11-14.

4. The literature on learning from experience, both individually and in organizations, is vast. A brief summary of the standard learning cycle can be found in P. Senge, et al., *The Fifth Discipline Fieldbook*, pp. 59–65. Other classic references include the "PDCA cycle" of quality improvement; see W. F. Deming, *Out of Chaos* (Cambridge, Mass.: MIT Center for Advanced Engineering Studies, 1982), p. 88; D. Kolb, *Experiential Learning: Experience as the Source of Learning and Development* (Englewood Cliffs, N.J.: Prentice-Hall, 1984); and E. Schein, *Process Consultation Revisited: Building Helping Relationships* (Reading, Mass.: Addison-Wesley, 1999).

5. See, e.g., J. P. Kotter, *Leading Change* (Boston: Harvard Business School Press, 1996), and P. C. Nutt, *Managing Planned Change* (New York: Macmillan, 1992).

6. J. Jaworski, *Synchronicity: The Inner Path of Leadership* (San Francisco: Berrett-Koehler, 1996), pp.176–179, pp. 182–185. See also J. Jaworski, "Synchronicity and Servant Leadership," in *Focus on Leadership: Servant-Leadership for the 21st Century*, L. C. Spears and M. Lawrence, eds. (New York: John Wiley and Sons, 2002), pp. 287–294; and J. Jaworski, "Destiny and the Leader," in *Insights on Leadership: Service, Stewardship, Spirit and Servant-Leadership*, L. C. Spears, ed.(New York: John Wiley and Sons, 1998), pp. 258–287.

7. See C. O. Scharmer, "Presencing: Learning from the Future as It Emerges," paper presented at the Conference on Knowledge and Innovation, May 25–26, 2000, Helsinki School of Economics, Helsinki, Finland, www.ottoscharmer.com. C. O. Scharmer, "Self-Transcending Knowledge: Sensing and Organizing

Around Emerging Opportunities," *Journal of Knowledge Management*, 5, no. 2 (2001): 137–150. C. O. Scharmer, W. B. Arthur, J. Day, J. Jaworski, M. Jung, I. Nonaka, and P. Senge, "Illuminating the Blind Spot: Leadership in the Context of Emerging Worlds," summary paper on an ongoing research project, www.dialogonleadership.org. See also a comprehensive presentation of the U theory in Otto's forthcoming book, *Theory U: Leading from the Emerging Future* (www.ottoscharmer.com). See also Otto's earlier work on the foundations of the U published in C. O. Scharmer, *Reflexive Modernisierung des Kapitalismus als Revolution von innen. Auf der Suche nach Infrastrukturen einer lernenden Gesellschaft* (Reflective Modernization of Capitalism: Toward Infrastructures of a Learning Society) (Stuttgart: Schäffer-Poeschel, 1996). See also the work of our European colleague Friedrich Glasl, who developed a different but related version of a U process: F. Glasl, *The Enterprise of the Future* (Stroud U.K.: Hawthorn Press, 1997), pp. 67–71; and F. Glas, *Confronting Conflict* (Stroud U.K.: Hawthorn Press,1999), pp. 154–156.

The U theory developed here draws on integrating three different bodies of methodology: phenomenology (precise observation), Eastern and Western contemplative practices (primary knowing), and fast cycle innovation and creating (rapid prototyping of living examples). The sources of inspiration for this synthesis are manifold, but probably the most important one for both Otto Scharmer and Glasl has been the work of the Austrian philosopher Rudolph Steiner (1861–1925), who integrated the Goethean approach to science in his spiritual science (Anthroposophy). See R. Steiner, *The Philosophy of Freedom* (London: Rudolf Steiner Press, 1988).

8. Behavioral scientists call this "cognitive bias" and "anchoring" perceptions on past experience. See, e.g., D. Kahneman, P. Slovic, and A. Tversky, *Judgement under Uncertainty: Heuristics and Biases* (Cambridge, U.K.: Cambridge University Press, 1982).

9. The noted organizational theorist Karl Weick gives a powerful example of this in his analysis of the death of the Mangulch forest firefighting troupe who were unable to "drop their tools" and flee when a fire suddenly took a surprising turn: see K. Weick, "Prepare Your Organization to Fight Fires," *Harvard Business Review* (May-June 1996), pp. 143–148. Henry Mintzberg has made similar points in his analysis of effective strategy as emergent: see H. Mintzberg, "Crafting Strategy," *Harvard Business Review* (July–August 1987), pp. 66–75.

10. The Bhagavad-Gita, or "The Lord's Song," translated by Annie Besant, reprinted in R. Ballou, *The Bible of the World* (New York: Viking, 1939).

Chapter 7

1. Matthew 19: 24.

2. Eleanor Rosch, "Spit Straight Up–Learn Something! Can Tibetan Buddhism Inform the Cognitive Sciences?," in *Meeting at the Roots: Essays on Tibetan Buddhism and the Natural Sciences*, B. A. Wallace, ed. (Berkeley, Calif.: University of California Press) (forthcoming).

3. Ibid.

4. "Conversation with Eleanor Rosch: Primary Knowing: When Perception Happens from the Whole Field," interview by C. O. Scharmer, University of California, Berkeley, Department of Psychology, October 15, 1999, www.dialogonleadership.org.

5. Nishida was the first modern Japanese philosopher who profoundly integrated Eastern wisdom traditions and Western philosophical thought; see K. Nishida, *An Inquiry into the Good*, trans. M. Abe and C. Ives (New Haven, Conn.: Yale University Press, 1990).

6. "Conversation with Eleanor Rosch: Primary Knowing: When Perception Happens from the Whole Field," interview by C. O. Scharmer, University of California, Berkeley, Department of Psychology, October 15, 1999, www.dialogonleadership.org.

Chapter 9

1. The full letter can be viewed at www.solonline.org

2. Maria von Trapp was one of the daughters of the Austrian navy captain Baron von Trapp and his first wife. After her mother's death, her father eventually remarried a former novitiate and nanny for the children, whose name was also Maria. Baron von Trapp's second wife, Maria, is the heroine of the *Sound of Music* story.

3. With the help of Maurice and Hannah Strong and several other associates, John Milton founded the Sacred Land Trust, which has so far succeeded in setting aside about 360 acres so that this land will be protected from all development.

Chapter 10

1. G. B. Shaw, "Dedicatory Epistle," *Man and Superman* (New York: Penguin, 1950).

2. See R. Fritz, *The Path of Least Resistance* (New York: Ballantine Books, 1989), and R. Fritz, *Your Life as Art* (Newfane, Vt: Newfane Press, 2002).

3. Fritz's term "structural tension" is called "creative tension" in the Fifth Discipline books (see, e.g., P. Senge, *The Fifth Discipline*).

4. *Lao Tzu, Tao T. Ching*, Gia-Fu Feng and Jane English translation (New York: Vintage Books, 1972), Chapters 29, 48.

5. M. Buber, *I and Thou*, p. 59.

Chapter 11

1. R. Bache, *Dark Night, Early Dawn* (Albany: State University of New York Press, 2000), pp. 188–189.

2. See "Conversation with John Kao, Interview by C. O. Scharmer" in *Reflections: The SoL Journal,* 2, no. 4, 10–20; see also www.dialogonleadership.org.

3. See R. Fritz, *Your Life as Art* (Newfane, Vt: Newfane Press, 2002).

4. Well-known examples are the World Business Council for Sustainable Development (www.wbcsd.org), CERES (www.ceres.org), and the United Nations Global Compact (www.unglobalcompact.org).

5. For a complete account of the "Lakes Story," the team's internal identification, see M. Hotchkiss, C. Kelley, R. Ott, and J. Elton, "The Lakes Story," *Reflections: The SoL Journal*, 1, no. 4 (2000), 24-31.

6. J. Jaworski, *Synchronicity*, p.88.

7. W. H. Murray, *The Scottish Himalayan Expedition* (London: J. M. Dent and Sons, 1951).

8. R. Bache, *Dark Night, Early Dawn*, pp. 189–196.

9. Ibid, p. 183.

10. Ibid, p. 185.

11. Ibid, p. 183.

Chapter 12

1. See P. Mirvis, K. Ayas, G. Roth, *To the Desert and Back: The Story of the Most Dramatic Business Transformation on Record* (New York: Jossey-Bass, 2003).

2. Dee Hock, *Birth of the Chaordic Age* (San Francisco: Barrett-Kohler, 1999), p. 124-125

3. Ibid, pp. 134-135

4. Ibid.

5. Ibid., p. 140. The principles are:

   It should be equitably owned by all participants.

   Participants should have equitable rights and obligations.

   It should be open to all qualified participants.

   Power, function, and resources should be distributive to the maximum degree.

   Authority should be equitable and distributive within each governing entity.

   No existing participant should be left in a lesser position by any new concept or organization.

   To the maximum degree possible, everything (such as exiting the association and use of commonly held property) should be voluntary.

   It should induce not compel change.

   It should be infinitely malleable yet extremely durable.

6. "Democratic Vistas," *The Portable Walt Whitman*, M. van Doren, ed. (New York: Penguin Books, 1979), p. 348.

Chapter 13

1. See D. Chatterjee, *Leading Consciously* (Massachusetts: Butterworth-Heinemann, 1998), and *Light the Fire in Your Heart* (New Delhi: Full Circle, 2002).

2. See N. Huajin, *A Light Talk on the Original "Great Learning"* (Lao Ku Culture Foundation, 1998).

3. For an exposition written for Westerners on the Buddhist concept of self, see M. Epstein, *Thought Without a Thinker: Psychotherapy from a Buddhist Perspective* (New York: Basic Books, 1995).

4. In D. Whyte, *The Heart Aroused* (New York: Doubleday/Currency, 2002), p. 295.

Chapter 14

1. A similar observation has been made by Jakob von Uexküll, who claimed that the globally extended effects of our actions (*Wirkwelt*) are no longer linked and

fed back by a similar extension of our perception (*Merkwelt*). See J. Uexküll and
G. Kriszat, *Streifzüge durch die Umwelten von Tieren und Menschen* (Frankfurt
Main: Fischer Verlag, 1970).

2. D. Peat, *Infinite Potential: The Life and Times of David Bohm* (Reading, Mass.:
   Addison-Wesley, 1999), p. 1.

3. See J. Jaworski, *Synchronicity* (San Francisco: Berrett-Koehler, 1996), pp.
   79–89; private conversations with Bohm (London, July 28, 1980).

4. See, e.g., G. Cajete, *Native Science: Natural Laws of Interdependence* (Santa Fe,
   N.M.: Clear Light Publishers, 1999).

5. D. Bohm and M. Edwards, *Changing Consciousness: Exploring the Hidden Source of
   the Social, Political and Environmental Crisis Facing the World* (San Francisco:
   Harper, 1991), p. 6.

6. Ibid.

7. For example, systems family therapy arose in reaction to this, arguing that the
   greatest insight and leverage lay in understanding larger patterns of interpersonal relationships. In other words, if you want to help a teenager in difficulty,
   you need to understand what's happening between the teenager and the parents as elements in a family system. See D. Kantor and W. Lehr, *In the Family*
   (San Francisco: Jossey-Bass, 1975).

8. See, e.g., D. Ancona, "Bridging the Boundary: External Activity and
   Performance in Organizational Teams," *Administrative Science Quarterly* (1992,
   37), pp. 634–664.

9. H. T. Johnson and A. Broms, *Profit beyond Measure* (London: Nicholas Brealey
   Publishing, 2000), p. 45. See also H. T. Johnson, "Reflections of a Recovering
   Cost Accountant," SoL Research Forum, January, 1998, www.solonline.org.

10. Johnson and Broms, *Profit Beyond Measure*, pp. 103–110.

11. F. Capra, *The Hidden Connections. Integrating the Biological, Cognitive, and Social
    Dimensions of Life into a Science of Sustainability* (New York: Doubleday, 2002),
    pp. xvi–xvii; see also F. Capra, *The Turning Point* (New York: Bantam Books,
    1982).

12. J. S. Bell, "On the Problem of Hidden Variables in Quantum Mechanics," *Review
    of Modern Physics*, 38 (1966): 447–452; J. T. Cushing and E. McMullin,
    Philosophical Consequences of Quantum Theory: Reflections on Bell's Theorem (Notre
    Dame, Ind.: Notre Dame Press, 1989).

13. D. Radin, *The Conscious Universe* (San Francisco: Harper, 1997), p. 278.

14. D. Bohm, *Wholeness and the Implicate Order* (London: Ark Paperbacks, 1984), p 129.

15. R. D. Nelson, D. I. Radin, R. Shoup, P. Bancel, "Correlation of Continuous Random Data with Major World Events," p. 10, http://noosphere.princeton.edu. See also R. D. Nelson, D. I. Radin, R. Shoup, P. Bancel, "Correlation of Continuous Random Data with Major World Events," *Foundations of Physics Letters*, 15, no. 6 (2000): 537-550; D. I. Radin, "For Whom the Bell Tolls: A Question of Global Consciousness," *Noetic Sciences Review*, 63 (2003): 8-13, 44–45; D. I. Radin, "Exploring Relationships Between Random Physical Events and Mass Human Attention: Asking for Whom the Bell Tolls," *Journal of Scientific Exploration*, 16, no. 4 (2002): 533-548. Summary of probabilities in the network on 9/11: observed network variance - 0.003, observed autocorrelation - 0.001, and observed internode correlation - 0.0002. Direct inquiries to R. D. Nelson, Department of Mechanical Engineering, Princeton University.

16. See Jaworski, *Synchronicity*, pp. 79–80, 177–180; see also L. McTaggart, *The Field: The Quest for the Secret Force of the Universe* (New York: HarperCollins, 2002).

17. H. Maturana and F. Varela, *The Tree of Knowledge* (Boston, Mass.: Shambala Press, 1987).

18. Ibid.

19. Capra, *The Hidden Connections*, p. 261.

20. Private conversation with David Bohm (London, July 28, 1980).

21. A. Zajonc, *Catching the Light: The Entwined History of Light and Mind* (New York: Bantam Books, 1993).

22. "Investigating the Space of the Invisible: Conversation with Arthur Zajonc," interview with C. O. Scharmer, Amherst, MA, October, 2003. www.dialogonleadership.org. See also: A. Zajonc, *Goethe and the Science of His Time: An Historical Introduction*, in *Goethe's Way of Science: A Phenomenology of Nature*, D. Seamon and A. Zajonc, eds. (New York: State University of New York Press, 1988), pp. 15–30.

23. Goethe, 1823, quoted in A. Zajonc, *Goethe and the Science of his time: An Historical Introduction*, in *Goethe's Way of Science: A Phenomenology of Nature*, D. Seamon and A. Zajonc, eds. (New York: State University of New York Press, 1988), p. 27.

24. It is a sign of the emerging confluence of the two epistemologies that the National Science Foundation is funding the planning process and is a potential funder of the center.

25. According to von Thater-Braan, the term "native science" is controversial among mainstream scientists. In private correspondence, she defined it as "a body of knowledge gathered, evolved, and held collectively by the worlds' Indigenous peoples and passed orally from generation to generation since pre-history. Until recently this knowledge was dismissed as 'primitive.' In actuality it continues to prove itself to be quite sophisticated and complex. With the recognition of the severity of the environmental crises we face, indigenous knowledge/science is being sought and valued by scientists in many disciplines."

26. Quoted in P. Senge, *The Fifth Discipline*, p. 170: "[the human being] experiences himself, his thoughts and feelings, as something separate from the rest—a kind of optical delusion of our consciousness. This delusion is a kind of prison for us, restricting us to our personal desires and to affection for a few persons nearest to us. Our task must be to widen our circle of compassion to embrace all living creatures and the whole of nature in its beauty."

27. See Humberto Maturana, "Metadesign," www.inteco.cl/articulos/metade-sign_parte3.htm.

28. See P. Senge, *The Fifth Discipline*, or P. Senge, et al., *The Fifth Discipline Fieldbook*, pp. 135–140.

Chapter 15

1. I. Nonaka and H. Takeuchi, *The Knowledge-Creating Company: How Japanese Companies Create the Dynamics of Innovation,* (Oxford: Oxford University Press, 1995).

2. T. Berry, *The Dream of the Earth* (San Francisco: Sierra Club Books, 1988), p. 123.

3. R. Greenleaf, *The Servant Leader Within: A Transformative Path* (Mahwah, N.J.: Paulist Press, 2003).

4. M. Buber, *I and Thou*, trans. Ronald Gregor Smith (New York: Scribner, 1958).

5. This theory is central to Mahayana Buddhism, the school of Buddhism that came from India and has been particularly influential in China, northern Asia,

and Japan. See, e.g., *The Awakening of Faith* (attributed to Asvaghosha) trans. with commentary by Y. S. Hakeda (New York: Columbia University Press, 1967).

6. The interview *The Blind Spot: Hitler's Secretary* is available in DVD with English, French, and Spanish subtitles through www.amazon.com.

Epilogue

1. D. Quinn, *Ishmael* (New York: Bantam/Turner Books, 1992).

2. Ibid, p. 56.

3. See www.fredfoundation.org.

4. Emoto's method builds on earlier work of Dr. Lee H. Lorezen. M. Emoto, *Messages from Water* (Tokyo: IHM General Research Institute, 1999), p. 139. Also see www.hado.net. Books are available through Source Books, (615) 773-7691.

5. For example, see the review by Dr. Ho of the Institute of Science and Society (ISIS) at www.i-sis.org.uk/water4.php.

6. Emoto, op cit, p. 139.

7. Emoto's basic procedure is to take one hundred samples from the same source. One drop from each sample is frozen in a separate petri dish, and then photographed. The photographs in his book show crystals that are representataive of the one hundred samples from each experimental condition. He also shows how the multiple samples from one source or for one experimental condition show features similar to one another yet quite different from those from another source or condition.

Acknowledgments

The four of us have worked together in different combinations for over two decades, but what made this project so special were the many additional friends and colleagues who were involved.

One unique feature was the input and inspiration of more than one hundred and fifty leading scientists and social and business entrepreneurs who agreed to be interviewed by Otto and Joseph. These interviews typically began with a simple question—"What question lies at the heart of your work?"—and invariably opened up a deep territory of introspection and caring. If any of us ever doubted that a shift was occurring in the dominant worldview, talking with these remarkable individuals renewed our faith that the future can indeed be different from the past. Without their willingness to open themselves and become vulnerable to our simple questions, this book would not have been possible.

In the initial stages of the project, Michael Jung and Jonathan Day of McKinsey Europe, and Ikujiro Nonaka of Hitotsubashi University joined with us in making sense of these interviews. As the ideas began to form into this book, a few of those we interviewed also helped more extensively, including Eleanor Rosch, Francisco Varela, Bill Torbert, and especially Brian Arthur, who met with us on several occasions and gave us feedback on the entire book. We are indebted to Sigrun Bouius, Goran Carstedt, Khoo Boon Hui, Ante Glavas, Sherry Immediato, Seija Kulkki, Manuel Manga, Diane Senge, Ursula Versteegen, Barbara Stocking of Oxfam, David Chapman of Shell, Vivienne Cox of BP, and Ann Murray Allen of HP, all of whom read earlier versions of the manuscript and provided valuable comments. Adam Kahane, whose work represents another embodiment of the ideas here, read and re-read multiple versions of the work in progress.

We also want to thank the regional co-interviewers who helped us complete the final set of interviews conducted around the world: Glennifer Gillespie and Beth Jandernoa (South Africa and the U.S.), Elena Diez Pinto (Guatemala), Tacito V. Nobre and Fabiola M. Nobre (Brazil), Darshan Chitrabhanu (India), Jacqueline Wong (Singapore), and Fabio Sgragli (Europe). A special thanks to Susan Taylor, who handled the logistics of setting up interviews for the book, and transcribed many of the tapes.

John Milton has been an inspiration and teacher to us all; without getting to know him we would undoubtedly never have appreciated just how closely these ideas connect to ancient wisdom about understanding nature and ourselves as inseparable facets of the universe's generative dance.

Nina Kruschwitz took the manuscript and suggested a streamlining of the overall structure we had been unable to see for ourselves. She also helped edit the book, and shepherded it through the design and production process.

The presentation of conversations in the book follows the spirit and general flow but not the details of our meetings. Most of the meetings occurred in the home of Otto and his wife and partner, Dr. Katrin Käeufer, in Cambridge, Massachusetts. Katrin became an important thinking partner in the whole enterprise, serving as a coresearcher focused on cross-sector dialogue, such as the Guatemala project, and on network leadership, as described in the German healthcare story.

Initial funding for the interview project came from McKinsey & Company. Additional funding was provided by the MIT Fund for Organizational Learning, Generon Consulting, SoL, and anonymous individual donors.

About the Authors

Peter Senge is a senior lecturer at the MIT Sloan School of Management, and the Founding Chairperson of the Society for Organizational Learning (SoL). He is the author of the widely acclaimed book, *The Fifth Discipline: The Art and Practice of the Learning Organization* (1990), which has sold a million copies worldwide and was identified as one of the seminal management books of the last seventy-five years by *Harvard Business Review* in 1997. He is coauthor of *The Fifth Discipline Fieldbook* (1994), with colleagues Charlotte Roberts, Rick Ross, Bryan Smith, and Art Kleiner; a second fieldbook on sustaining change, *The Dance of Change* (1999), with George Roth as an additional coauthor; and the award-winning *Schools That Learn* (2000), coauthored with Nelda Cambron-McCabe, Timothy Lucas, Bryan Smith, Janis Dutton, and Art Kleiner.

Peter is widely known as one of the most innovative thinkers about management and leadership in the world, translating the abstract ideas of systems theory into tools for better understanding economic and organizational change. His work today focuses on fostering collaboration among diverse business, governmental, and nongovernmental organizations in order to address long-term systemic change that is beyond the reach of individual organizations.

He received a B.S. in engineering from Stanford University, a M.S. in social systems modeling, and a Ph.D. in management from MIT. He lives with his wife and children in central Massachusetts.

C. Otto Scharmer is a Senior Lecturer at the MIT Sloan School of Management. He is also a Visiting Professor at the Center for Innovation and Knowledge Research, Helsinki School of Economics. An international action researcher, he is a cofounder of the Society for Organizational Learning and has consulted with multinational firms, international institutions, and NGOs in the United States, Europe, and Asia.

Scharmer holds a Ph.D. in economics and management from Witten-Herdecke University, Germany. His article "Strategic Leadership within the Triad Growth-Employment-Ecology" won the McKinsey Research Award in 1991. His most recent work has included research in the form of dialogue interviews with 150 eminent thinkers on leadership, strategy, and knowledge creation. A synthesis of this research has resulted in a theoretical framework and practice called presencing, which he elaborates in his forthcoming book, *Theory U: Leading from the Emerging Future*. With his colleagues, Otto has used presencing to facilitate profound innovation and change processes both within companies and across societal systems.

He lives with his wife and their two children in Boston, Massachusetts.

Joseph Jaworski is the Chairman of Generon Consulting and cofounder of the Global Leadership Initiative. Joseph has devoted much of his life to exploring the deeper dimensions of transformational leadership. He began his professional career as an attorney, specializing in domestic and international litigation at Bracewell & Patterson, a large Houston-based law firm where for fifteen years he was a senior partner and member of the executive committee. In 1975 he was elected as a fellow of the American College of Trial Lawyers. In addition, he ran a successful horse-breeding operation (Circle J Enterprises), and helped found several organizations, including a life insurance company and a refining company.

In 1980, Joseph founded the American Leadership Forum, a non-governmental organization responsible for developing collaborative leadership. Ten years later, he was invited to join the Royal Dutch/Shell Group of companies in London, to lead Shell's renowned team of scenario planners. Thereafter he returned to the U.S. as a senior fellow and a member of the Board of Governors of the MIT Center for Organizational Learning, and was a founding member of the Society for Organizational Learning.

Joseph is the author of the critically-acclaimed book *Synchronicity* (Berrett-Koehler, 1996), an explication of generative leadership based upon his lifelong work and experience. He and his family divide their time between Boston's north shore and rural Vermont.

Betty Sue Flowers is the Director of the Johnson Presidential Library and Museum in Austin, Texas, a position she was appointed to in 2002. Prior to that, she was the Kelleher Professor of English and member of the Distinguished Teachers Academy at the University of Texas at Austin. She is a Senior Research Fellow of the IC2 Institute, an Honorary Fellow of British Studies, a recipient of the Pro Bene

Meritis Award, and a Distinguished Alumnus of the University of Texas. She is also a poet, editor, and business consultant, with publications ranging from poetry therapy to the economic myth, including two books of poetry and four television tie-in books in collaboration with Bill Moyers, among them, *Joseph Campbell and the Power of Myth*. She hosted "Conversations with Betty Sue Flowers" on the Austin PBS-affiliate and has served as a moderator for executive seminars at the Aspen Institute for Humanistic Studies, consultant for NASA, member of the Envisioning Network for General Motors, Visiting Advisor to the Secretary of the Navy, and editor of Global Scenarios for Shell International in London and the World Business Council in Geneva (on global sustainable development and, most recently, on the future of biotechnology).

Betty Sue received her B.A. and M.A. from the University of Texas and her Ph.D. in English Literature from the University of London. She lives in Austin, Texas, with her husband and son.

About the Organizations

SoL (The Society for Organizational Learning, Inc.) is a nonprofit membership organization that connects researchers, organizations, and consultants around the world. Founded in 1997, SoL's purpose is to create and implement knowledge for fundamental innovation and change. By providing a variety of forums, projects, courses, and virtual infrastructures, SoL enables individuals and institutions to expand their capacity for inspired performance, creating results together that they could not create alone.

SoL publishes an e-journal, *Reflections*, that is available by subscription or as a benefit of membership. A portion of the net proceeds from SoL publishing sales are reinvested in basic research, leading-edge applied learning projects, and building a global network of learning communities.

More information about membership, professional development opportunities, events, and publications can be found on the SoL website, www.solonline.org.

The **Global Leadership Initiative** (GLI) is a nonprofit that creates living examples of successful innovation by applying the U theory of social change to vital global challenges. Founded in 2002, GLI is launching ten international Leadership Labs—focused on critical issues like AIDS, water, malnutrition, sustainable food production, and climate change—over the next five years.

The organizers of GLI—from Generon Consulting, SoL, and the Massachusetts Institute of Technology—bring extensive experience in dialogue-and-action projects, scenario planning, leadership development, and action research. By simultaneously engaging leaders from corporations, government, and civil society, GLI is dedicated to building leadership capacity while producing concrete results.

For more information on programs, projects, and research see www.globalleadershipinitiative.org.

Index

for authority figures, 119–221

and awareness, 203

in globalization, 229

maintenance of, 158–62

with nature, 173

in quantum theory, 194–195

scientific worldview of, 189

water crystals and, 244, 245–46

control, surrender of, 96–97, 102–3

"Conversations with Betty Sue Flowers" (Flowers), 270

corporations

auto makers, 152, 193

leadership of, 186

merger of, 94–95

union-management relations, 33–35

corporations, global

accountability of, 132

executive meeting, 118

living, 147

and NGOs, 125

see also institutions, global

Cottrell, John, 33–34

creativity

impediments to, 31, 39, 146

source of, 11, 30–31, 94, 101

see also innovation; prototyping

"Creativity and Personal Mastery" (Rao), 134-35

culture, modern

assumptions of, 125

integrative thought in, 211

new global, 6

separation in, 214–15

shifting the burden, 203–09, 205

culture, organizational

learning-oriented, 118

in meetings, 47–49

culture, traditional

goals for, 211

knowledge in, 54–55, 179–80

proximity in, 208–09

threats to, 6

Deming, W. Edward, 72, 195

democracy, 167, 170, 172–74

Descartes, Rene, 189, 195

destiny/purpose, 114, 220, 235–39, 247

Dewey, John, 86–87

dialogue

between leaders, 122

with prototyping, 148, 152–53

quality of, 33, 34

economy

national, 31, 36–37

network, 35–36

economy, global

political agendas and, 6

who benefits from, 6, 118, 165

education

deeper levels of, 108, 145–46, 161–62

fragmentation of, 190, 198

industrial-age, 7, 8–9

standardized tests for, 193

Einstein, Albert, 189, 197, 203

elder wisdom, 178–79

eleven direction ceremony, 58, 59–60, 61, 63–64, 130

Elter, John, 152

emotions

avoidance of, 39–40, 224–30

group expression of, 40

love, and intelligence, 197, 210

suspension of, 138

Emoto, Masaru, 241, 243–46

entrepreneurs

commitment of, 103, 130–35

emerging ideas of, 8, 10–11, 137–38, 142–43

environment

global, 6, 22–24

local vs. distant, 208–209

perception of, 54

see also sustainability

environmental movements, 55, 166, 238

Executive Champions Workshop, 118, 125, 246

farming, 108–9, 166, 236

Fast Company (Taylor; Webber), 32, 135, 140, 153

feedback, 36, 152, 153–54

fire story, 79–81, 89–90, 103, 143

Flowers, Betty Sue, 13, 269

Ford Motor Company, 152

Foundation for Industry Research, 265

Foundations of Physics Letters, 195

fragmentation, 190–93, 198, 209

freedom, types of, 222–24

Freud, Sigmund, 191

Fritz, Robert, 139, 149

Fuller, Buckminster, 4, 212

future, emerging, 83–84, 86, 89–91, 219–21

Galileo, 189, 195

Gandhi, Mahatma, 147

Gardner, Howard, 30

Gates, Bill, 84

Gauguin, Eugene Henri, 190

Gell-Mann, Murray, 37

General Motors, 192

generative moment, 90, 103–4, 145–46

Generon Consulting, 265, 269, 272

Germany, 105, 229–30

Getty, J. Paul, 24

Geus, Arie de, 5, 29

Global Leadership Initiative (GLI)

genesis of, 125–26, 222, 233, 272

New York meeting, 163–67

and Theory of the U, 129, 167

"Global Requiem" (Miles), 24

Global Scenarios, 270

globalization

Reader Comments

To share your own comments, join the *Presence* mailing list,
or access reader resources, including *The Presence Workbook*, visit
www.presence.net

~

Rather than just introducing a set of new tools, *Presence* reminds
us of our purpose. The book is also important because it is very
brave. It talks about how most of us feel, but do not know how
to express or explain—even to ourselves.

— *Evrim Calkavur, Su Consulting, Istanbul*

I loved the book. It's a remarkable synthesis and a great read that
fills an even greater need. I'll spread the word.

— *Diana Chapman Walsh, President, Wellesley College*

I spend a lot of time reading what could be called the more
sophisticated end of general management literature and *Presence*

is dramatically different in layout and approach. It is reflective and discursive, with a lot of forays into philosophical thinking and developments in scientific theory. Those who are used to a diet of "how to's", sidebars, summaries, and highlighted key points are likely to find it hard going. However, these are probably precisely the people who most need to absorb the ideas in the book. The argument of the book as a whole asserts that total reliance on dispassionate analytical rationalism is a sure path to the wrong answer and that we (individually and collectively) need to find ways to see the wholeness of life and to use our hearts and our intuition to become "part of a future that is seeking to unfold." While this worldview is still radical in business circles, it is not new, and in fact is part of a growing movement. The authors take a valuable further step both in explaining why a change is necessary and in sketching an approach to learning the profound transformations in perspective that are needed.

— *Bill Godfrey, Change Management Monitor Review Site, Australia*

Many people in northern developed countries, and in the U.S. in particular, have little awareness of the problems with the global food system, or even that such a system exists. They don't know, for instance, that the average pound of food travels some 1500 miles before sale in the U.S and in so doing crosses many national and international borders. As food systems have become global, large farms and multinational food businesses apply technology and market power to continually drive prices lower and production higher, a pattern repeated again and again for agricultural commodities from corn, to coffee, to forest products, to fish. Falling prices and production driven beyond environmentally sustainable levels are now a primary source of both poverty and deteriorating food ecosystems worldwide. Rich country governments respond by spending $500 billion a year for farm subsidies but poor governments don't have this option.

No one intends to produce a system that is unsustainable, but individuals are making decisions in a system that is critically fragmented. Fortunately, more and more people see that without fundamental changes, many agriculture and fishing businesses may not even exist in a decade or two. But doing something about sustainable food requires bringing parties together that normally do not cooperate.

We formed the Sustainable Food Lab to use the U process to build new networks of leaders capable of working together to address these systemic dysfunctions. Leaders from more than 30 organizations — including multinational food companies like Unilever and SYSCO, small farm cooperatives and local NGOs in half a dozen countries, global NGOs like Oxfam and World Wildlife Fund, and government officials from Europe, the U.S. and South America — have, with the help of four foundations and the Dutch Ministry of Agriculture, reached the point of prototyping initiatives. We are just at the outset, but the relationships among leaders across normal boundaries might be the most crucial ingredient to major change.

— *Hal Hamilton, Director, The Sustainability Institute; Co-Leader, The Sustainable Food Lab*

No one yet knows how to foster the kind of collaboration that will be needed to transform global food systems. Creating sustainable food systems will require real changes in company strategies and in national policies. But the larger change we are seeking is in our individual and collective mindset, and for that we will need leaders with a deep sense of trust, mutuality, and real commitment to change. I've never seen a process quite like the U for bringing a very diverse group of people to a profound place of connection with one another and with their common purpose.

— *Oran Hesterman, Food Systems and Rural Development Program Director, the W. K. Kellogg Foundation, and team member, The Sustainable Food Lab.*

The authors articulate a message that is fundamental to people everywhere: the connectedness of all things. Their discussion of parts and wholes resonates both intellectually and emotionally; it confirms what I have found in my conversations with people around the world, and in my own work. By opening ourselves to the world and to the living systems that sustain us, we can create meaningful and lasting change. This may sound idealistic but it is extremely practical, indeed it is a matter of survival – for individuals, organizations, and societies.

— *Elena Díez Pinto, Director of the United Nations Development Programme's Democratic Dialogue for Latin America and the Caribbean*

Presence makes a fresh and provocative contribution to organizational learning theory. For deep organizational change to occur, there must be an ongoing synergy between the personal and the collective. Generating new options depends both on the inner development of individuals and on collective processes in which they mutually enact the field of the emergent future. Organizations, from small working groups to global companies, can be fertile ground for cultivating a life-serving societal transformation. *Presence* serves as a personal and collective compass to guide us into this new land.

— *David I. Rome, The Greystone Foundation*

The authors have illuminated, instructed, and brought hope and opportunity with this work. *Presence* is marked with a clarity fueled by humility appropriate to the mystery of the topic and the gravity of the times.

— *Rose von Thater-Braan, The Native American Academy*

Thank you for *Presence*. Increasingly I believe that the best thing we can do for MBA and other students of management is to teach them some sort of mindfulness practices, so that they will become more aware in general, and more aware of the impacts of their decisions and actions as managers and leaders.

— *Sandra Waddock, Professor of Management, Boston College*

I took what I learned by going through the U process and led a transformation project in a refinery that was the worst performing one of the eight in our system on all measures. Within two years it went from worst to first. After nine straight years of losing an average of 20 million dollars a year, it made 38 million the year after the transformation process. There is no doubt in my heart that the whole idea of absorbing and being mindful of what's going on-not just jumping in right away with a decision-is the best way to operate. We couldn't make a wrong decision. It was effortless. The U Process is real powerful stuff!

— *Gary Wilson, Former Operations Manager of major oil refinery*

Presence is remarkable in at least three ways. First, the authors' work has extraordinary emotional as well as intellectual impact; it continued to affect me long after my initial reading. Second, I found that the insights I gleaned from the work depended on what was happening around me. I suspect I will take away different messages each time I read it. Third, the authors somehow opened me to unexpected messages and opportunities in my own life. My reading of *Presence* coincided with many seemingly chance encounters that in very real and specific ways have been essential to my own work, helping me find new ways to connect with colleagues, customers, and the larger community.

— *Darcy Winslow, General Manager, Global Women's Footwear, Apparel, Equipment, Nike, Inc.*

www.presence.net